D0899835

Milton: a study in ideology and form

CHRISTOPHER KENDRICK

Milton: a study in ideology and form

Methuen
New York and London

First published in 1986 by
Methuen, Inc.
29 West 35th Street
New York NY 10001

Published in Great Britain by
Methuen & Co. Ltd
11 New Fetter Lane
London EC4P 4EE

© 1986 Christopher Kendrick

Phototypeset by AKM Associates (UK) Ltd
Ajmal House, Hayes Road, Southall, London
Printed in Great Britain
at the University Press, Cambridge

All rights reserved. No part of this book may be reprinted or
reproduced or utilized in any form or by any electronic, mechanical or
other means, now known or hereafter invented, including photocopying
and recording, or in any information storage or retrieval system,
without permission in writing from the publishers.

Library of Congress Cataloging in Publication Data
Kendrick, Christopher, 1953–
  Milton: a study in ideology and form.

  Bibliography: p.
  Includes index
  1. Milton, John, 1608-1674——Religion.   2. Theology,
Puritan, in literature.   3. Milton, John, 1608-1674. Paradise Lost.   4. Milton, John,
1608-1674. Areopagitica.   5. Great Britain——History——Puritan Revolution,
1642-1660——Literature and the revolution.   6. Revolutionary Literature, English——
History and criticism.   I. Title.
PR3592.P8K46   1986   821′.4   85-25982

ISBN 0-416-01251-5

British Library Cataloguing in Publication Data
Kendrick, Christopher
  Milton: a study in ideology and form.
  1. Milton, John, *1608-1674*——Criticism and
  interpretation
  I. Title
  821′.4   PR3588

ISBN 0-416-01251-5

To my parents

Contents

Acknowledgments

My debts are many; I can only mention a few of them here. This study is an amended version of a doctoral dissertation which was advised by Leslie Brisman, whose acute patience stood us both in good stead, and Fredric Jameson, whose presence, then, as well as whose written work, was a very great influence. I am also thankful to Professor Joseph Kramer of Bryn Mawr College for his criticism and enthusiastic support of the manuscript at various of its stages, and to Margaret Ferguson of Yale for her encouragement.

The book owes much to ongoing discussions with close friends and peers. Kasturi Haldar provided moral counsel through the dispiriting phase of revision. Joseph Loewenstein and Jon Haynes told me about the Renaissance. John Guillory and Richard Halpern discoursed upon Milton. John Rieder and Steven Shaviro kept me abreast of many recent theoretical developments. Carl Freedman provided theoretical guidance, read what I wrote, and offered comradely criticisms upon the whole.

Last but not least, I would like to thank my editors – Janice Price (but for whom the book might not have seen the light of day) for her kindness and care in the early stages of the editing process; and Merrilyn Julian (but for whom the book might have had no cover) for her meticulous attention to the later stages.

Needless to say, those weaknesses and distortions that remain in the book are wholly owing to my own mistakes and limits.

The authors and publishers wish to thank the editors of *English Literary*

History for permission to publish chapter 2, which was originally published, in a slightly different form, as 'Ethics and the orator in *Areopagitica*' in the Summer 1983 issue of the journal.

Milton: a study in ideology and form

1
Introduction: reformation and ideological transition

It is generally recognized that Milton's life work is the product of a cultural revolution. Most of those who deny that the Puritan revolution of the 1640s was a social revolution would still admit that the cultural face of England was irrevocably changed by it. And virtually no one would contend that Milton would have produced what he did in the absence of cultural upheaval. Yet most Milton criticism has failed to see the centrality of this upheaval to any understanding of Milton's work. This failure has been nowhere more apparent than in the criticism of the two works with which this book is concerned, *Areopagitica* and *Paradise Lost*. *Areopagitica* has been fashioned into the stuff of journalism courses, where it is read for its eternal prescience as a landmark argument against censorship. *Paradise Lost* has been canonized as an assertion of monolithic Christian tradition, if not of eternal Christian verities; the most authoritative recent edition of the poem would seem to have poetasting divinity students in mind as Milton's fit audience.[1] Both works have been detached from the cultural revolution that inspired them and read as the work of an isolated Great Man. I hope in the present study to "correct" this traditional interpretation by attempting to see Milton's works both in relation to the collective agency of revolution and as determinate acts within that agency, as symbolic revolutionary acts themselves.

Yet the focus of this work is not so much on the cultural revolution itself, not so much on the moment of solidarity and conscious collective accomplishment, as it is on the dispersal of revolutionary energies, on the alienated effects of what had been collective action. As the reader will presently become aware, little of the blood and sweat of the Protestant transformation makes its way into the language of this study; Protestantism is considered less as a revolution than as an ideological transition. The narrative of transition unfolds under the aspect of social determination rather than that of class agency: its characters are not classes which become conscious of their own interests as opposed to those of other classes and act upon the world in the name of these interests;[2] its chief agents, rather, are material structures beyond the reach of consciousness which combine, in the case at hand, to determine changes in the ideological map of English society, and more particularly in the constitution of the individual subject. My readings of *Areopagitica* and *Paradise Lost* take as their main focus the determined emergence of a discrete ethical framework of thought within the dominant theological code of these works. This discrete framework of thought may be described as an ethical *problematic*: by this I mean that it is composed of a system of concepts and questions possessed of their own proper unity[3] apart from theology – a unity which is founded on the presupposition of an ethical subject, an individual free to make ethical choices on the basis of "personal experience." The appearance of this problematic is coterminous with that division of politics from religion which stands out, in historical retrospect, as the most consequential ideological accomplishment of Milton's age. The crucial unit of Milton's own ideology to be dealt with, which both determines and manifests the dislocation between theological and ethical modes of thought, is the heresy of monism, Milton's radical Protestant concept of the unity of body and soul. I will be primarily concerned, however, not to perform a straightforward ideological analysis of this heresy's ramifications in Milton's texts, but to show how it determines the form of these works, and thus to depict Milton as a transitional poet or cultural figure.

I am conscious that my relative neglect of the collective agency of the Puritan revolution constitutes a major limitation of my work. Nonetheless, in spite of its tendency to omit agency, the study works, I hope at every level, within the Marxist framework, and depends upon the as yet unfinished problematic of historical materialism. I would propose that the antithesis I have evoked between collective agency and structural determination is not in fact an opposition between mutually exclusive modes of explanation, but rather a matter of alternative historiographic codes or genres with which to describe the past. These genres would seem to complement one another, if only because they appear antithetical, and yet their precise relation will remain a problem, at least in our own time, for any historical work of consequence. "Men make their own history, but . . . under the given and inherited circumstances with which they are directly confronted."[4] The two halves of Marx's axiom hold these codes in suspense, and pose a conundrum for historiography which will be impossible to overcome in practice, according to classical Marxism as I understand it, until man has mastered the social conditions of his existence. Until that time the social historian will necessarily prefer one of these genres over the other, and this selection will continue to know its own historical determination. The best example from the past of this inevitable determination of the historian is perhaps to be found in Marx's career itself, in the well-known opposition between the revolutionary and the scientific Marx. On the one hand, there is the Marx of the later 1840s, who announced in the *Communist Manifesto* the entrance of a new collective agency onto the contemporary historical stage, and who attempted to make that entrance decisive. On the other hand, there is the Marx of the European Restoration, who devoted himself in *Capital* to the painstaking construction of the structural laws of capitalist development. My own "spontaneous" preference for the retrospective code of structural determination over the more "humanist" and sympathetic one of collective agency is not very difficult to explain, given the situation of revolutionary – or indeed of progressive – politics in the United States today. But there is perhaps also a less political, more strictly intellectual reason for my determinist predisposition: the view of history or historical subtext that I presuppose in what follows has been most rigorously formulated in structural rather than collective or cultural terms. The best case for the superior explanatory power of Marxism in dealing with this period is made by the rich literature on the economic transition to capitalism, all of which stems from and attempts to expand upon Marx's groundbreaking work in *Capital*.[5] Since the Marxist view of seventeenth-century English history will be unfamiliar to some readers, I will begin by giving a bare historical overview of this transitional period, basing my summary on the results of the transition debate as I understand them.

The transition period is defined as the period of primitive accumulation, in which the original mass of capital, and with it the conditions requisite for capital's self-reproduction, were gradually prized from out of the feudal polity. The transition spans centuries, and includes fairly distinct phases of primitive accumulation: it dates roughly from the fifteenth century, the period of the rapid disintegration of high feudalism, to the late seventeenth century, the main (or second) period of manufacture, in which a politically established capitalism was beginning to transform the forces of production. Capitalism arrived in England as the dominant mode of production in the late sixteenth century, when wage-labor – which is to say, capitalist productive relations – attained predominance in the most basic sectors of production.[6] So long, however, as primitive accumulation continued to be necessary for capitalism's security, so long as the accumulation of capital was secured not only or even mainly by capitalist production itself, but rather by forms of direct political exploitation such as were intrinsic to feudal and postfeudal production and exchange, then capitalism, though dominant, remained *emergent*. Emergent capitalism designates the phase in which capitalism was dominant but not yet assured and in which the category of capital itself had a double status. On the one hand, capital was deployed within capitalist relations of production, upon an expanding and at least potentially autonomous market: it took on, in this respect, a productive, strictly economic function. On the other hand, capital was not yet fully responsible for its own self-expansion, but depended on residual forms of political exploitation for its growth; it was in this respect a direct effect of class struggle and thus clearly remained a political category. This is the period, so vividly evoked in the last pages of Volume I of *Capital*,[7] in which capital had not yet learned to feel guilty about its origins, but which came to represent the repressed bad conscience of later capitalism. I will treat Milton as an ideologist and poet of emergent capitalism.

From an analytical point of view, the crucial factor in the emergence of capitalism is the separation of economy from polity, of production and exchange from direct coercion; the main problem for any study of the transition is to determine how that separation took place. It is one of Dobb's main accomplishments to have stressed that the decline of feudalism and the rise of capitalist relations was not solely due to an increase in foreign trade and market interactions generally.[8] To say simply that an increase in commodity production and market relations transformed feudalism is to project capitalism as exterior to feudalism, and its emergence as an invasion from without.[9] This is historically and analytically inadequate to both feudalism's decline and capitalism's emergence, because it simplifies both modes of production.

To understand the transition, it is necessary first to comprehend the general disintegration of feudal relations on its own terms. This disintegration was brought on, not by extrinsic changes in the sphere of trade, but by the contradictions defining the feudal mode of production, the main one being the political-economic conflict between landlords and peasants.[10] One may then explain the emergence of capitalism as the general effect of the contradictory tendencies inherent in the late feudal relations of production, organized in large part around petty commodity production, which followed feudalism proper. The emergence of capitalism is no more explained by spontaneous market forces than is the disintegration of feudalism. It seems to have been the outcome, rather, of the more or less direct struggle for the various forces of production which was enforced by the general disintegration of feudal ties. Here, too, as more recent work on the transition has shown, it was the struggle in the country that was of decisive importance.[11]

There are two salient aspects or stages of the conflict on the land: first, the conquest by the peasants of their "freedom," or correlatively the disenserfment of the laboring class; and second, the consolidation by the dominant landholding class, in the face of the peasant threat, of sovereign control over the land – in other words, the prevention of the peasant smallholding. The result of the conflict was a freeholding agrarian laboring class which was nevertheless deprived of traditional possession of the land, and thus peculiarly susceptible to expropriation. Such a class was the necessary condition for the crystallization of capitalist relations of production and the appearance of the capitalist farmer. This latter transformation was itself the condition for what might be considered a technological revolution on the land, by which the efficiency of agricultural production was increased dramatically.[12]

It is only an apparent paradox that the growth of agrarian capitalism chronologically preceded that of commercial and industrial capitalism. The establishment of agrarian capitalism, in an England whose production was still overwhelmingly agricultural, underwrote the growth of trade and industry, providing the free labor force (in the form of a surplus population) and creating the markets indispensable to the capitalization of these sectors. Even though commerce and especially industry were comparatively underdeveloped and heavily monopolized, there were major changes during the late sixteenth and early seventeenth centuries in the structure of trade and industry. Internal trade, regularized by the creation of a carrying system and of specialized markets, expanded greatly; foreign commerce boomed in the early seventeenth century, after the formation of the joint-stock companies in the 1580s and 1590s.[13] emergence of the capitalist mode of production constitutes the ultimate differentiation of the artisan class and the breakup of the guild structure can be dated from this period.[14] This restructuring of the main industrial class contributed to the freeing of capital, and was partly responsible for the attack on monopolies which was so important an issue in the prewar years. There was generally, and especially in London, an impressive growth in the amount of fluid capital; capitalist circulation, however restricted, must have begun to appear as a total social phenomenon. The growth of deposit banking with scriveners and goldsmiths was sign and symptom of this qualitative difference.[15] Milton, the son of a thriving scrivener, grew up in the midst of this new abundance of circulating capital.

The interdependence of the agrarian and the more urban forms of capitalism is perhaps clearest when we turn to the political history of the period, where it seems that something like a national economic interest, independent from and partly in conflict with the interests of the state (or more properly of the monarchy), begins to manifest itself. Consider the cloth business, far and away England's largest. The prosperity of the cloth trade, as Stone has pointed out, was a vital interest not only for merchants but also for the new class of landowners producing wool for the market and for the artisans who turned wool into cloth.[16] Indeed, it was chiefly because of the new productive importance of trade for all sectors that an opposition began to materialize in the House of Commons, composed of both gentry and commercial bourgeoisie. The main aim of this group was to counteract the economic exactions of the Crown, but to do this was in effect to redress the balance of power between Crown and Parliament. The ultimate effect of the opposition was to precipitate, in the 1630s, a renewal of the drive toward absolutism which had begun with the early Tudors, and of whose enforced curtailment the rule of king in parliament, the mixed monarchy so scorned by Hobbes, was the very sign. It was the renewal of this contradictory drive which united the opposition against sundry forms of political regulation, leading to the breakdown of the government in 1640, and finally to the revolution itself.[17]

It is impossible and unnecessary to give a detailed account of the political developments of the revolutionary period. What is more important is to outline the general form according to which politics is here understood. From any properly Marxist point of view, I think, the emergence of the capitalist mode of production constitutes the ultimate context in relation to which the revolutionary events of the mid-seventeenth century are to be grasped; more precisely, emergent capitalism *determines* the political developments of the period, not in the sense of causing them, but rather in the sense of providing the limiting context to which the revolutionary phenomena must be seen as necessarily responding, and thus in terms of which they attain their ultimate intelligibility. The crisis of political power that culminated with the breakdown of government in 1640 should be understood as a result of the contradiction between capitalist social relations and a neo-feudal form of political rule; and the forces that created the conditions for the parliamentary opposition may likewise be taken as the ultimate motor of the revolutionary attack on the monarchy that followed, and that wound up securing the political entrenchment of capitalism even if it failed on its own terms.[18]

These terms were of course mainly religious ones. The process by which the revolutionary nature of the conflict between Crown and Parliament revealed itself was one in which religion came to the fore as its single prime mover. "Religion was not the thing at first contested for," said Cromwell, "but God brought it to that issue at last."[19] We ought not to disregard the sense of fatality in his words. There is a strong sense in which the political revolution was *made* by the cultural revolution that preceded it and which provided the very conditions for revolutionary class praxis.[20] In order to understand the transition to capitalism for which the revolution at midcentury represents the single most decisive agent and point of no return, we must attempt to understand what Milton called reformation as a crucial ruptural force in that process. But to do this last, we must grasp Protestantism not only as the consciously determining agent of revolution, but also as the unconscious and determined condition of the transition to a secular culture. The study of the socioeconomic transition should be complemented by a study of Protestantism as the paradoxical revolutionary agent of the co-determining ideological transition.[21]

There is no body of Marxist literature on the Protestant transition comparable to that on the socioeconomic transition. The main question to which any such study must address itself, I think, is that of how the unity of religious ideology, or what I call *theology*, was dissolved, and hence how the dominance of ideology itself was eclipsed.[22] I work with the supposition in the following study, and attempt to prove in the case of Milton, that this dissolution and restructuring of religion may best be understood in terms of the appearance of a discrete ethical framework within theology, and that the basis for this appearance was the new socioeconomic situation of emergent capitalism, in which the means of production was formally subsumed under capital, and thus in which the form of bourgeois civil society itself, with its abstract interpersonal relations between producers now thrown upon their own devices, began to exert its force.

The notion that the ethical orientation of religion was crucial in the secularization of the world is of course not an original one. It was one of Weber's main contributions to have emphasized the role of the Protestant ethic in undermining Protestantism itself.[23] He did this from what we may call an immanent point of view; that is, he attempted to understand the process of secularization from within the logic of religion itself. This, I think, is what makes his study so useful, even as it marks off its limits. For Weber, the Protestant ethic was a way of theorizing and responding to the new immediacy of God's relation to the individual subject or believer, of Providence become predestination. The Reformation eventually came to terms with predestination by domesticating it, by channeling it into the worshipper's everyday activity, whose events thus became signs or indices of the believer's spiritual state and hence of God's will. Protestantism "sanctified" everyday life and work in order to mediate the relation between man and God and thus re-secure Providential stability in quotidian ritual. The main support for this displacement of predestination was economic activity: vocational work assumed a new and privileged function in insuring the stability of the true believer. By what was then an inevitable paradox, work secretly became the bearer of free will, creating what was in effect a new form of human autonomy. The Protestant valorization of work proves to be one with "the spirit of capitalism;" it determines the rationalization of economic activity which, for Weber, constitutes capitalism. Thus the opposition between predestination and free will encoded in the Protestant ethic is set in historical motion: the vocational work that begins by signaling God's will ends as the support of the rational capitalist subject's freedom. It performs the function of historical mediation between two radically different forms of social life, between what are in Marxist terms two different modes of production.

From a Marxist point of view, Weber's interpretation of Protestantism is hampered only by its basis in an oversimple equation of rational activity with capitalism. This equation permits Weber's polemic against the Marxist axiom of the determination of consciousness by social being, for it leads him to say that Protestantism determined capitalism because it *preceded* it.[24] A comprehensive correction of Weber's anti-Marxist bias would have to undertake an examination of the social origins of Protestantism, which are to be found in the breakup of the feudal system. But for our present purposes it is enough to argue that whatever the determining conditions of Protestantism, the Protestant ethic can only represent the mediating contradiction between two modes of production if the material conditions for such mediation are in place. If the conditions for the competition of individual capitals do not exist, if capitalist relations of production are not at least incipient, then the Protestant ethic can hardly hale them into the world, but will rather remain more or less seamlessly imbedded in the theological framework which determines it. This was the case, for example, in Sweden, where Protestantism, far from determining the advent of capitalism, was rather put in the service of an absolutist state machine.[25] Only when a discrete socioeconomic level inheres in the relations of production to serve as a vehicle for its stabilizing signification can the repressed dialectic between predestination and free will, in which predestination serves as the basis for the will which then proves it, assume the revolutionary transitional function of lifting the capitalist subject free of its theological hindrances.

Such, I believe, is the function this dialectic assumes in Milton, who lived out the clash between predestination and free will in an extreme form, and who wrote his best poetry from it. Milton, more than most Puritans, believed in predestination and free will at the same time; it should come as no surprise, therefore, that this contradiction is clearly manifest in his notion of poetic "work," or what we might call his vocationalist poetics. On the one hand, Milton was orthodox in believing that God predestined his saints and inspired his true poets: his early conception that the ambitious poet must be pure in every part, must make his life a true poem, made ascetic purity into the sign of God's inspiration. On the other hand, he was a heretic in holding, with Arminius, that the individual believer played a decisive part in saving his own soul, and that the true poet spun his verse from his soul by a total act of will, out of a kind of natural inner necessity. The myth, latent in Milton's early chastity fetish,[26] of organic poetry, a poetry attached to the poet's bodily state as if by an umbilical cord, is primarily an Arminian willful myth, a poetic of total responsibility and control.

Milton's Arminianism has long been recognized to be peculiar, not just for being linked to a poetic vocation, but also for being imbedded in a private heretical system or complex (Arminianism, antitrinitarianism, materialism, thnetopsychism, monism).[27] I would argue that the main purpose of this complex is to give adequate figuration to the dialectic between predestination and free will, and that monism, the doctrine of the utter unity of the soul with the body, is the logical nucleus of this figuration. We can attain a clearer sense of what monism consists of as a doctrine, and see how it addresses the antinomy of predestination and free will, if we consult Milton's direct exposition of this doctrine in chapter 7 of *De Doctrina*. But before turning to this chapter, I would note that monism should in fact be understood, in my opinion, less as a "bodiless" doctrine than as what Raymond Williams has called a "structure of feeling," a living response to determinate social conditions. Only when grasped as a lived structure will the ultimate significance of monism, as a necessarily imperfect "semantic figure" for the experience of emergent capitalism, appear.[28]

In chapter 7, having argued that God created the world "not out of nothing but out of himself," out of a primal matter which "originated from God at some point in time" before the creation, Milton is led to address the questions of the relation between body and soul, and of the origin of the soul.[29] The argument here evolves out of and extends the argument for materialism. First Milton proves from Scripture that God created soul and body at the same time, making a point of this "in case anyone should think that souls . . . really existed beforehand." In proving that soul and body were created at the same time, he also proves his monism, which he carefully explains:

When God breathed that breath of life into man, he did not make him a sharer in anything divine, any part of the divine essence, as it were. He imparted to him only something human which was proportionate to divine virtue ... when man had been created in this way, it is said, finally: *thus man became a living soul.* Unless we prefer to be instructed about the nature of the soul by heathen authors, we must interpret this as meaning that man is a living being, intrinsically and properly one and individual. He is not double or separable: not, as is commonly thought, produced from and composed of two different and distinct elements, soul and body. On the contrary, the whole man is the soul, and the soul the man: a body, in other words, or individual substance, animated, sensitive, and rational. (pp. 317–18)

The logic of the argument now requires Milton to clarify his materialist concept of creation by working out a view of the generation of the soul which will square both with the primacy of matter and the indivisibility of body and soul. Thus he proceeds to argue – first from Scripture, and then from reason – that "the human soul is generated by the parents in the course of nature, and not created daily by the immediate act of God." He is most specific as to the mode of the soul's generation in his rational arguments – especially in his resort to the Aristotelian-scholastic notions of the soul as the form of matter and of an informing "power of matter":

> By what sort of law could we make a soul answerable for a crime which Adam committed, when that soul was never in Adam and never came from him? Add to this Aristotle's argument, which I think a very strong one indeed, that if the soul is wholly contained in all the body and wholly in any given part of that body, how can the human seed, that intimate and most noble part of the body, be imagined destitute and devoid of the soul of the parents, or at least of the father, when communicated to the son in the act of generation? Nearly everyone agrees that all form – and the human soul is a kind of form – is produced by the power of matter. (pp. 321–2)

The "power of matter" is an inherent informing potency put by God into the original matter (which is conceived as passive substance and not as the abstract, pure potency of the Aristotelians[30]); after having taken up lodging, it would seem to acquire a kind of relative autonomy, so that the power of matter itself shapes the body-soul: "the human form, like all other forms," is "propagated and produced as a result of that power which God had implanted in matter" (p. 325). God does not intervene in the process of propagation. The power of matter is, then, a category crucial to Milton's notion that soul and body are one, that not only the soul is "for God." At the same time, precisely in assuring Milton's monism, it secures the integrity of the theological subject vis-à-vis God. In the power of matter, God's will makes itself the basis for, and creates in the form of a potency, man's free will. The power of matter thus represents the abstract activity through which predestination and free will are rendered into discrete forces, through which the human soul cancels predestination in proving it.

The theological importance of monism resides, I think, in this crucial separation. Monism represents an attempt to think of the soul in its relation to God (and secondarily to nature and the fall) in a way such that freedom of the will might definitely be preserved. I do not wish here to go into the contradictions in which Milton immures himself in setting forth his materialism and monism; it should be obvious that the doctrine of monism, in retaining the categories of matter and spirit, body and soul, necessarily perpetuates the division that it attempts to abolish. Suffice it to say, then, that the doctrinal apparatus involved provides no very adequate theory of the soul's freedom. Neither would it seem to do justice to that *feeling* for the subject or self which may be inferred as motivating the conceptual development of monism.

But one of the curious things about this apparatus as a way of thinking about the soul is that, considered seriously, it confesses its own inadequacy precisely insofar as it is merely an intellectual apparatus; it asks to be taken, indeed, as something like a "structure of feeling." For the informing power of matter generates the whole man, both body and soul; the humors of the body and the faculties of the intellect are thus indissolubly linked, and true self-knowledge implies a self-conscious harmony of body and soul, of the whole man through all his senses and faculties; it approximates to poetic knowledge, which in Milton's terms (and he weighed his words) is "simple, sensuous and passionate."[31] One gains a clear vision, at this point, of how Milton's sense of vocation – expressed earlier in his career in the chastity cult and in an emphasis on temperance in general, in the desire to make his entire life a poem – is intimately bound up with his monism, and how monism itself is geared toward the production of organic poetry.

Why should the poet's defense against predestination take the form of such an organic poetic? How can Milton feel the cumbersome doctrine of monism to be at all satisfactory or coherent? These are primary questions, whose answers I can hope fully to provide only in the complex argument of the chapters that follow. But it will perhaps prove useful, at this point, to offer a necessarily abstract and skeletal résumé of these "solutions", and to anticipate the course of the argument, which moves, roughly speaking, from considerations of ideology to considerations of form, or – somewhat more precisely – from a focus on the form of ideology (in *Areopagitica*) to a focus on the ideology of form (in *Paradise Lost*).

In brief, then: I hold that Milton's monism testifies to the existence of that discrete socioeconomic level which was ignored by Weber, or in other words to the emergence of capitalism in England. To put this somewhat more precisely and fully: I argue that Milton's organicism of the soul seemed forceful because it responded to the commodification of the individual subject's powers by emergent capitalism, and marked what was in effect a paradoxical *identification* with the capitalist market. It was by identifying the soul's powers with those of the free commodity, by likening its creative movement to the movement of the integral market formally instated by capitalism, that Milton felt himself free. The privileged Miltonic work in which to study such identification and its contradictory effects is *Areopagitica*, with its argument for limited deregulation of the market in books. I contend in chapter 2 that Milton's strongest case against licensing identifies the movement of book produc-tion or authorship with the movement of the free market, a conflation that is crucial both to the uncentering or fragmentation of the tract's rhetorical subject and to the crystallization of an ethical problematic.

Part II delineates the structure of this problematic and situates it in its ideological context. The central point to be made in this section is that the advent of this identificatory ethical problematic brings with it a new form of narrative figuration for the subject, in which the commodity or commodified body serves as the subject's secret vehicle. According to this "possessive individualist" narrative, the subject represents the body at once as objective sign and as sheer subjective agency: in the same movement, the subject distances itself from the body, making the body represent what it *lacks*, and yet figures itself in terms of its immediate unity with bodily forces, in terms of possession. This narrative represen-tation is curiously neutral; the givenness of the initial possessive movement permits no questions to arise as to the adequacy of narrative representation to its referent. I hold that this neutral narrative not only

14 *Milton: a study in ideology and form*

institutes commodity reification into the sphere of the unsuspecting subject, but also attempts to cancel, through the very neutrality of possession, the distancing of the subject from itself determined by that reification. Milton's monistic poetic repeats this paradoxical narrative valorization of abstract bodily immediacy, and thus might be seen as a version of a possessive individualist poetic: in defending against pre-destination, it also defends against the abstraction of the subject's powers determined by emergent capitalism.

But this latter defense is no longer a strictly theological defense carried out in the name of a collective organization (the church); it is rather a psychological-ethical defense carried out in the name of individual freedom and concreteness. The appearance of such an ethical possessive individualist narrative finally spells the eclipse of theology as *the* ideology, the dominant and encompassing problematic, in the ideological formation. This is not, of course, to say that theology disappears; it obviously does not, and has not. Instead, its structural place in the total social and ideological framework is modified, and undergoes a relative marginalization. The master code or necessarily controlling ideology of *theology* turns into *religion,* with its psychological and ethical motivations and justifications.

Finally, I hope to indicate in what follows the relation of Milton's ideology, or of the form of this ideology, to literary form. It is indeed one of my main concerns to study the formal effects of the moment of ideological transition in Milton's work, and I do this by focusing, especially in the analysis of *Paradise Lost* in Part III, on Milton's use or practice of *genre.* The results of this part of the study do not lend themselves to concentrated summary; but – especially given the practical nature of the generic criticism in these chapters – a word concerning the general theory of genre with which I am working will perhaps be welcome.

The critics to whom I am most heavily indebted for this theory are Terry Eagleton and Fredric Jameson. In Eagleton's *Criticism and Ideology,* genre is theorized as an essential element in the literary "means of production," providing both raw material and technical "machinery" to the process of narrative construction.[32] But while genre may seem neutral or indeterminate to the writer, it nonetheless comes to him preformed and possessed of determinate meaning. In other words, it is *ideological* by its very nature. I take this to mean, with Jameson, that genres always bear the mark of their origins upon them, that they testify in their very form to an original relation to a definite social situation or mode of production.[33] When we speak of the ideology of a genre or generic system, we are speaking of the formal remnants of an original relation, which can finally only be understood and specified through a reconstruction of the relation between genre and its native social situation. So it is that in order to consider Milton's resurrection of classical epic, I am led, in Part III, to discuss the "original" determination of classical epic by the slave mode of production.

The generic ideology uncovered by such a reconstruction is not, of course, simply a constant: it does not exist in some immutable realm "above" its later incarnations. Rather this ideology, as rendered free-floating and quasi-eternal by the autonomy of the generic institution, is necessarily worked upon and modified by subsequent generic renderings or productions. It is always a question, then, in any given generic analysis, of uncovering within the form itself the intersection of at least two ideologies or ideological constructs. Thus I argue that *Paradise Lost* modifies and transgresses against the form of classical epic in the very attempt at re-embodying its spirit. It does this by introducing the form of the possessive individualist narrative, with its psychological-ethical orientation, into the more politically and humanistically oriented narrative of epic. It is in this formal sense that I would see *Paradise Lost* as the epic of emergent capitalism.

At a still more general formal level, I argue that the appearance of an individual-ethical problematic works to set the various generic "means of production" off from the subject as abstract forms of fixed representation. Genres are thus picked up and used as if from a distance by the possessive individualist poet; they are converted into meta-genres, and made to serve as vehicles for the subject's fragmented narrative force. Aesthetic forms of narrative are thus marked by the same contradiction that we have seen to exist within the subject-narrative of possessive individualism. Meta-genres represent, on the one hand, a reification of genre, a casting of generic form as something existing over against the writing subject and to be "used" by him. Yet, on the other hand, the very "use" of genre as a sign of abstract power attempts to overcome the division between the subject and its generic representations by making these latter peculiarly the subject's own. Insofar as this defense against generic reification is understood to be a representative one, the subject's attempt to triumph over genre may be understood as a symbolic collective act; insofar, that is, as meta-genre becomes a new genre in its own right, then it may be said to redress the abstract isolation of the subject in its very form as a collective means of representation. It is at this point that the code of collective agency can be seen to rejoin that of determination, and Milton's poem appears to assert the force of cultural revolution.

PART I

Revolution in a pamphlet

2
Areopagitica: rhetoric, ethics, and the dislocation of the subject

Areopagitica is in many respects exceptional among Milton's tracts - not least for its strategic acuteness. Written in late 1644, during the crucial period in which the "win the war" party was coming to dominance in Parliament, it responds to the exigencies of its political context more subtly and perhaps more comprehensively than any other of his pamphlets. For this reason, and more especially because its strategic acuteness conditions the "release" of Miltonic ideology in a relatively "pure" or "raw" state, making possible a more or less unmediated, secular reading of the monistic ideologeme, *Areopagitica* is a privileged text, a natural starting point, for a Marxist analysis of Milton. That is why I begin with it here.

But to understand Milton's strategy and its consequences, we cannot, of course, look simply to *Areopagitica* itself. We must begin by describing briefly the tract's context of intervention, which is both political and biographical, or (to put it in the terms Milton would have used) domestic and civil. In 1643–44, the basic question facing the parliamentary party was whether to endeavor to negotiate with the king or to defeat him in open combat. This question came more and more clearly to be one with the question of toleration, and was in large measure fought out in the toleration dispute. For it appeared impossible, at least to such as Cromwell, to defeat the king without invoking the aid of heretical elements of the population located, for the most part, in small crafts and trade. The toleration dispute gave mediation, then, to a dispute over the possibility of class hegemony, or in other words over the ability of

Parliament to affiliate itself with heretical factions and still dominate them.[1]

The Licensing Act of 1643, against which *Areopagitica* is written, had as its main end the scotching of the spate of radical texts that appeared upon the effective disappearance of the censorship. Its passage represented a minor triumph for the Presbyterian over the opposing Independent or "win the war" party. But neither party could control Parliament by itself, so coalition politics was in order. The largest single parliamentary faction or group "in the middle" was that of the Erastians, who were amenable to winning the war, on the whole, but not to the separation of church from state which would likely ensue on victory if the radicals played a major part.[2]

Milton's procedure in *Areopagitica* responds to the parliamentary impasse, and is shaped by an immediate political strategy: that of splitting the Erastians in Parliament off from the Presbyterians and winning them over to the tolerationist camp.[3] This strategy, which forbade Milton the use of *jure divino* arguments such as he had relied on in the antiepiscopal tracts and was forced to resort to in *The Doctrine and Discipline of Divorce*, can in fact be seen as partial explanation for Milton's selection of the Licensing Act as the occasion for entering the toleration controversy. For this selection locates the tract in the civil terrain, and enables Milton to bypass the questions of the divine institution of the church and church doctrine, and of the relation between state and church; he thus steers clear of the Separatist argument (which would of course alienate the Erastians), takes for granted the unity of the national interest with that of the church, and tends to imply that nation and church are in fact, and should be, one.

At the same time, as Arthur Barker has shown, Milton's marital problem, and the turn in his intellectual development that it induced, also dictate the manner of his intervention in the toleration dispute. For the argument in *Areopagitica* furthers the trend begun in *The Doctrine and Discipline*, where emphasis is placed on natural as opposed to divine law, or more properly, where divine law is made to accord with the dictates of nature.[4]

This peculiar conjuncture of domestic and civil straits leads Milton to cast his argument in primarily ethical, or ethical-epistemological, terms: the focus of his principal argument is on the conditions of ethical knowledge, and on the natural process of ethical cognition that he spontaneously represents as providing those conditions. My own principal argument in this chapter, maintained in its very form, will be that this focus determines the nature of the orator or rhetorical subject in *Areopagitica* as a chief point of interest in itself. Keeping Milton's strategy well in mind, let us now turn our attention to the rhetoric of his tract.

Disruptive heresy: Milton's soulful books as monistic figures

Areopagitica is one of the few Miltonic tracts to keep before the reader a fairly well-defined argumentative structure; here, at least, one's attention is prevented from being absorbed by the periodic intricacies of Milton's style. We may read this structural definiteness as testimony to the strategic aim proper to the coalitional moment. Each of the pamphlet's four main arguments would seem calculated to sway the Erastians; and the very form of its discourse – the traditional and civil one of the classical oration – seems peculiarly suited to the advocates of a strong state. Nonetheless the strategic overarching argument is not left to do its work alone, but is rather supplemented by a series of extremely dense passages scattered through the tract which give it summary and pregnant expression, crystallizing Milton's entire position. These summaries are often located at critical junctures; for example, each of the four basic arguments is clinched by one. I wish to concentrate especially on two such passages: the defense of books that serves as the keynote to the argument proper, and the description of the "true warfaring Christian," which projects in its clearest form the process of ethical cognition mentioned above.

The former of these passages follows directly on the short program (in rhetorical terms, the partition) with which Milton concludes his introductory address to Parliament. "I shall now attend with such a Homily," he says, "as shall lay before ye, first the inventors of it to bee those whom ye will be loath to own; next what is to be thought in generall of reading . . .; and that this Order avails nothing to the suppressing of scandalous, seditious, and libellous Books . . . Last, that it will be primely to the discouragement of all learning, and the stop of Truth."[5] Rather, however, than taking up straightway with the first part of this homily, Milton introduces his whole topic by telling what is to be thought of books in general. The audience is tacitly widened to include the general public as he modulates into a mode resembling the essay:

> I deny not, but that it is of greatest concernment in the Church and Commonwealth, to have a vigilant eye how Bookes demeane themselves, as well as men; and thereafter to confine, imprison, and do sharpest justice on them as malefactors. For Books are not absolutely dead things, but doe contain a potencie of life in them to be as active as that soule was whose progeny they are; nay they do preserve as in a violl the purest efficacie and extraction of that living intellect that bred them. I know they are as lively, and as vigorously productive, as those fabulous Dragons teeth; and being sown up and down, may chance to spring up armed men. And yet on the other hand unlesse warinesse be us'd, as good almost kill a Man as kill a good Book; who kills a Man kills a reasonable creature, Gods Image; but hee who destroyes a good Booke, kills reason it selfe, kills the Image of God, as it were in the eye. Many a man lives a burden to the Earth; but a good Booke is the pretious life-blood of a master spirit, imbalm'd and treasur'd up on purpose to a life beyond life. 'Tis true, no age can restore a life, whereof perhaps there is no great losse; and revolutions of ages doe not oft recover the losse of a rejected truth, for the want of which whole Nations fare the worse. We should be wary therefore what persecution we raise against the living labours of publick men, how we spill that season'd life of man preserv'd and stor'd up in Books; since we see a kinde of homicide may be thus committed, sometimes a martyrdome, and if it extend to the whole impression, a kinde of massacre, whereof the execution ends not in the slaying of an elementall life, but strikes at that ethereall and fift essence, the breath of reason it selfe, slaies an immortality rather then a life. (pp. 492–3)

The paragraph contains the gist of the argument to follow. To preface the four-part argument with such a definition is to shift attention, for the moment, from the rhetorical apparatus outlined above to the inherent nature of books themselves, which thus appear to dictate, to incorporate in their very substance, the principles of their own regulation. But the definition also renders prominent the figure of the orator, whose impassioned pronouncements indicate an active knowledge that exists independently and as if out of the reach of the structure of discourse by and through whose orderly movement the oratorical persona itself is supported and realized. Thus the definitive formation of the oratorical ethos occurs at a moment of argumentative overflow – in a place, that is, where we meet with more argument than we expected. This may perhaps be laid down as a kind of law operating throughout the tract: excessive argument marks the spot where ethos becomes prominent.

But the moment of excess in which ethos is made prominent also marks the spot in which this ethos reveals itself as having two dimensions or levels. For the reasoning in the above passage is excessive, not only because it had not been called for by the program, but also, as has been implied, in its relative intensity. Oratorical passion is so strong as to suggest a rift in strategic ethos even as it foregrounds that ethos as such; passion serves as the rhetorical support for a discrete level of intensely personal ethical feeling that I will here designate as "self-validating" ethos.[6] The official ethos that is founded in the structured movement of the oration and apparently constitutes its stable center is suddenly overshadowed by the emergence of the more passionate self-validating ethos, whose sign and chief testimony is an influx of rhetorical vigor that resists methodical discourse. It is important to stress that this rhetorical movement, by calling into question the adequacy of methodical discourse to the tract's lofty argument, does not supplant the official ethos but opens up a rift within it. Official ethos does not abdicate its function in the face of rhetorical passion, but is a constant presence in the tract, even when, as in the passage at hand, it is momentarily thrown from the apparent center of the discourse. Thus the literary subject or total ethos of the tract is neither the strategic nor the self-validating ethos, but is constituted by the mutual articulation of these separate rhetorical levels.

The "decentering" movement through which the self-validating ethos is brought to the fore is most evident in the three sentences that make up the first period in the paragraph quoted above. Milton writes this period for what seems mainly a strategic reason: he wants to remove the possibility that his audience misinterpret his aim as that of arguing against all censorship whatever, not only licensing. Since the Erastians were in favor of a strong state, such misinterpretation would be fatal to the tract's political success. From a later historical vantage point, then, the period seems to be introduced to avert that liberal misreading – made so frequently, as John Illo has argued, by subsequent critics of Milton – according to which *Areopagitica* represents the prototypical statement of the case for freedom of thought and speech.[7] But Erastian suspicion and liberal misreading are to some degree encouraged by the curious eccentricity of Milton's prose. This eccentric movement manifests itself in the case at hand as a tendency for the definition of books offered in the second and third sentences of the period to "absolutize" itself – to detach itself, that is, from its immediate rhetorical context, whose purpose is to establish the power of books to be malefactors, and to create a context within this context, an ethic beneath or discontinuous with the ethical motives of the rhetorical moment. For books, as they become vigorous through the intensifying permutations of the definition, come to incorporate in themselves a counterargument that anticipates the warning against the unwary persecution of books with which the remainder of the paragraph is occupied.

> For Books are not absolutely dead things, but doe contain a potencie of life in them to be as active as that soule was whose progeny they are; nay they do preserve as in a violl the purest efficacie and extraction of that living intellect that bred them. I know they are as lively, and as vigorously productive, as those fabulous Dragons teeth; and being sown up and down, may chance to spring up armed men. (p. 492)

The liveliness and productiveness of books is restated in successively more extreme senses: from being as active as that soul was that bred them, in the second clause of the first sentence, books come to be identified, in the next clause, with the quintessence of their authors' powers; then, in the second sentence, where classical citation is aptly used in order to convey their potential force across gaps of historical time, books manifest a seemingly autonomous power. Indeed, they conclude – after being metaphorically embodied in the citation of the dragon's teeth which was introduced as an analogy – by generating men. Thus the figure with which the definition began, that of books as the offspring of men, is turned inside out, and this reversal, this cyclical movement, reinforces the tendency of the definition to jerk itself loose from the subordinate place in the argument that it seemed initially to have been allotted, isolating itself to form an as-if self-enclosed – eminently quotable – whole. The reference to the dragon's teeth does continue, at a certain level, the ostensible rhetorical function of the definition, by exemplifying the danger of books left alone. But this function, attributable to strategic ethos, is scarcely felt, not only because the ambiguity of the citation tends to obscure it,[8] but mainly because its exemplification of the potentially harmful effects (political rather than moral) of books' power is consumed by what is felt as an intensely ethical valorization of these powers in and for themselves. Such is the self-referential character of the movement here that the citation is hardly felt as a public gesture, as an external allusion to a commonly possessed tradition, at all. Instead, the demonstrative "those" seems to single out an item activated in the artificial orator's memory, and the assimilation of books to teeth in the final clause ("and being sown up and down . . .") suggests a mental association previously or spontaneously formed. Thus the citation functions primarily as "personal" citation, and imposes itself most forcefully at the level of self-validating ethos.

One feels, already, that this militant ethical ethos *motivates* the more comprehensive and containing strategic ethos in its progress through the tract as a whole. Nonetheless, self-validating ethos remains a separate category, and exists at a level discontinuous with the programmatic argument. The measured, careful syntax at the beginning of the next sentence ("And yet on the other hand unless warinesse be us'd"), reminding one of the subordinate position of this definition in the flow of the argument, reinstates the official ethos, and highlights the discontinuity. For the impression given the reader as he encounters the caution against unwary censorship is that this argument has not only been made already, but has been made in more radical fashion; and only in those eccentric passages which follow in the paragraph does the argument in fact catch up with itself.

The practice of excessive definition and eccentric periodization is of course not an anomalous phenomenon. Both traits are characteristic of the anti-Ciceronian style that emerged in the late sixteenth century, and which Morris Croll has argued was geared toward the expression of a qualitatively new and more complicated sense of individual and social reality.[9] Its loose periodization made possible the simultaneous articulation of distinct registers or areas of experience whose unantagonistic relation was no longer provided by a coherent hegemonic religion. Indeed, it may be said to be in the nature of the eccentric or imbalanced period to take on a momentum of its own, and to express in dislocated form the fractured referent to which it responds. As such a monolithic agent in its own right, the eccentric or anti-Ciceronian style may be taken as a privileged expression of Renaissance prose, in which what must be called sheer periodic writing characteristically assumes a governing formal function, and thus in which the very concepts of individual subjectivity and authority are constantly exposed as problematical and secondary.[10] If there is a paradigmatic generic vehicle of eccentric prose, it must be the Renaissance anatomy, that paradoxical compendium, at once scholastic and empirical, which methodically and to the point of tedium sets about the dispersal of whatever scraps and fragments of knowledge and reflection the writing subject has previously shored against its ruins. I will argue later that the text of *Areopagitica* partially realizes the anatomy form, but would emphasize here in advance its compromising of this genre. While *Areopagitica* does know its anatomical moment, the gravity of its political aim and oratorical conventions prevents the removal of the subject from center stage. Insofar as the eccentric style appears as an agent in its own right, it works to push Milton's political desire from its strategic channel and to the "left" in making apparent what I must still at this point call his personal-ethical desire.[11] The absolutizing or self-referential movement of eccentric writing renders into extreme form both Milton's radicalism and his "individualism," which are thus revealed at this level to represent one and the same impulse. The rhetorical register of the self-validating ethos exposes Milton's politics in their most scandalous dimension for the contemporary Erastian audience, and in what is generally taken as their most liberal aspect by the modern reader. Anti-Ciceronian syntax can most clearly be seen as the carrier and producer of this radical yet isolationist impulse in the closing period of the above quotation: what begins as a measured concluding statement ("We should be wary therefore what persecution we raise") gives way to a rapid series of subordinate and appositional clauses, each exceeding the last in expressing the sinfulness of the suppression of a good book, which culminates with the unnatural image of the suppressed book as a slain immortality.

Thus far the self-validating ethos has been described as an absolutizing rhetorical movement which determines and is one with a peculiarly ethical or personal content, a content that one feels to have a pressing relevance for Milton himself. It is now time to begin asking what motivates this ethos, what it is that produces the sense of personal urgency in these excessive passages.

We need not look far for a partial explanation of the personal urgency.

For it seems clear that Milton's sense of vocation – seldom far beneath the surface in any of the early tracts – expresses itself in the valorization of good books. The hopes and fears attending on this sense of vocation must have been particularly acute during this period, when Milton had apparently thrown all his efforts into the cool medium of prose after having been unable, in the midst of the revolutionary situation he entered on returning to England in 1639, to make progress on any major poetic work. It is these hopes and fears which are registered within and against the more politic official ethos to yield the passionate eccentricity observed in the above passage. The one great work which was Milton's early and constant ambition through life speaks here before its time, and protests its worth.

But Milton's vocational idealism, while it helps explain the urgency manifest in the defense of books, can hardly explain by itself an important aspect of the form this defense takes: its characteristic figuration of spontaneous "embodying" or incorporation, which itself seems to kindle Milton's imagination and spur on the eccentric rhetorical movement. We notice, for instance, that, in the closing period of the above passage, the clause in which the figure of incorporation is reintroduced ("how we spill that season'd life of man preserv'd and stor'd up in Books") seems both to begin the movement into eccentricity and away from the balanced period, and to trigger the rapid series of subordinate clauses that follows in which the body metaphor is extended and purified into an immortality. Similarly, in the period where a good book becomes the incarnation of reason, the particularization of the metaphor results in the argument's exceeding itself: "as good almost kill a Man as kill a good Book," Milton says at the beginning of this period, but by the time the good book has become the eye of the image of God, it seems to be the more indispensable of the two, or rather to deny the propriety of any such implied comparison of value. We will return to the question of the relation between these corporeal figures and the rhetorical movement, but at present it is necessary to focus more precisely on the figurative activity itself.

This is not easy to do, since the figures used to define books in the quoted paragraph are curiously indefinite, characteristically hovering between metonymy and metaphor, or shifting from one into the other. Thus, to return to the first period in the above passage, an originally metonymic relationship between books and their creators (in which books-as-progeny represent or equal their authors) is transformed into a metaphoric relationship (in which books embody their creators' living powers), with the analogy between books' powers and souls' powers (according to which books are "as active as" souls) serving as a kind of bridge effecting the transition between these two figures. The point of the figurative work set in play in the eccentric movement of the prose in this place appears to be to transform a metonymy into a metaphor, and thus to literalize or defigure it, making books into the actual embodiment of creative energy.

The effect of this figurative process on the "imagery" of the passage is to render it correspondingly shifting and indefinite. The relationship between books themselves and the images used to define them is curiously elastic, is indeed something like what is in psychoanalysis called a transitivistic relationship, where the distinction between exteriority and interiority is constantly being eclipsed. The transition from analogy to metaphor, for instance, turns a relationship of likeness, in which books see themselves, so to speak, in the imagery, into a relationship of identity, in which books are incorporated in the imagery. This elasticity of relationship contributes to our impression that the successive corporeal images presented and re-presented by the language are in constant spontaneous motion. In fact – and this is not surprising, since Milton is clearly defending literary creation in defending books – the common denominator of the imagery must be defined as much in terms of its characteristic activity as in terms of the kinds of objects that fill this activity. For the objects that are at the root of the imagery remain either nebulous or indescribable. The chemical and birth metaphors, which tend to denote gradual processes rather than determinate objects, are not wholly picturable; while the vagueness of the two main vehicles – the seed and the human body – implies that these objects, too, are stages in a spontaneous activity immanent within them. The body, or the body-in-seed, remains, however, here and elsewhere the predominant image, serving a kind of coordinating function and affecting our experience of the entire range of figures in the tract.

This spontaneous activity manifests itself within the "images" or signifieds of the figures as a kind of insistent inner pressure: it is as if the referent of these signifieds, the body itself, were making its power felt. It may be that my immanent analysis has uncovered a tendency within all figuration; but I think the figuration of incorporation [12] is unique for projecting the force of the referent as strongly as it does, in such a dense and conflictual fashion, and for casting it predominantly in the form of a raw bodily movement. This movement features, in one version or another, a dialectic of container and contained, and seems to possess two polar moments: a metaphoric moment of condensation, in which an abstractly defined fullness is formed; and a metonymic moment of generation or dissemination, in which the full body disperses itself in fragments or breaks onto a new plane of existence. The book is a vial of concentrated energy possessed of its proper eschatology; it may erupt into new and comprehensive significance at any moment.

To describe the figures in the above passage is to indicate the quality of the figuration throughout *Areopagitica*. For in this as in other of Milton's tracts, one becomes aware while reading of a *network* of figuration, in which all figures are implicated. This figurative network has been studied in separate essays by Alan Price and John Evans.[13] Though I must emphasize that I do not mean by "figurative network" quite what they mean by "imagistic argument" (and I will return later to this difference), I do think that these critics have convincingly shown that there is an imagistic logic working in the tract to relate all figures into one complex. The prime source of this figural affiliation lies, as Evans has noted, in the "natural" activity which the figures body forth – that is, in the curiously vivid and indeterminate activity of the "imagery" which claims to represent the natural logic of things in themselves. The figure of the "field of this world," for instance, which sets the stage, in the most famous passage in the tract, for Milton's advocacy of an active knowledge of evil, naturalizes and renders more militant the quietistic apocalypticism implicit in Jesus' parable of the wheat and tares: it posits a process of conflictual definition in all external reality, and implies an informing principle at once plenary and disintegrative which is analogous to the vital principle incorporated by books in the keynote passage.[14] In the final part of the tract, where Milton widens his argument into a (qualified) defense of religious liberty, the figure of Truth reincarnates in successive appearances this sense of the dense vitality of external reality. The central passage of this section features the dissemination of Truth:

> Truth indeed came once into the world with her divine Master, and was a perfect shape most glorious to look on: but when he ascended, and his Apostles after him were laid asleep, then strait

> arose a wicked race of deceivers, who as that story goes of the
> *Ægyptian Typhon* with his conspirators, how they dealt with the
> good *Osiris*, took the virgin Truth, hewd her lovely form into a
> thousand peeces, and scatter'd them to the four winds. From that
> time ever since, the sad friends of Truth, such as durst appear,
> imitating the carefull search that *Isis* made for the mangl'd body of
> *Osiris*, went up and down gathering up limb by limb still as they
> could find them. (p. 549)

The use of the pagan myth to invigorate Milton's Protestant myth of
original catastrophe in the holy community renders the actual catastrophe, the dismemberment of Truth ("took the virgin Truth, hewd her
lovely form into a thousand peeces, and scatter'd them to the four winds"),
curiously attractive in itself. Again, the figurative activity appears to
valorize and detach itself from the ethical perspective which it has been
introduced to corroborate. This means that Truth itself, partly by its
association with pagan myth and partly by its being enfigured, seems to
contain a latent power: though the repetitive phrases in the last clause
("up and down," "limb by limb") connote a homogeneity in Truth's
dispersal, nonetheless there is the sense that any individual limb might
radically differentiate itself, might spring (like seed) to life, in any
moment.

   Truth appears in other forms in the latter part of the tract. The
corporeal figure tends to be grafted onto each of the major (commercial,
military, and light-dark) figurative patterns of the final section.[15] In a
period occurring just before the great vision of England "rousing herself
like a strong man after sleep, and shaking her invincible locks," the "waies
of Truth" are seen to be like the operations of the healthy body:

> For as in a body, when the blood is fresh, the spirits pure and
> vigorous, not only to vital, but to rationall faculties, and those in the
> acutest, and the pertest operations of wit and suttlety, it argues in
> what good plight and constitution the body is, so when the
> cherfulnesse of the people is so sprightly up, as that it has, not only
> wherewith to guard well its own freedom and safety, but to spare ... it
> betok'ns us ... entring the glorious waies of Truth and prosperous
> vertue destin'd to become great and honourable in these latter ages.
> (p. 557)

As a testimony to excessive energy, England's state of military and intellectual warfare is a sign of radical health in the body politic, and betokens great changes. The phrase "waies of *prosperous* vertue" introduces a commercial aspect into the organic and military contexts: the commercial situation which corresponds to a state of bodily health is one in which all the various conduits are flowing freely, in which circulation is at a maximum. At another point Milton complains of "the incredible losse, and detriment that this plot of licencing puts us to, more then if som enemy at sea should stop up all our hav'ns and ports, and creeks, it hinders and retards the importation of our richest Marchandize, Truth" (p. 548). The ways of Truth tend to be one, on this plane, with the ways of the "free" competitive market. That the movement of the market is naturally vigorous and free is implied by the necessity of stopping up all the possible avenues of Truth's entrance: Truth will come in by creeks if not by havens and ports.

I will return to this conflation of market with bodily power in a broader interpretive context later on. For now I will content myself with again posing, in simply personal terms, the question of what motivates the self-validating movement in which the entire figurative network from which I have just given a few examples plays a constitutive part. And here it seems legitimate to insist on the importance of the analogy between the self-validating register of Milton's text and the self-validating or isolationist aim of his theory of the soul. I would claim, indeed, that the peculiarly volatile figurative axis of this register, in which the raw force of book-bodies appears to dictate or coincide with their own repeated representation, is *motivated* by Milton's heretical representation of the body-soul dichotomy as a relationship of simple unity in which the body serves as a kind of literal metaphor for the soul. The natural activity posited by the network as its basis, and seemingly constitutive of eccentric self-validation itself, may be read as the figurative extension and displacement of Milton's heretical sense of the subject to all of reality. We may thus trade in the term "self-validating ethos" for the somewhat less cumbersome, if unfortunately esoteric, "monistic ethos."

It is perhaps appropriate at this moment of the argument to account for what may seem the esoteric nature of my own emphasis on Milton's monism. Arthur Barker argued some time ago for the importance of monism in Milton's thought, granting it a central place in the complex of his heresies.[16] Although I cannot do so in this study, I would want finally to argue over and above this that Milton's monism is part of a vital seventeenth-century ideologeme or cultural figure, which traverses the works of orthodox and nonorthodox writers alike (Donne, Herbert, Marvell, Hobbes, Bacon). Nonetheless the general significance of monism – both in Milton's works and in those of his approximate contemporaries – remains comparatively unstudied and undervalued. Part of my aim, then, is to begin to consider this significance, insofar as it is revealed in Milton's writing. Obviously a certain danger of distortion attends such a project. In the sections and chapters that ensue I have tried to avoid overemphasizing the theological figure of monism by contextualizing its role in terms of different (semantic or historical) frameworks. The reader will decide how far I have succeeded at this.

Let us return, now, to the keynote passage in defense of books and consider more closely how monism informs the text. Nowhere is the tract's profession of monism so clear as in this passage, which amounts not only to a displacement of Milton's monism but also to a secret argument for it. Milton's description of literary creation represents a displaced version of the generation of the soul, and the imagery of spontaneous incorporation that so vividly expresses his feeling for the sanctity of literary creation operates as a hidden metaphor for the potency of matter, that incorporating movement producing the body-soul itself.[17] The analogy that the creation of books bears to the creation of the soul is at some points detailed. We can see, for instance, that the "potency of life" which active spirits impart to books, occupies the place of the power of matter in creation. More important and interesting is the appearance of the human seed in both kinds of creation. In a passage from *De Doctrina* quoted above, Milton calls the human seed "that intimate and most noble part of the body." When he argues that books "preserve as in a violl the purest efficacie and extraction of that living intellect that bred them," he appears at first to be mixing chemical and birth metaphors; but the metaphors may not be so mixed as all that: "extraction," in all probability, literally refers to the human seed (the production of which is conceived in chemical terms). There is also a class connotation to the word (as in "of noble extraction"),[18] which thus compresses into little space the attitude toward the human seed expressed in *De Doctrina*.

Monism's individual soul thus impinges upon Milton's defense of books mainly through monistic connotation, which in its very density alludes to the substantiality of the subtext it displaces. The extreme compression of the monistic figure appears to recapitulate, at the level of the figurative "sign," the conflictual density that it projects at the level of the figurative referent, "beneath" the text. This impression is not simply a matter of multiple puns, but also of a high degree of "underground" figurative communication. The reference to seed in "extraction," for example, seems to spawn the citation of the "fabulous dragon's teeth," which spring up armed men and are thus human seeds of a sort. It would appear that part of the function of the rhetorical figure of gradual amplification or excessive definition lies in its allowing the imagery to take on a logic as if independent of syntax. Thus the libertine syntax, as carrier of the monistic imagery, contributes to the subversion of syntactic logic, and assists in producing the impression that Milton's "real" argument somehow exists beneath, and remains untouched by, the movement of the discourse itself.

Let us consider further this apparently mysterious impression. How can an argument seem to occur, or seem to wish to occur, *beneath* the discursive text in which it is made? The answer lies, I think, in the curiously "negative" implication of the figurative axis with the discursive argument, or in what we might alternatively call the non-relationality of the monistic ethos. The discursive argument from nature makes it clear that the spontaneous activity occurring throughout the tract at the figurative level is natural: the movement within figuration that we have described professes to be a natural logic. But at this level, at the level of the "imagistic argument," the argument of the tract is not *from* natural law, considered as a conceptualized system, but rather is constituted by the figurative movement of that law. The absolutizing tendency of this constitution splinters the text by positing a system of connections existing, not in an active, but in a predominantly *passive* sense. The figures do not implicate themselves in a coherent, patently designed network. They do not simply compose a second level of discursive argument, existing beneath and elucidating the "rational" one. Instead, it is more proper to say that the individual figures *are implicated* in a larger network. The figures do not look beyond themselves, and their self-regard results in a militantly anti-discursive system, a network punctuated by discrete units each of which communicates much the same message. The text of the tract is perforated by the monistic figuration and the subversive ethos that it helps to construct. It is precisely this subversion or perforation which is blurred over by both Evans and Price, whose essays, in their concern to show a coherent and quasi-discursive argument at the level of the imagery, remake the text according to New Critical canons. The figurative network does not run parallel to the superstructural argument, providing it with effective corroboration and a secondary level of quasi-discursive support. Rather that network exists at a level of textual reality different from that of the superstructural argument: it is actively anti-discursive. Thus the production of natural law at the figurative level tends to "deconstruct," at the same time that it supports, the superstructural argument (the argument from natural law), for this latter argument appears to be *reducible* to the anti-discursive level insofar as it is transparently motivated by it. The superstructural argument, that is, impresses us as being collapsible onto a subliminal argument – though it is in fact ineradicably different from that argument – and thus takes on a redundant aspect.

We have arrived here at a basic problem posed for criticism by Milton's prose, which K. G. Hamilton has well summarized in his statement that Milton's periods "jump up and down in one place."[19] In the prose before 1653, one often has the irritating sense that Milton repeats himself in each section of his argument, and that each such section expresses the same deep-lying mental set. What this amounts to is that Milton does not submit himself to discursive argument so readily as New Critical principles tend to require, with their emphasis on the necessary mutual qualification of all the elements of a literary work. The perforation effected by the figurative axis at the level of monistic ethos represents precisely an attempt to deny such mutual qualification. The breaks attempt to posit the text as an impulsive non-relational power, as the very force of signification. But this force itself is not distinguishable, I would argue, from a determinate *narrative* figuration of the subject. The ruptures which permit this narrative force to appear are paradoxically textual efforts to escape textual relationality, and thus to fulfill the dictum implied in Milton's definition of books by making the text an adequate stand-in for that autonomous "ethical ego" which it is precisely the purpose of Milton's monism to secure.

These efforts are paradoxical because it is obvious that the mutual qualification imposed by textuality cannot really be overcome. Thus, to return to the level of imagistic logic whose emergence is permitted by the libertine syntax, it is clear that syntax, even at the moment of its subversion by the figurative movement, does retain an importance, not as a system of constraints placed on this movement, but simply as the bearer of verbal time. For when the figures are read as symptoms of monism, it becomes apparent that an important function of the scheme of redefinition or amplification is to permit the metaphorization of metonymy by which the figurative referent itself appears as raw figuring power. In its sheer capacity as bearer of time, it permits the transformation of official natural law into a movement of discontinuous mediation, and thereby lets the book-body become its own justification.

Wider horizons: the Imaginary and emergent capitalism

Before turning to the form of Milton's ethic, the question of the motivation of the monistic ethos needs to be considered in a more general context.

The production of monism in the text of *Areopagitica* helps us see that Milton does not adopt into his theology the Aristotelian notions of the potency of matter and of the soul as form without changing them in the process. The Aristotelian view of the form-content relationship as the determinate imposition of *actus* on the pure and abstract potency of matter is transformed, in Milton, into something approaching an *immanent* view of form, where form is understood as evolving out of and expressing what has now become a determinate potency of matter, or in other words a content possessed of its own logic. It is not enough to say that this amounts to a secret Platonizing of Aristotle, without pointing out the specific traits and emphases of Milton's implicitly held version of the form-content relationship, which distinguish it from most Platonic or neo-Platonic theories of processional or emanational creation, as well as from the transcendent Aristotelian notion. These distinguishing traits are evident in the natural activity produced on the figurative plane. Logic of content, on the one hand, is imaged by that conflictual density seemingly inherent in the incorporating activity of the figurative referent. Form, on the other hand, depends for its existence as an entity independent of content on the gap emerging from this movement, which it was the business of the rhetorical amplification discussed above to express in exacerbated form. Thus form – whatever its own manner of operation, whatever its own process of self-definition – is nothing but content itself, distanced and displaced from its original locus.

Chronologically viewed, it is content "seasoned" with age and hence relatively autonomized. This autonomy frees the category of form or of the soul itself, and is therefore crucial for Milton.

When we see the monistic figuration in this light, it becomes the sign of a subjective experience of reality, indeed of a feeling for the subject itself, which cries out for explanation. Up to this point, we have tended implicitly to explain monistic ethos and figuration in mostly personal terms: the monism which we know to be Milton's personal philosophical solution to the theological problem of the soul's relation to God, receives more adequate – because more affective and hence personally satisfying – expression through the imagery and rhetoric of *Areopagitica*. Such personalist explanations themselves require explanation, and seem to point in two different directions. On the one hand, the materials in question seem to indicate a unique psychological – almost a bodily – experience on Milton's part, calling for interpretation in something like psychoanalytic terms. On the other hand, however, the feeling for the subject expressed in the monistic representation of the form or soul as immanent solicits an explanation in terms of some historical event or transformation, as a reflection of and response to which it may take on comprehensible meaning.

I do not intend here to attempt an extended psychoanalytic reading of *Areopagitica*, but only to indicate where such a reading might begin. I will simply suggest that the level of the text that I am calling monistic ethos enacts or re-presents what Lacan calls the Imaginary order – that preverbal axis or register of experience whose mode of entrance into or coordination with the Symbolic order (roughly, the order of language) fixes the subject as such, formalizing its relationship with the Real.[20] The Imaginary marks the initial stage of objectification, at which the body and its parts are libidinally invested and, as projected onto the external world, become perceptual apparatuses of a kind. Primary narcissism, aggressivity, and transitivism (i.e. childlike identification) come into being at this juncture; consequently, relationships in the Imaginary, if we may so speak of them, are characterized by a kind of loving violence, a will to absorb all definitions, all forms of otherness. In a textual or symbolic situation (which is always post-Imaginary), the mark of the Imaginary can be detected in any self-valorizing or absolutizing tendency, in any attempt to deny relationality. Thus the absolutizing movement of the monistic ethos, its disregard for the discursive argument, can be seen to be a properly Imaginary phenomenon, and the conflictual density, the militant plenary movement of the figurative network, appears to manifest the narcissistic-aggressivistic instincts inherent to this order.

This equation between the monistic ethos and the Imaginary register should provide support for my argument that the monistic ethos represents a discrete and unassimilable level of ethical feeling, a kind of incipient ethical ego. For the Imaginary order, in Lacan's scheme of things, is the basis of all ethics, since all ethical systems are grounded in and may be reduced to the narcissistic gesture by which one's own position is valorized and set off against that occupied by an abstract Other.[21] It would be idle at this point to use the monistic ethos to debunk the pretense made by the strategic argument of having "everyone's" interest at heart. Some such Imaginary pretense, it is clear, will be made by any text with an Imaginary component in it. Only when we raise the question of ethics to the political level, and ask what group or class the ethical "everyone" represents, is it useful to expose its pretense. We are already on our way toward politicizing Milton's ethic if we note a more interesting problem that is raised by the appearance of an Imaginary discourse within a strategic or consciously Symbolic language. This is the whole issue of the place of Imaginary "instincts" in the formation of the subject, that is, of the proper coordination of Imaginary and Symbolic orders. This question is raised at two levels. It is posed, on the one hand, simply by the problematical relation between the distinct rhetorical registers of monistic and strategic ethos, which, I am suggesting, correspond roughly to Imaginary and Symbolic orders. But it is also generated, from another angle, within monistic ethos itself. If what is going on in such moments of Milton's prose is a retreat to the Imaginary, it must be emphasized that this retreat or resurgence occurs in and through language or the Symbolic order, which, through the redefining process which unleashes the natural-corporeal impulse, appears to accommodate itself gradually to Imaginary logic, enabling a kind of replay of the drama by which the Imaginary enters into the Symbolic. The end of this drama, which we saw before to be the reconstitution of the gap by which form (or the soul) achieves its freedom, now also appears as the reconstitution of that gap which marks, for Lacan, the subject's entrance into language – as if to remake that gap, knowingly and properly, were to remake the subject in its true form, that is, in apocalyptic or revolutionary guise.

For it is a question, in *Areopagitica*, of the nature of the revolutionary or reforming subject: the great vision of England as "a noble and puissant Nation rousing herself like a strong man after sleep" should by itself make it impossible to forget that the tract was written at a time when God was shaking his kingdom and preparing it for a new period of reformation. We might read the reregistration of Imaginary and Symbolic orders as taking symbolic part in that reformation, as anticipating and commending a subject of the reformed future. Such a reading, which is clearly no longer dealing with an abstract individual subject but with a subject conceived in historical and perhaps even collective terms, might be said to be encouraged by the psychoanalytic categories (Imaginary, Symbolic, Real) used here. A main virtue of the Lacanian model is that it insists on the situational articulation of the subject, and thus without absorbing historical discourse tempts one to construct the historical situation to which the subject's actions and representations at some level must respond.[22]

What, then, is the significance of the Imaginary refiguring of the subject in Milton's text? To what situation does it respond? The immediately significant context is that of political ideology or ideological struggle, a context in which the formation of ideology appears as an inherently relational and differential activity. I have already suggested that the monistic ethos produces that which, understood in directly political terms, is most radical in Milton's argument, that which is most anti-Presbyterian and which would be most scandalous to the strategic audience. At this level, then, the foregrounding of the Imaginary in *Areopagitica* can be seen to coincide with and motivate what is most cogently grasped as an anti-Presbyterian innovation precisely in the realm of ethics. Milton's monism opens the way for his Arminianism: the transformation of the Aristotelian notion of form amounts to an attempt to "save" the instincts, and reconstruct – against and in place of the dominant Puritan ethic of calculated repression – a more truly hegemonic ethic of purification or sublimation.[23] The message of Imaginary access is that innate instincts may be submitted to education, that straightforward repression is unnatural. The hegemonic aim of this reinsertion of spontaneity into ethics can be seen most sharply in that it casts Milton in dialogue with those radical groups whom Hill has depicted, in *The World Turned Upside Down*, as questioning the Protestant Ethic at the very moment of its definitive establishment. Milton's radicalism is fairly distinctive, however, because it is apparently one with all that is residual or conservative in his constitution. The form that his purificatory ethic takes, inasmuch as it implies a kind of natural bodily uniqueness that has nothing in common with the strictly compensatory privileging of one's own functions peculiar to the entrenched bourgeois,[24] justifies the epithet of "aristocratic" so often applied to Milton. He is reviving something resembling "spontaneous nobility," and clothing it in saintly garb. So that at this point, monism may be seen as an attempt to reappropriate aristocratic ideology for the hegemonic revolutionary ends of the oppositional class. The incursion of the Imaginary in Milton's text thus marks the site of a complex class struggle in the realm of ideology or culture.

This radically differential perspective on Milton's ethics permits us to see the very manifestation of the Imaginary as an ideological statement in its own right. But the ideological struggle in the realm of ethics cannot be said fundamentally to determine this rather pure appearance of the Imaginary; nor can it be said to determine the immanent view of form which is instrumental in its ethical innovation. To establish the essential lines of force conditioning the differential development of any such crucial figure or notion as monism – to determine the actual content of such a notion – one must refer outside ideology to the primary historical structures which condition it, namely to the modes of production.[25]

This is the place, then, in which the textual or rhetorical analysis of monism is forced, in order to understand its object, to refer to the emergence of capitalism. The fact that Milton's heresy rewrites the Aristotelian concept of form – an idea first formulated, of course, under conditions imposed by a completely different mode of production – makes convenient a contrast that may help us to explain what monism and capitalism have to do with each other. The Aristotelian view of form was born and flourished in societies where commodity production was not generalized, and where the technical means of production and the market for which the craftsman produced were both relatively stable and fixed quantities. Accordingly, Aristotelian form implied a static, crafts-manlike view of production and of the subject. With the emergence of capitalist class relations, capital becomes for the first time a dominant and determinant force in its own right, and production – though retaining its regulated and fixed *technical* basis – is put at capital's disposal: it is socially unfixed, so to speak, or rearranged from without. Only at this stage does the economy come to appear as a determinate and discrete system with its own laws of motion, which manifest themselves primarily in the sphere of national commerce, but which also begin to govern domestic production. In this way the development of capitalist class relations alters the whole of society, revolutionizing it from the bottom up; and in doing so not only makes possible but also impels notions of production and of the form-content relationship as possessed of their own immanent dynamic.[26]

It is as such a total "ontological" phenomenon or process that the emergence of capitalism should be understood to establish the conditions for the dynamic sense of the subject expressed in the monistic ethos. But I believe the pressures set up by this process are closer to the tract than the term "conditions" would seem to allow. Indeed, the economic process seems to provide monistic ethos and figuration with their very fabric, and thus to register itself within them in a most concrete way. To see how this happens, we must turn to the capitalist market.

The formation of a unified market is a critical development in the transition to capitalism, and under capitalism the market takes on an unwonted importance in the life of the individual: the individual's relation to society comes to be obscurely mediated by the market – governed, that is, by the reified market categories which now take on a dynamic of their own. It is one effect of this reification that the market itself acquires a natural metaphorical power; thus the market apparatus comes to secrete a corresponding ideological apparatus, what will much later be called "the marketplace of ideas," which is not so much an idea as a mental set or structure for the entertainment of ideas. *Areopagitica* is a landmark, in its way, in the formation of this market ideology, and this fact, I think, is how one may account for its continuing ideological force. The essential argument of the treatise is for a free circulation of ideas: "Truth is our most valuable commodity," Milton argues, and it must not be monopolized. But Truth's entrance into the commodity form is an ambivalent one: the whole tract, beginning with the defense of books, might be read as a protest against the commodification of human activity:

> I cannot set so light by all the invention, the art, the wit, the grave and solid judgement which is in England, as that it can be comprehended in any twenty capacities how good soever, much lesse

that it should not passe except their superintendence be over it, except it be sifted and strain'd with their strainers, that it should be uncurrant without their manuall stamp. Truth and understanding are not such wares as to be monopoliz'd and traded in by tickets and statutes, and standards. We must not think to make a staple commodity of all the knowledge in the Land, to mark and licence it like our broad cloath, and our wooll packs. (pp. 535–6)

Truth and understanding are not *such* wares. Yet, at least on the literal level, they are wares. In fact, part of Milton's rhetorical strategy is to make all human activities appear in the light of the commodity form. Each sphere of activity is capable of being monopolized, its natural movements bottled up and stapled, and the monopolization of books logically leads to or implies the fetishism of other areas. If books are to be licensed, the third part of Milton's argument goes, then manners, recreation, music, balconies must also be regulated. The regulation of these areas is regarded as a patent impossibility, since they are not really commodities, not really "things" offering themselves to monopoly. Like books, the activities of these areas have a kind of human power that simple wares cannot have. Or so we are left to infer. But this does not change the fact that in being depicted as monopolizable, they have been seen under the aspect of the commodity. And inasmuch as there tends to be an implicit analogy drawn between the naturally deregulated state of such activities and the free movement of commodities on the market, Milton has fetishized these activities, instilling them with the abstract or reified power of the market, in the very process by which he intends to demonstrate their incommensurability with mere "wares." Thus the commodity places its shadowy imprint on much of the imagery in the tract; as a result, market ideology comes to be inscribed most intimately within Milton's argument, and to motivate its very figuration. For from this angle, it looks as if the conflictual density, the Imaginary movement of the monistic imagery, negatively registers what is still felt very clearly as the alienated "human" power of the commodity. Such negative registration should be taken as a privileged symptom of Milton's moment, the moment of emergent capitalism in which the power of human production, though having passed the brink of reification, though having been transcoded into the abstract and quasi-transitivistic logic of the market, still knows its former condition, and stands ready to reinstate itself as neither use- nor exchange-value, but as concrete and qualitatively specific activities.

We have outlined now what is indeed an extremely overdetermined situation.[27] If the figurative axis does indeed register, in its very form and pressure, the Imaginary, on the one hand, and the commodity, on the other, and if both the commodity and the Imaginary motivate, in some way, the ethic of Milton's tract, then we are faced with the question of how to articulate the relation between what at first sight appear to be radically discontinuous dimensions of experience. On a general level, it stands to reason that the historical process which makes possible a new sense of the subject, and which throws the subject upon its own resources, should also bring about such a revolutionary access of Imaginary instincts as occurs in Milton's imagery. But although this makes a certain historical fitness appear in the conflation of Imaginary and commodity movement, it does little to help us understand the specific way in which this conflation works in the text. The key to this double-coding seems to lie in the curious way in which the commodity comes to inscribe itself in the figures. As we have just seen, though books and cultural activities are "not such wares" as can be stapled, they are "not uncommodities," that is, they are not averse in their very essence to the commodity form. They thus come to harbor a fetish-like potency, and consequently Milton's protest *against* the commodification of Truth – for at some level *Areopagitica* must be read as such a protest – is harnessed to the power of the fetish itself, and to the dynamic of the market which expresses that power. The coincidence of the Imaginary and the commodity codes begins to be more comprehensible when this situation is fully realized. For at this point the Imaginary appears partly as a reaction against this power of the fetish: its accession amounts to an attempt to absorb the fetish which supports it and provides it with a language, and to reinsert a logic of substance into the alienated market logic. Put another way, the Imaginary code attempts to stand as a kind of metaphor for the commodity code, and the point of its metaphoric vigor is to abolish the shadowy fetish to which it is strapped.

Milton's politics of the moment:
the temperate return of reformation

A review of our interpretation of the self-validating register of Milton's text is now in order. I began by suggesting that this ethical level spoke of personal anxieties, of Milton's sense of vocation and the not unrelated question of freedom of the will. Such anxieties we saw to express an access of self-regarding Imaginary instincts within "Milton." But this accession is not merely a personal problem. Rather it is to be taken as an ideological figure, as a response to a determinate ideological conjuncture: Milton recommends an ethic of purification to the revolutionary class. Such anticipatory figuring of a new subject must not only be seen at the conjunctural political level, but must also be taken more generally as a specific reaction to the major social transformation of Milton's time. The ethic of purification produces a dynamic and empowered bourgeois subject and reacts against its recent reification. This latter contradiction, which institutes a struggle between the commodity and the Imaginary at the figurative level, may be said to be the basic contradiction of Milton's tract, and determines an ambiguity or aporia at the heart of the soul-body relation which reappears at a number of levels of the text. This aporia, manifesting itself generally in the form of an antinomy between quality and quantity, or qualitative and abstract power, informs and qualifies the tract's pivotal ethic of purification, to which it is now time to turn.

This ethic is centrally located in the argument for the beneficial effects of books promiscuously read, the second of Milton's four arguments. There is once again, in this section, a shift in the rhetorical register on which the argument is pitched, and it is possible to see the same essential ambiguity appear on both strategic and monistic levels. Toward the beginning of this section (pp. 509–12) Milton stages a trial by visions. He cites two dreams (recorded by the "primitive doctors" Jerome and Eusebius) that contradict each other on the permissibility of unholy reading, and argues that Dionysius Alexander's dream in favor of free reading is the more authoritative. Milton's rhetorical method here seems to mirror the ethical method that he is to advocate shortly: the trial by contraries frees reason, since the conflict disburdens reason of the weight of authority, making choice possible. It also generates an authoritative reason, since the quotation from Paul with which Dionysius Alexander

corroborated his own vision calls to mind another Pauline quotation –
"To the pure all things are pure" – from which Milton now proceeds to
argue. This famous antinomian topos tends to imply a homogeneity in
external objects as well as in the human instincts themselves, which
would seem to disable any ethic of purification. Milton is immediately
concerned to deny this implication: "For books are as meats and viands
are: some of good, some of evill substance; and yet God in that
unapocryphall vision, said without exception, Rise *Peter*, kill and eat,
leaving the choice to each mans discretion" (p. 512). Abstract qualities of
"good" and "bad" pertain to substances; qualitative choice is thus possible,
and the will may direct the instincts or passions. But when Milton
returns, a little further on, to this argument that God "left arbitrary the
dyeting and repasting of our minds" when he enlarged the physical diet,
so that every man is now free to "exercise his owne leading capacity," he
suddenly diverts his flow into an exordium on temperance, as the oration
seems to cross paths with the sermon:

> How great a vertue is temperance, how much of moment through
> the whole life of man? yet God committs the managing so great a
> trust, without particular Law or prescription, wholly to the
> demeanour of every grown man. And therefore when he himself
> tabl'd the Jews from heaven, that Omer which was every mans daily
> portion of Manna, is computed to have bin more then might have
> well suffic'd the heartiest feeder thrice as many meals. (p. 513)

Temperance appears here to be a kind of quantitative choice, and
replaces qualitative choice. But though temperance regulates quantity, it
is a "humorous" virtue which rides the crest of quality, signifying a
tunedness of the instincts with respect to which all things, now, are
indifferently pure. So the regulatory logic of temperance seems to
contradict, even as it makes possible, the qualitative logic of choice; and
it is noticeable that, with the appearance of temperance, choice, defined
as a function of arbitration between positive qualities of good and bad,
disappears momentarily. This latent antinomy between temperance and
reason, between abstract and positive definitions of good and evil,
reproduces, at the level of the strategic argument, the ambivalence
imposed by the struggle between the commodity and Imaginary instincts
at the level of monistic ethos.

Milton's argument thus far in this section is based on the authority of the Gospel, and offers itself as an interpretation of Scripture. He now continues the process of detaching reason from authority by citing two other places in Scripture which at first glance appear to contradict his position; reason is freed from Scripture itself, and Milton's argument is thus transformed into its own text. In the passage that follows, Scriptural authority is incorporated, as it were, into monistic ethos – the parable of the wheat and tares (Matthew 13. 24–30) determines the reasoning as if from within, imparting a latent apocalypticism to it – as Milton attempts to limn more concretely the ethic which has remained abstract on the strategic level. It becomes apparent that the absolutizing movement of the monistic ethos is a temperate movement, and that the antinomy between (qualitative) choice and temperance is contained within this temperate movement itself. Temperance is truly a virtue of great moment for Milton – as we shall see, a timely virtue indeed.[28]

> Good and evill we know in the field of this World grow up together almost inseparably; and the knowledge of good is so involv'd and interwoven with the knowledge of evill, and in so many cunning resemblances hardly to be discern'd, that those confused seeds which were impos'd on *Psyche* as an incessant labour to cull out, and sort asunder, were not more intermixt. It was from out the rinde of one apple tasted, that the knowledge of good and evill as two twins cleaving together leapt forth into the World. And perhaps this is that doom which *Adam* fell into of knowing good and evill, that is to say of knowing good by evill. As therefore the state of man now is; what wisdome can there be to choose, what continence to forbeare without the knowledge of evill? He that can apprehend and consider vice with all her baits and seeming pleasures, and yet abstain, and yet distinguish, and yet prefer that which is truly better, he is the true warfaring Christian. (pp. 514–15)

I do not want to read this passage, but rather to analyze the ethical logic that it presents and enacts. I would note first that this is an ethic with a decided epistemological bent: what it dictates is a way of actively knowing the world. But this active knowing is itself governed by that immanent informing principle, that objective process of differentiation, which we have seen to be integral to Milton's monism. The reference to the apple above, for instance, implies that a differentiating principle is contained in the object *ab origine*, and that it is this immanent principle which, when released, gives birth to differential knowledge. Thus the process of differentiation by which good and evil are antithetically defined appears to be at once substantial and cognitive. Even as Milton inquires into the substantive conditions of ethical knowledge, he is tracing the path of a properly ethical cognition; the epistemological orientation of the strategic argument is in fact only the first impulse in the movement of ethical cognition, which is itself never called into question. The knowledge which emerges from and is purified in this cognitive process is clearly full of feeling; vice must be apprehended as well as known. The instincts must thus be understood to play a crucial part in ethical cognition, in the development of reason itself. Instinctual temperance makes possible and is in turn made possible by the purification of reason. We may say that Milton's purificatory ethic adumbrates, in attempting to enact as the solution to its dilemma, some sort of dialectical relationship within the body-soul between the instinctual virtue of temperance and the cognitive function of reason, a kind of concrete reciprocity, within "substance" itself, between quantity and quality. The dialectic between reason and temperance settles the question of toleration; that between quantity and quality answers the problem set by the economic situation – the advent of the commodity form.

I am arguing then that Milton does indeed solve his ethical problem in practice, and in all its manifold repercussions. He does this through the very *act* of constructing an ethic of suspense, of waiting. The ethical construction itself effects a reversal: a state of indecision, in which the individual is determined by his situation, is turned into a state of decisive empoweredness. But this solution, now and throughout Milton's career, remains a strictly momentary one; all one need do to expose the dilemma that it contains or forcibly resolves is analyze the moments of the cognitive process projected by the virtue of temperance. What should be emphasized first, however, is that Milton's ethical solution is not just a personal one but rather addresses a class problematic. The sense that Milton is spokesman for a whole class is paradoxically never so strong as at the level of monistic ethos. Although the ethic of purification is obviously modeled on the operation of an individual consciousness, it is not decisively located there, but possesses an ontological-social status, and is figured most vividly as the ethic of the collective subject of reformation. We will see in a moment that it is precisely this overdetermination of the reformative code that permits the clear registration of ideological dislocations and conflicts within the sphere of the subject of the tract. For now it is enough to say that if Milton is writing from and for a collective subject of a sort, then to expose the aporias contained in his ethical resolution will likewise be to disclose the contradictions forced upon and played out by the revolutionary bourgeois class.

The virtue of temperance is located at a logical crossroads: it marks the place where both substantial and abstract logics are generated, and, by that humorous act of will that is the act of ethical construction, it appears to hold these logics in solution. Three distinct logical moments – those of substantial, differential, and distinctive or presence-absence logic – can be separated out here, and each of these moments may be read as representing or corresponding to political moments or stages, both in Milton's career and in the career of the bourgeois revolution. The first of these moments, the moment of substantial logic, exists beneath the text, so to speak, and is represented only in the bodily movement of the monistic imagery. Though it is figured as motivating the ethical process, as its instinctual bottom level, it cannot be depicted in the text itself. The world of complex qualitative differences in terms of which such a logic would work can only be gestured at or connoted, it cannot be grasped by the binary ethical categories of good and evil. It is thus present only as absent, and owes its appearance as raw ethical power to the very abstract logical categories that it generates. This reversal then can be read as a figure of desire, of the utopian wish, abstract though it be, to achieve, beyond and through the ethical construction itself, genuinely concrete categories, and a truly collective vision. It thus represents the moment of the revolution's solidarity with itself, the moment in which Milton betrays his closest affinity with the heretical classes and class factions without whose support bourgeois rule could not have been instated.

But the logic which is uppermost in Milton's ethic, in the above passage and throughout the tract, is the differential logic according to which the abstract qualities of good and evil progressively define each other in a total combat, in terms of a total (ontological and epistemological) process in which the good is called radically into question in every moment of its existence. The purification of knowledge here involves an incessant activation and reactivation of the soul-body through all its powers, a constant dialectical dispersal and collection of consciousness through the various faculties and affections, directed toward the restraint of an evil qualitatively, if latently, present within them. It is evident that such a logic, when applied to the social formation, implies the extension of toleration to at least all those groups willing to submit themselves to the strenuous process of purification which it valorizes. Just as all of the instincts and faculties are potentially good, or are "not ungood," so all the various sects might contribute to the activation of the good and the true. This thus constitutes the progressive moment in Milton's ethic, since the question of whether or not the sects were to be tolerated was one, at this point, with the question of whether the king's party was to be beaten or compromised with.

Yet this process by which the good gradually defines itself against and purifies itself of evil necessarily brings into being that presence-absence logic which the ethical construction itself is based on. The emergence of this logic coincides with the crystallization of reason. For good and evil are antithetical qualities and may inhabit the same terrain only as potencies. The determinate act which realizes reason expels the evil potency and turns it into a determinate lack of being by whose absence the good defines itself. That this strictly distinctive logic in fact *founds* the cognitive-ethical process, rather than appearing only at its logical end, is abundantly evident when one recognizes that the differential moment itself can be nothing other than "good." Insofar as reason acts by constructing the ethic of suspense, then the very absence of the state of activation which it dictates is condemned as the evil other. All those of implicit faith – most notably, of course, Catholics – are relegated to the ashcan of reformation. Hence the presence-absence logic projects a view of the progressive definition of truth and the good different from that implied by the differential logic. According to the latter logic, each stage in the progress of truth involves a dialectical activation of the body of Truth in which all the "segments" of Truth are radically called into question and redefine themselves in the context of the totality. The presence-absence logic, by contrast, tends to make the progress of truth into an additive process: the way to determine the truth content of a new idea is to compare it with the determined body of Truth, and the Truth will presumably manifest a growth proportionate to the degree of equivalence which the new idea displays with it. The advent of reason, then, reifies the body of Truth at the same time as it frees it through all its members. Thus it is that Milton's ethic (as is the case, perhaps, with all strictly ethical positions) is ultimately antitolerationist, and in this its conservative moment – the moment which corresponds to the time when the revolutionary middle class, in order to protect its position, turns against those elements which have brought it to power – the ethic of purificatory waiting reveals most clearly its strictly ideological component, the potential class bias built into it from the beginning.

Milton's purificatory ethic of suspense constitutes, then, a response to and reconstruction of two very different kinds of social contradiction, two discrete sources of anxiety within the subject. On the one hand, it temporarily resolves the political contradictions in process of being lived out by the revolutionary party; one wants to add that the strategic argument, in which distinctive logic is more prominent, tempers the tolerationist bias of the monistic argument in deference to the Erastians and, I think, to Milton's own class feelings. On the other hand, the monistic ethic casts the basic antinomy set for it by market logic, that between abstract-quantitative and qualitative power, as two indispensable halves of the same substantial process; the paradoxical desire of the economic subject for the concrete is most clearly situated and most adequately allayed at the level of self-validating ethos. The tendency of these two anxieties to manifest themselves most distinctly on different rhetorical registers testifies, I think, to their objective distance from each other in the "text" of social experience to which *Areopagitica* responds. The political desire for class rule and the economic desire for concreteness, for all their complex interconnectedness, are radically different desires, and show themselves to be such.

How then is it possible for Milton's monistic ethic to respond to such different anxieties, to manage a conjuncture of desire, in one and the same movement? I have already touched upon the answer in pointing out that the ethic of purification is not only an individual ethic, or rather that precisely as an individual ethic it is also the ethic of reformation. Monism is, after all, a heresy, an individual transgression or choice against the collective theological code. As such a heretical concept or figure, it can attempt to resolve the ideological anxieties and dislocations in one strategic and overdetermined move, since these problems may be presumed to be already registered within the reformational code, even if that code is not capable in its canonical form of adequately managing these anxieties, of channeling all desire into its nominally seamless domain. Milton's monistic (hence in fact heretical) ethic of suspense responds to what is felt first then as a theological inadequacy. It is not only or primarily a way of living political or economic anxieties; rather it is a way, and counsels a way, of living predestination, of attending divine signs in the face, in the very script, of such anxieties. The correlated economic, political, and ethical antinomies are felt as indeterminate manifestations of God's will in the body itself, whether this be the individual body or the body politic of the nation-church. It is thus the centrality of the predestinary code within reformation theology that permits and enforces such a unified symbolic response as is contained in the monistic ethos to a crisis highly conjunctural in character. At the same time, we can see that the presence of this unifying code also enforces on the subject such radical dislocations, such a manifest uncentering, as it undergoes in *Areopagitica*.

But even if predestination enforces the latent fissuring of the subject's desires, it is not finally responsible for that fissuring. The master code of reformation may rule in *Areopagitica*, but it does not reign. Not theology but ethics governs the viewpoint of the tract, and this focus determines the emergence of a new content within the theological subject itself. All we need do to make this clear is to point out that there is no obvious reason within theology for predestination to be located within the body, for its antinomies to be "resolved" in the figuration of raw bodily movement or power. To understand why this should be, we must return, at least in the context constructed by *Areopagitica*, to the desire for the concrete established by the emergence of capitalism. Considering Milton's ethic of predestined suspense in the light of its historical moment leads us to realize once more the paradoxical importance of the aristocratic element in Milton. It is precisely the recrudescence of spontaneous nobility within a generally Puritan framework of thought that allows Milton to register the contradictions deriving from an essentially bourgeois (hence progressive) problematic in what seem "immediately lived" terms. We may take the bodily vigor of the directly ethical argument to signal, then, a new and privileged status for ethics within the ideological formation of emergent capitalist society. In this view, the division between strategic ethos and monistic ethos marks a definitive stage in the separation of ethics from religion.

That ethics is not thoroughly controlled by theology may more clearly be understood when we see that the ethical focus of the tract throws its official theological position into contradiction with itself. The central problem here concerns the specification of the category of "things indifferent," that is, of those beliefs and actions which were neither inherently good nor evil and which therefore could be tolerated by the church. Milton makes it clear, especially toward the close of the tract, that there are certain fundamentals of the faith which cannot be breached, although he does not indicate precisely what these fundamentals are:

> I mean not tolerated Popery, and open superstition, which as it extirpats all religions and civill supremacies, so it self should be extirpat ... that also which is impious or evil absolutely ... no law can possibly permit ... but those neighboring differences, or rather indifferences, are what I speak of, whether in some point of doctrine or of discipline, which though they may be many, yet need not interrupt the *unity of Spirit*" (p. 565).

The intended theological position of the tract, then, is vague; but the ethical focus distorts this position and renders it yet more ambiguous because the progressive impulse which is uppermost in this ethic entails a radical redefinition of truth in every moment. According to this view, so well conveyed in the great city and nationalistic passages, society is in process of rebuilding itself from its very foundations, so all truths are equally to be tested, and everything is *prima facie* indifferent. Putting the problem in terms of this theological ambiguity helps us not only to see the problematical position – both nationalist and Congregationalist – which the tract adopts with respect to the church,[29] but also has the effect of clarifying the contradiction in the ethical focus itself. It does this last, however, at the expense of diverting attention from the central event in the tract, which is not the operation of a theological discourse, but the creation of a literary subject that registers, through its uncentered ethical orientation, the full weight of a specific personal and historical juncture.

PART II

The subject and primary reification

3
Possessive individualism, genre, and ethics

I have thus far argued, primarily through the use of immanent analysis, that the rhetorical subject of *Areopagitica* is uncentered by the appearance within it of a properly ethical level of argument figured in terms of the dynamism of bodily forces. *Areopagitica* has long been felt to be the most purely "Miltonic" of Milton's tracts, and I would venture that it is at its most Miltonic in its rhetorical imaging of this ethical subject, which is also, in the tract's implicit theological context, a heretical subject. The orator's house has many mansions: I have also argued that the ethical subject exists as a discrete level because of its virtual unity with an emergent economic level, that of the "capitalist subject."[1] In this chapter I wish to situate the "event" constituted by the appearance of a capitalist subject, which, it stands to reason, was not created in a vacuum. If my analysis in the last chapter is not to appear suspect, comparable happenings in the sphere of the subject should be discernible in other ideological areas. The main example of such a happening, I will argue, is to be found in the "philosophy of possessive individualism,"[2] which presents in its clearest and most basic form the ideological unit or framework of which monistic ethos and monism are peculiar variants. Possessive individualism lays bare the "new" problematic which the ethical subject of *Areopagitica* constructs and attacks all at once, and which remains central to the major work of Milton's career. In the process of establishing the context of the problems found in *Areopagitica*, I hope to justify my collocation of *Areopagitica* with *Paradise Lost*, so that this exceptional tract will eventually be seen in its very exceptionality to prove the rule of Milton's literary practice.

I should emphasize, however, that I am not about to suggest that Hobbes' philosophy is an "influence" on Milton's argument in *Areopagitica*. The ideological determinants that appear once we leave immanent analysis behind are much older and more authoritative than possessive individualism, which was elaborated during the revolutionary period. Milton legitimates his heretical attack on licensing through the strategic articulation of three distinct ideologies: classical republicanism, Pauline antinomianism, and popular anti-monopoly sentiment. The first of these ideologies, republicanism, is communicated primarily by the tract's classical form. That the Greeks, used as models, will make England strong is an unspoken message in *Areopagitica* – unspoken because the classical notions of citizenship and of political liberty are written into the very concept of the oration. Although these notions are crucial to the treatise – and to Milton – they were not typically linked with a dynamic sublimative ethic such as we have discovered in Milton's pamphlet. The classical orator projects a stable morality, and his passion speaks of the unity between virtue and rhetorical power, not of some untouchable virtuous process whose real integrity exists only beneath written speech.[3] Ideological justification for Milton's ethic of purification is found, then, not mainly in republicanism, but in Pauline theology's transgressive concept of law and the correlated impulse to "prove all things." One may read Milton as recasting in ethical and Arminian terms Paul's ontological notion that evil may purify itself only if it is made to know itself as evil through transgression or the temptation to transgress.[4] Paul's ethical antinomianism, however, rendered unto Caesar what was Caesar's: it connoted neither economic nor political freedom, nor was it imaged in terms of the natural movement of the market. The strategic determinant of this element of Milton's ethic was the crusade against monopolies, so crucial to the parliamentary forces' original unification, which was carried out in the early stages of the revolution.[5] Milton clearly enlists popular anti-monopoly sentiment to corroborate his argument for free trade in books, and to suggest its inevitability.

We must allow that this last distinction between Pauline and anti-monopoly ideology is in a basic respect artificial. For anti-monopoly sentiment, though originally a distinct phenomenon, was in effect incorporated into the reformation religion that revived Paul, as one aspect of its attack on idolatry. Milton's deployment of anti-monopoly sentiment in his argument against licensing is in fact a logical extension of his attack on prelacy in the earlier pamphlets: monopolies are to the body politic what prelatical paraphernalia are to the church – obstructions and hindrances to the all-important dialectic between predestination and the individual or group will. I mean to raise no question here concerning the transcendent importance, in the revolution and in the political stabilization of capital's economic rule, of Protestantism's attack on the various idols of absolutism; nor do I question the predestinary code's crucial significance in the formation of the bourgeois class and personality. In *Areopagitica* we have, indeed, a vivid example of how the Protestant attack on idols could lead to the valorization of a "free" market and subject. But I do not think that this example is typical of the attack on idols in the economic sphere. Milton's projection of a free market and figuring of market movement as the locus of ethical value goes beyond that attack. Protestant anti-idolatry, though it surely responded to the emergence of the capitalist market, nonetheless did not tend to picture it in free movement or as the generative source of value.⁶ Thus, though Protestantism is the main determinant of Milton's ethical argument, we cannot sketch in it the form of the particular problematic to which Milton's argument adheres.

In other words, Milton in deploying anti-monopoly sentiment takes it to an unusually progressive extreme. This progressiveness lies in the dramatic and seemingly unmediated relationship that exists between the commodity and Milton's ethical epistemology. Milton's argument for free trade in books as a condition of ethical cognition is most vigorously made precisely through the presentation of ubiquitous commodity movement. We have already noted the paradox inherent in this "imagistic" argument. On the one hand, the commodity structure informs the monistic argument and affords it a basic ontological rationale, inasmuch as the natural energy that actively constitutes the monistic argument comes to be conflated with, or to serve as a kind of signifier for, the movement of commodities, in all its problematical ambivalence: books should not be subject to licensing, it is implied, because this disrupts the healthy flow of the market. On the other hand, the "false concrete" of the commodity, its intrinsically reifying structure, is repeatedly attacked and exploded, in quasi-allegorical fashion, by the volatile monistic figuration: the argument implied by this attack is that books should circulate because they are not commodities like other commodities, because the power of book production is not commensurable with the commodity form, and to regulate it as if it were is unnatural, even impossible. Ethical, political, and theological antinomies all follow from the central epistemological aporia posed by the ambiguous commodification of book production.

Precisely this allegorical significance of the commodity and the correlated progressiveness of *Areopagitica* become a source of anxiety when we begin to think of turning to the analysis of that consummately "right-handed" Miltonic work, *Paradise Lost*. The importance of the commodity theme in *Areopagitica* is, in a sense, an accidental importance. In no other of Milton's pamphlets do "wares" figure as a major thematic element; nor, of course, do they appear in the poetic works. The symptomatic relation of ethical, political, and theological antinomies to the ambivalent status of the commodity in *Areopagitica* thus cannot obtain in any of these works; the socioeconomic contraries immanent to the commodity theme can only have a mediated significance with regard to a work like *Paradise Lost*. To bring out this significance, to fill in the apparent distance between the "absent" commodity and Milton's literary practice, it is necessary to situate both the category of the commodity itself and the contradictions to which it is linked in *Areopagitica* more concretely in the area of ideology. The commodity as theme or as signifier, that is, must itself be seen as a crucial ideological category – not, as I have tended to see it, as the place of truth in the tract, but as the product, finally, of determinate social relations. The reification of human power thematized by the commodity must be conceived not as an emanation of the commodity, but as a determinate or categorical structuring of action effected at the level of the socioeconomic relations of the emergent capitalist mode of production.[7]

The work of contextualization has already begun, of course, in the preceding chapter; as will have become obvious to those who "believe" in immanent reading, I do not finally think that such interpretation is desirable or even possible. One always approaches a text with predispositions, with unscrupulous referential intentions of one kind or another. Simply in order to construct the commodity theme, I found it necessary to refer it to the capitalist market that was developing in the seventeenth century, and to interpret the dynamism of the subject that it signified as an effect of the autonomy of the capitalist economy. My reference to the quasi-eternal aspects and ideological effects of the capitalist market now needs historical qualification. It is the consensus among historians that an "organic" or generalized market, developing in pace with the disintegration of the petty mode of production, was in place by the early seventeenth century.[8] Especially important in this connection is the development of the home market, which was closely tied to the capitalization of agriculture.[9] Yet it should not be concluded from the fact of its emplacement that this generalized market was homogeneous or uniformly developed; nor is it precisely correct to imply, as I have tended to do in chapter 2, that this organic market was consciously perceived as a dynamic, self-regulating entity.

Let us consider this last matter. The reigning political economy of Milton's time on into the eighteenth century was mercantilism, and one should look to it, I think, for a clear indication as to the basic apprehension of the commodity and the commodity market in this period. Mercantilism assumed, in all its permutations, the necessity and the naturalness of positive regulation of the market. It thus posited the commodity as an essentially political category.[10] One may explain this by reference to capitalism's uneven development in England: English mercantilism's political definition of the commodity and of the market was mainly attributable to the dominance of commercial and agricultural capital, and to the (partly correlative) underdevelopment and political subordination of specifically industrial capital within the English social formation.[11] For it is industrial capitalism that forms the most basic and "typical" instance of the entire complex system of capitalist production: in it, the commodity stands forth most clearly as capital, as self-producing value, and it is thus in it that a "conscious" ideology of economic autonomy is ultimately based. But in spite of the fact that such an ideology of autonomy was not yet present in coherent form, it nonetheless did receive fragmentary and *ad hoc* expression both within mercantilism itself and outside it, in the popular movement against monopolies already mentioned. As Dobb has shown, the as yet absent ideology of autonomy had its resonance within mercantilism in the form of a tacit antagonism between official and implicit concepts of the market – between notions of the market as static and externally regulated, on the one hand, and as dynamic and organic, on the other. Although mercantilism did not alter its most basic assumptions about the nature of the economy itself, it certainly did in its later emphases – first, on the terms as against the balance of trade, and second, on full domestic employment (and hence on industrial expansion) – make concessions to industrial capitalism, and thus to the ultimately organic logic of the capitalist market.[12] We may read *Areopagitica* as anticipating this antinomy in later mercantilist writers between organic and static views of the commodity and of the market, provided we allow and emphasize that this conflict is most manifest at the ethical level of Milton's tract, in the paradoxical split between differential and presence-absence ethics. The figurative free market in *Areopagitica* gives particularly lucid expression to the incipient free market ideology, and to the still necessary transparence of the compromised character of such ideology, even though it images an ethical process, and is hence primarily an ethical market.

This ethical valorization of the free market, this registration of economic contradictions within a primarily ethical-political discourse, would seem to be virtually inevitable, though it will only emerge over course of time why this is so. In the first place, the polemical context and intent of the tract practically insure the taking of an ethical focus on the monopolized market. Anti-monopoly sentiment, of which *Areopagitica*'s argument is an "intellectualist" extension, was "by nature" ethically charged. Inasmuch, however, as this sentiment derived from contradictions within feudalism, the ethical feeling involved was naturally grounded in the feudal social structure, and was directly political in character.[13] Anti-monopoly sentiment was not typically cast in terms of a dynamic immanent to the market and, by extension, to nature; nor did it necessarily posit the ethical subject as constituting itself through its production of or reaction to a homologous dynamic: it did not typically give the subject an essentially, if ambivalent, economic definition and infer its motivations from its economic situation. Rather the attack on monopolies tended to aim for an immediate loosening of the flow of trade on behalf of a politically entitled subject.[14] So Milton's conscious polemical use of anti-monopoly ideology does not in itself determine his figuring of free economic flow, nor does it entail the specific form of his ethical (and other) contradictions. It may be supposed that the absence from anti-monopoly ideology of a politically progressive extrapolation from socioeconomic relations such as we find in Milton, and its consequent failure to posit the subject in terms of economic entitlement, was due primarily to the importance of its fusion of the economic and political in its revolutionary political role. It was the critical location and immediate function of anti-monopoly sentiment within a hegemonic Puritanism that gave it a static and symbolic character, discouraging any extrapolation from the socioeconomic situation to which this sentiment was in part a response.

But if its progressive political function strait-jacketed anti-monopoly ideology, preventing the radical generalization from economic relations which would have transformed its economic content, such an extrapolation could and did take place, in however cryptic and concealed a fashion, within the realm of political theory, in Hobbes and those who came after him. Hobbes' philosophical radicalism doubtless had its positive foundation in the revolutionary turmoil of which anti-monopoly sentiment was one manifestation.[15] However, it also had an important and immediate *negative* determination: it was precisely the relative distance of philosophical discourse from the dust and heat of ideological struggle, or, in other words, its highly mediate nature, which permitted possessive individualism's more or less coherent elaboration of the market in terms of political relations.

It is the ambiguous significance of this elaboration for the status of the philosophical subject that is of main interest here. As C. B. MacPherson has demonstrated, in *Leviathan* Hobbes silently posits the political subject as an economic subject in the first instance.[16] The nasty and brutish state of nature on which Hobbes bases his political reasoning, and from which he derives and justifies his absolutism, represents, for MacPherson, an abstraction from special social relations: the predominantly market relations of a competitive and atomistic bourgeois commercial world. Indeed, from a retroactive or total perspective on Hobbes' argument, we can see that his political subject comes into being, or is "superadded" to the economic subject, only because of the contradictory tendencies inherent in the (natural) economic subject: because its drive to wealth and power ultimately conflicts, on the social plane, with the will to self-preservation.

But in another sense – from what might be called an immanent perspective – the political subject is related to the economic plane in a much more immediate way; for the political subject comes into being specifically *as* the economic subject, which structures it and provides it with its basic motives in the very act of taking cover "under," or of being absorbed by, the political subject. The individual's possession and control of his own labor power – which, for MacPherson, represents the secret foundation and starting point of liberal political philosophy – is grasped and thought as *sovereignty*, as an immediately legal and political right to the "free" use of one's bodily forces.[17]

This legal-political definition of a "free producer" must be seen, from our own perspective, as marking the definitive commodification of the economic subject by emergent capitalism. It thus splits the subject even in the act of giving it a legitimate unity, conferring on it the same ambivalence that Marx imputes to the commodity form. On the one hand, the subject's freedom, its very status as an independent unity, depends upon the freedom of the body; the relationship of possession is an immediate one, the subject existing as such insofar as he is one with his bodily power. On the other hand, the ascription of sovereignty to the subject clearly reinforces the administrative connotations which were already implicit in the absent concept of possession itself, and thus instrumentalizes the body while now casting the subject as a separate, controlling ego or administrator, as a disengaged proprietor of its own labor power. From the proprietor's point of view, the body, itself nothing other than property, retains its uniqueness as the initial instrument of appropriation; production itself, defined as individual activity, is conceived as personal appropriation, occurring only under the aegis of, and necessarily reproducing, the relation of proprietorship.

It is easy to see that this conception of proprietary production not only separates the individual producers from one another, but also puts them finally in competition with one another. Thus Hobbes' state of nature features a life and death struggle among all the members of humanity for the very conditions of existence.[18] More than this, however: the separation of the subject from labor power reveals the class character of this philosophy, inasmuch as this separation, this objectification of labor power, not only renders labor power alienable in theory, but, more importantly, sanctions its alienation in reality. Consequently, when the philosophy of possessive individualism defines the individual subject, it is also defining a class subject. It speaks for the class which controls its own labor power, and posits it as against the class of wage-laborers which was in formation throughout the seventeenth century.[19] The political definition of the subject as the sovereign of his personal forces lays claim, it is true, to political neutrality; nonetheless, and especially in this period of fear and loathing of wage-labor,[20] it exposes that subject as being politically determined from its beginnings. For it is not a question (as

MacPherson at times implies) of the subject's self-definition merely by way of some bare quasi-metaphysical cognition of the isolation imposed by market structures. Rather such reified cognition is only one aspect (the commercial moment, if you will) of the subject's definition, which is at the same time transparently motivated by the social division of labor which supports generalized isolation. Possessive individualism's open contempt of wage-labor, its lack of bad conscience about defining itself against this degraded Other, marks it as the liberalism of an early phase of capitalism, in which class struggle has not yet been neutralized by the free working of the economy. It should perhaps be added that this emphasis on the class derivation of possessive individualist ideology is not meant to imply that this ideology is inflexibly class oriented, that it is always and everywhere bourgeois ideology *tout court*. Indeed, as was the case with market ideology, possessive individualism is less an ideology proper, less a concrete and specific content, than it is a general apparatus or structure which performs its ideological work in the act of being filled in or papered over by specific ideologies, and which assumes its precise class bearing in this process of ideological interaction.[21]

We may read in this sheerly formal character a second feature which places possessive individualism as an early capitalist ideology. The split in the subject instituted by possessive individualism remains for the most part merely logical in character, and is resolved in advance by being set in motion, by being cast in the form of an initially unproblematical – political – subject-narrative. The contradictions involved in the subject's definition do not present themselves in the realm of the subject itself, in the form, say, of some division between the subject's internal and external workings, between its private and public spheres. They turn up, and are worked out and transformed, in the highlighted areas of this philosophy, in the theories and justifications of political structures and of government in general.

The seamlessness of the split in the possessive individualist subject, its unproblematical narrative status, testifies to the emergent state of capitalism in England at this time, and to the comparative dominance of commercial capital within it. On the one hand, simple possession is the mode of subjectivity corresponding to primitive accumulation: capital itself not yet having become the main source of accumulation, not yet having attained anything like apparent autonomy as the motor of production, the division between exchange-value and use-value has not yet asserted its full force in the domain of civil society, and the subject is left free to do his own – and not capital's – work, even while working to accumulate. On the other hand, the merchant's work is peculiarly unscathed by this division, even should it be in force, because for him the use-value of his product lies exactly in its exchange-value. Nonetheless we can see clearly in the merchant, that privileged archetype of the capitalist subject, that the division between use- and exchange-value constitutes this subject's chief structural condition. It is this division which determines the "logical" split in possessive individualism between possession and proprietorship, and is, indeed, identical with that split insofar as the body is seen in the quality of labor power, as itself a commodity.

We now come to what I take to be a main paradox of the emergent capitalist ideology of possession – that it constitutes a response to and protest against the commodity reification of capitalism itself. The paradox is clarified when we see possession as a transitional or displaced notion. For possession originally designates the immediate and unquestioned relationship between producers or producing units and their means of production which characterized feudal relations. It thus defines the feudal producing unit's immediate place or mode of membership in the parcelized and territorialized feudal formation.[22] Possessive individualist "possession," on the other hand, expresses in pure fashion the general commodification of labor that marks the constitutive moment of the bourgeois or capitalist subject – the point at which it distinctly *separates* itself from the normative subject of post-feudalism, which was still largely defined by its immediate relationship with its means of production. Nonetheless it *rewrites* feudal possession in breaking with it, casting possession in terms of the individual's control over his only remaining means, his bodily powers. The possession of the free producer assumed by possessive individualism is an economic abstraction: it removes the subject and his labor from the social conditions which determine individual labor in its very essence, and thus redefines the very concept of production by casting the individual's creative powers or abilities into the category of labor power. At the same time, however, as it institutes abstraction, possession advertises itself as the moment of the concrete, and makes insistent allusion to the unreified production, the social abilities, inherent to the feudal economy. That Hobbes, the apologist for absolutism, "invented" possessive individualism is perhaps no accident, for possession is in a strong sense still a feudal category, or at least aims at an impossible resurrection of feudal labor on a capitalist basis. Possession is thus a doubly split concept: not only does it commodify the subject, thereby establishing a division between (abstract) bodily immediacy and proprietorship of the body's powers, between use- and exchange-value; it also, through the creation of use-value or abstract labor power, alludes to the "real concrete" of feudal labor which its very appearance wipes from the ideological map.

Thus is determined the ambivalence of the ideological unit which I will call the possessive individualist narrative and which must be understood as at once constructing the capitalist subject and symbolically reacting against it. I prefer the term "narrative" to that of "concept" or "structure" for two reasons. First, I want to emphasize that what I have isolated in possessive individualism is not simply relevant to philosophy or official discourse, but is constitutive of social experience, as a kind of inchoate fantasy or germinal narrative that controls the social collective's figuration of its own mode of operation. Second, the "unit" of possession is defined even in possessive individualism itself less as a rigorous concept than as a kind of raw and abstract impulse, which sets the conditions for the very possibility of both subjective and social representation. The subject is naturally in integral motion, a motion composed of the two indissoluble moments or – more properly, as we now can see – *drives* of possession and proprietorship. On the one hand, the possessive individualist narrative is founded in the subject's unity with the sum of its own power, in an impulse of bodily immediacy which knows no social circumscription and hence cannot be taken from the subject. On the other hand, the very abstractness of this impulse of bodily power puts the subject at a distance from the body, whose immediacy it can thus know only as an instrumentality, only in the mode of sheer control.

The paradox of this instrumental or proprietary drive is that, although it is founded by the will's separation from the body, it is at the same time a drive for immediacy, of which it retains the illusion. This illusory immediacy amounts to the displacement of possession itself, and marks the repetition of the original antinomy within its proprietary half. Possession takes the form, in proprietorship, of a neutral or noninstru- mental moment of sheer cognition. What impresses a modern reader most, indeed, about the possessive individualist narrative is its unprob- lematical and utterly cognitive character: its will – so prominent in the philosophical fables of Hobbes and his followers, who unquestioningly trace the path(s) of the series of appropriative individuals to its end in obligating social contracts and definite political structures – to pure description.

In describing the possessive individualist narrative, I am attempting to describe the peculiar form taken by the reification of social relations in emergent capitalism. The possessive individualist narrative institutes commodity reification into the sphere of the subject and objectifies all the subject's social relations. In creating a reified and reifying subject, it lays the groundwork for future onslaughts of reification. Its curious instrumentalization of the subject's powers may thus be termed the moment of "primary reification."

Let us establish this moment's uniqueness in broader terms before returning to Milton. Primary reification marks the point at which a general narrative form for the subject's activity appears for the first time, replacing the partial or collectively situated subject-narratives of feudalism. It thus tends to redefine the place of narrative: the force of narrative is located in the subject, in his self-sufficient appropriative movement, rather than in the site of social production or interaction, for example. If the emergent capitalist is distinguished from the feudal subject by the unqualified narrativization of its activity, it distinguishes itself from later forms of reified subjectivity by its purely subjective character. Though the possessive individualist subject is the logical effect of social reification, it appears the other way round. Reification emanates from the subject, most clearly visible not at the level of general socioeconomic processes (as will become the case in later capitalism, with the advent of mass production and mass consumption), but rather at the level of the individual producer, in the very transparency of individual "possession" and hence of "individuality." This is not to imply, of course, that such individuality does not persist as an informing structure in the ideologies of later periods; to the contrary, the commodi-fication of the subject, while undergoing modifications of specific structure and function with the gradual development of the social system, continues to determine individual activity and perception as the basic mode of access to the natural and social worlds, all the way up to the period of monopoly capitalism. It is possible, then, to speak of the reification of the subject as primary reification in a logical as well as a chronological sense. The commodification of the subject remains, under capitalism, a primary principle of structuration of all ideology. It is not overly reductive or "essentialist" to hold that, once capitalism is established, each individual must eventually define himself (and thus must be defined) within and against this primary reification. It goes without saying, however, that the subject's commodification may take very different forms in specific instances, so that it never wholly determines the subject but instead exists to be filled in by other ideological structures. Yet this does not mean that such secondary structures always function somehow *apart* from the commodity structure of the subject and may be separately ticketed and indexed. We need only recall the coexistence of the commodity and Imaginary codes in *Areopagitica*, their mutual articulation by the same textual and figurative movement, to see that this is definitely not the case. I would suggest that the close interdetermination between economic and psychological definitions of the subject in *Areopagitica* is paradigmatic of capitalist reification, such that we are always driven to speak of a conflation of codes if we are to speak comprehensively. I will return to the question of psychological overdetermination in a moment.

Meanwhile, the meaning should have become clearer of what was said above concerning the inevitability of Milton's argument from and for a free market. Milton's postulation of a free market, his implicit economic definition of the market, corresponds to the progressive market assumptions of possessive individualism, and we may assume it to have been arrived at by an analogous route. Just as possessive individualism could extrapolate from commercial relations because of its distance from the political arena, because of its comparative purity and generality as a discourse, so too Milton may be supposed to have imaged a free market not only or perhaps mainly because of his bourgeois background, but because of the "literary" and subjective focus of his argument, because of what is generally described as its humanist character. It was the quasi-humanist "distance from his age" cultivated by Milton throughout his career, and so often paired by critics with Miltonic idealism,[23] that drove him, once on political terrain, to hypostasize the market. But we must then read the Miltonic aloofness, in turn, not simply as a symptom of his peculiar vocation, but as the partial effect of possessive individualism, insofar as the free subject of this philosophy is inscribed in the autonomy of the market.

And this is the crucial point. Milton's argument not only corresponds to, but actually produces a version of the possessive individualist position. At the logical ground level, he makes an argument for a free intellectual market: licensing should be avoided because it is in the nature of intellectual production to enjoy its own integral movement, to appropriate its own audience. It is surely no accident that this argument is most apparent in the monistic passages which most frequently introduce commodity figuration. The movement of commodities serves as a figure for, and is indeed conflated with, the body and its freedom. Through its very ambivalence – both in its quality of raw representational power and in its quality as representative or emblem of that power – the commodity gives the free subject its firmest basis, representing it in its most radical form even while protesting against and questioning the very category of referential representation. Since the commodification of the subject is the hidden basis of the philosophy of possessive individualism, Milton, in commodifying the intellectual producer, expresses the truth of this philosophy more clearly than the philosophers do. In a sense, indeed, he goes beyond the philosophers, almost to the point of leaving possessive individualism behind; for expressly to commodify the individual's labor is at once to render the individual's freedom problematic and his activity manifestly social in character.

Thus Milton's monism takes on a deepened significance here, marking the place where the civil society of an emergent capitalism impinges most directly on Milton's theology. Monism is not simply an unusual way of handling an impossible theological place, though it is that; nor is it only a way of securing the necessary ontological underpinnings for Milton's revision of the dominant Puritan ethic into a repressive ethic of sublimation, though it is that also. It represents more fundamentally an eccentric construction of and response to the possessive individualist narrative, and therefore may be said to be negatively determined by that reifying narrative. Milton's location of (theological) freedom in the individual's body reduplicates, while at the same time expressing in an extreme or utopian fashion, the paradoxical valorization of the body, and of control over the body, which takes place in possessive individualism. He thus sets himself the same basic problem as is posed by the possessive individualist theory of the subject. Where and how does a knowledgeable will or reason which is one with the body distinguish itself as such and assume an independent directive function? The very generality of the question testifies to the abstraction of which the question itself is an effect: the question would not appear as a problem were it not for the abstraction of human power it presupposes (recall the strain put on the theory of the humors in *Areopagitica*, where the bodily heterogeneity that this theory implies can only with great difficulty – and abstractly – be made to fit in with the monolithic and all-determining faculty of reason). This problem of free knowledge is visible within Hobbes and Milton, and consistently haunts both forms of discourse. Yet it is never entertained as such but resolved in advance – ultimately by virtue of the seamlessness, the cognitive bias of the possessive individualist narrative; more immediately by virtue of their paradigmatic categories for possession. The logic of possession is refracted in different ways through these different substitute categories. Hobbes solves the problem of abstraction by resort to the metaphor of sovereignty; Milton handles it most convincingly by recourse to the immediacy of intellectual or literary creation.

I would suggest that the metaphor of intellectual production acted out in *Areopagitica* compromises the possessive individualist narrative more severely than it is already compromised, even while producing it as the basic ideology of the text. For on the one hand, the vocational aspirations written into this enactment are still explicitly social; the literary compulsion is communally oriented, and is clearly understood that way in *Areopagitica*. We might say that the manifest vocationalism of Milton's argument overdetermines the tract's basic individualism without obviously contradicting it. On the other hand, I think we must read the intellectual metaphor as *directly* affecting the tract's production of possessive individualism, in however hidden a fashion. The need for concreteness and for transparency of orientation involved in the operation of this metaphor works to exacerbate the desire for quality written into possessive individualism from its beginnings and deriving from the ambivalent abstractness of the commodity form itself. So it is that Milton winds up actually attacking this contradiction from within, as it were, by means of a number of explosive textual operations, the most basic of which involves the reproduction and thematization of the fetish itself, in an attempt, through figurative displacement, to embody and concretize its hidden dynamism.

But it is not only a matter, as should be clear by now, of the text of *Areopagitica*. It is my thesis that Milton in some sense *lived* the overdetermined contradiction in question, and that his monism is the sign of that living. If possessive individualism comes into the world silently protesting against the very reification of the subject that it both perpetrates and conceals, then Milton's monistic revision and theological upgrading of this nascent ideology renders its self-protest more or less audible, attempting, through the pure positivity of the body, to negate the very concept of possession and the abstraction on which it stands. If it is asked whence this negation is attempted, then one must answer that it comes from both sides of a kind of ideological divide within "Milton" – primarily from within the ideology of possession itself, basing itself on the paradoxical immediacy of the subject which this ideology creates; but also, as its theological status as a heresy proves, from without and from a distance, basing itself on those socialized aspects of religious and literary ideology which have not undergone reification and which are reified only by anticipation.

Psychoanalytical categories of explanation seem most pertinent to the former negation for it is in this negation from within capitalism itself that the Imaginary is visible as such. This means that what has been said concerning the struggle between the commodity and the Imaginary in *Areopagitica* may be extended to possessive individualism itself. The false immediacy of the subject determined by reification serves as a foundation for, and is expressed in terms of, a discrete accession of Imaginary discourse within the Symbolic realm, an accession that appears to produce the economic subject and at the same time to react against its abstractness. I mean to suggest here that capitalism, in commodifying the economic subject, restructures the psychoanalytic one: that capitalism sets out for the Imaginary a newly discrete prominence in the formation of the subject, and in so doing redefines the Imaginary, situating it more exclusively upon the "decoded" or freed body and assigning to it a privileged constitutive function in the realm of what is now a militantly individual subject. Imaginary instincts are fixed in narcissistic and aggressive play, not upon one of the places in the "social body," but rather by and upon the mirroring Other of abstract labor, which constitutes the subject's body at a remove from the subject, under the aspect of lack. This paradoxical Imaginary definition of the body as lack I would take, with Deleuze and Guattari, as the crucial defining feature of the psychoanalytic subject under capitalism: the decoded subject of capitalism, its productive moorings ripped from under it, knows even its own body as an imposed lack, and directs all its energies against this imposition.[24] The subject's Imaginary narrative force appears alternately to precipitate and to be motivated by its distance from its own concrete origins.

To say that reification restructures the psychoanalytic subject is not to imply that the categories of the Imaginary and Symbolic are ultimately determined by social-economic relations in any definite sense. I am assuming that socioeconomic and psychoanalytic objectifications of the subject are ultimately, in a logical sense, independent of one another. It is precisely for this reason that the accession of the Imaginary must be understood as actually producing the reified subject. I do wish to argue, however, that the socioeconomic register has a certain determinative primacy, both at the level of general theory, and (I think not by accident) within the text of *Areopagitica*. At the level of theory, the "eternal" character of psychoanalytic categories, as they are usually defined, tends to allot to History the role of a kind of compromised demiurge. History always supports and partially structures psychoanalytic categories, so these eternal categories must always be studied *in situ*, as partially determined by specific social relations. This determinative primacy of the socioeconomic is, in a sense, acted out or represented in *Areopagitica* by way of the conflation of codes, the overcoding of the commodity and the Imaginary, that we have already discussed. For the Imaginary has no proper historical vehicle. If the bodily imagery crucial to the monistic ethos were not largely merged with commodity figuration, then the body would implicitly be represented under the aspect of social units and territories, and would appear less as the source than as the function of Imaginary drives. The commodity code, in other words, seems to support the accession of the Imaginary, to provide it with a habitable substance, and thus partially to determine the alteration in the formation of the psychoanalytic subject of which this accession speaks.

Put more strongly, the economic definition of the subject as commodity absorbs the psychoanalytic definition of the subject in terms of material drives. Reification, as acted out and represented in the text, restructures the properly psychoanalytic problems of individual desire and its representations, and thus redefines the category of textual representation itself. This redefinition is exemplified in *Areopagitica* by the practice of the perforated text, by the disruptive devices of the eccentric style, which we saw to enact, on one level, an Imaginary defense against discourse, against the normative canons of textuality which would seem now to pose, with their assumption of difference and relatedness, a threat to the subject's Imaginary immediacy or homogeneity. Thus Milton-as-possessive-individualist writes against, as well as within, textual discourse; the possessive individualist narrative is partly defined by its apparent autonomy vis-à-vis the categories of representation. By an inevitable paradox, this division of the ego from its representations results in the complementary autonomy of discourse or representation from the subject. Since the initial narrative representation of the subject manifests itself as an unquestioned force, as prior to discourse itself, discursive representation takes on the same unquestioned and neutral immediacy vis-à-vis the subject, and indeed insures the subject's freedom through the display of its own autonomy.

If the Imaginary restructuring of the subject projects representation as a category external to the subject, and thus redefines all representation, in general terms, as something that adequates itself to the subject, then we may expect that this redefinition will work its effects upon the peculiarly traditional status of literary representation as well. This autonomy of representation is perhaps most brilliantly illustrated by the existence of the discrete stylistic universe of *Paradise Lost*, which Milton controls, in Coleridge's phrase, as if from a chariot and four.[25] But I would propose that the privileged category in terms of which to understand this transformation is that of genre, and that its main generic expression is to be found, not in the appearance of any specific genres, but in a way of practising genre as if from a distance, or in the prevalence of what is in effect a certain *kind* of genre, the *meta-genre*. In a situation where the subject feels itself to be one with the force of narrative, to be the privileged source of narrative, then the fixed narrative schemes which had before served as forms of collective representation, and which appear to us as signs of the contractual or collective nature of representation itself,[26] no longer seem concrete enough, no longer feel adequate to individualized social experience. They are accordingly disinvested of their status as fixed forms of social production by being overloaded with raw meaning, surcharged with the Imaginary energy set free once the poet ultimately fashions his work under the aegis of abstract labor power rather than under the sign of the generic contract. We want to distinguish such sundering of genre from its social moorings, from the ordinary definition of meta-genre, according to which any critical or ironic presentation of a generic scheme is meta-generic. The conventional definition applies well enough to "ordinary" periods of cultural crisis, in which generic contracts must be distorted and undermined in order to fulfill their social function.[27] But this ironic definition of meta-genre does not seem to be adequate for a period in which a radically new social content emerges in the form of generic practice. The poet writing under the aspect of labor power does not simply want to undermine and distort genre in a certain direction but to make it the straightforward sign, the living allegory, of the new narrative power of the individual subject.

Such a positive or allegorical practice of genre determines the uncentering of the rhetorical subject in *Areopagitica*, which I will now suggest corresponds to a disequilibrium between classical oration and Renaissance anatomy. The uncentering of the artificial orator occurs by way of a systematic exaggeration of the various parts and places of the classical oration, especially in the foregrounding of the figure of the orator and of the orator's passion. In classical oration, the orator's control over the variousness of his speech stands as a sign of the unity of political sagacity and ethical discipline with discursive power; the orator's passion is to consummate this symbolic argument by giving proof of the unity between ethical virtue and rhetorical power.[28] In Milton's oration, the rift between discourse and passion makes prominent the difference between political and ethical desire and casts the rhetor's real ethical force beneath the text of his argument. Milton's exaggeration of classical oration thus transforms oratory into a vehicle for a new kind of subject. But this transformation is one with the distortion of oration into something resembling the anatomy form, in which a host of different argumentative modes and devices are ironically detached from the subject who manipulates them, in such a way as to suggest the subject's final reducibility to a set of textual operations.[29] If the anatomy remains a loosely defined genre, this is because it is peculiarly meta-generic in the conventional sense of the term. It works by encompassing other genres, stripping them of their usual affect, and casting them into an ambivalently parodic vein. I have already given examples in passing of the generic oscillations in *Areopagitica*. The tendency for its discourse to fragment itself into a series of set pieces seems especially pronounced in the latter part of the tract, in which Milton dissects his opponents' arguments and the effects of licensing.[30] This generic parcelization goes beyond what is customary in oration, and represents the clearest evidence of the informing presence of anatomy in *Areopagitica* – an invasion, I think, that makes the tract rather difficult to parse in terms of the classical divisions or parts.[31] More crucially, the ambivalence of the tract's irony at the expense of those who would regulate thought as if it were any other commodity is partly a function of the anatomy's fragmentary and inherently fetishizing point of view, and thus an anatomical theme of a sort. But *Areopagitica*, of course, does not flirt with parody. Even if the rhetorical subject is uncentered and its argument fractured by the invasion of anatomy into its discourse, this does not result in a simple ironization of the oratorical genre. The congenitally ironic genre of anatomy is straitened in *Areopagitica* and made to signify, not the narcissistic melancholy of a textual subject in which no meaning can be fixed, but the ethical power of a subject figured as sheer narrative. Anatomy is thus converted from a genre in which textual representation reigns into a genre in which the Imaginary holds sway in the very excess of textual freedom.

But the Imaginary restructuring of the subject that determines this generic practice has its most decisive effects, not in the area of literary genre, but precisely in the domain of ethics. *Areopagitica*, as we have seen, argues for a free intellectual market, and by implication of argumentative excess valorizes the free and dynamic capitalist market. This valorization is, essentially and at its most immediate, an ethical valorization. The market structure itself is naturalized and its free working given an ethical value. Such an ethical encoding of market structures also takes place, not unexpectedly, in possessive individualism, where it is arrived at through assuming the primacy of the individual producer/appropriator's economic activity. The very existence of a number of individual producers hinges, of course, upon market relations, hence presupposing a market model of some kind; and the rights and duties of the individual, which become a central focus of attention in possessive individualist philosophy, are constructed to accord with some such model, are founded in abstract exchange. This validation of the market, then, allots to ethics a crucial role in political discourse. Even if possessive individualism obliterates or transcends an ethical perspective in its various theories of the state, nonetheless the state is justified by reference to a kind of individualized group ethics – by reference, that is, to the natural interests of a series of competitive producers in their individual relations with one another.

Thus possessive individualism defines for the ethical sphere of interpersonal relationships a new place and function within the ideological formation of seventeenth-century England, constructing ethics as a logically autonomous and primary area of discourse for the first time. This ideological redefinition, since it is based upon and presupposes the appearance of the isolated (economic) individual, necessarily implies a corresponding transformation of the place of ethics in the experience of the individual subject.

To put the matter in more general and more structural terms, the primary reification of the subject (of which possessive individualism is the contradictory production) determines a specifically ethical problematic. It determines this problematic not only in conditioning its existence and in giving it an experiential precedence in the subject's social relations. It also determines the structure of this problematic in accordance with the economic structure of the subject; accordingly the split between possession and proprietorship appears, in the realm of ethics, as a logical ambiguity or division between permissive and prohibitive, or spontaneist and administrative, ethics. We have already examined paradigmatic versions of these contrary ethics in *Areopagitica*. On the one hand, the moment of differential logic, which tended to define ethics in terms of an active and radically positive bodily process, represents a variant of permissive ethics, and corresponds, on the economic plane, to the moment of possession, when the subject is one with his body. The moment of presence-absence logic, on the other hand, in which ethics tends to be defined as a static process of selection "from above," represents a variant of prohibitive ethics, and corresponds to the economic moment of proprietorship for which bodily power is the ego's capital. Milton's paradoxical resolution to this ethical problem, his construction of a moment of suspense in which ethics is recast as a collective epistemological process, also constitutes the central means by which the subjective antinomies determined by primary reification are held together and in a sense overcome.

But the ethical encoding of the market involved here is complicated by its Imaginary overcoding. For the Imaginary in some sense motivates that ethical encoding: it is supported by and attached to the market, thus necessarily valorizing the market in duplicating its movement. In general terms, the reification that sets up a determinate ethical framework also recontextualizes Imaginary drives within this abstractly individualist ethical schema, in such a way as to give these drives a "purer" ethical expression. Yet in *Areopagitica*, the Imaginary reacts against the market movement which supports it; and this means that the ethical encoding of the market by the Imaginary is an ambivalent operation. The Imaginary not only validates, as it activates, the specifically ethical problematic in which it is set; it also negates and attempts to break out of that problematic in the very act of validation. And this ethical attack on ethics has the virtue of exposing the radically contradictory character of ethics in their inception.

I wish to argue that the same essential, eminently contradictory problematic as is central to the political argument of *Areopagitica* is also crucial to *Paradise Lost*. Its presence is clearest at the level of general narrative structure, where the division between spontaneist and administrative ethics is presented most clearly in the tension between the two ends of the story, between the image of God's plenty and the drama of the fall itself. These two polar moments tend to imply two different theodicical modes, and thus delineate, together, the ethical crossroads of Milton's epic. The image of creation justifies God's ways by reference to his original goodness and abundance, and in its various aspects comes to be associated with a correspondingly confident ethic of purification or natural development. This theodicy through creation forms a problematical supplement to the theodicy, obviously the more orthodox of the two, of the fall, which postulates the theological necessity of prohibitive ethics. Both theodicies are woven together in the actual plot of Eden and the fall. It is in this plot that they take shape as the halves of an ethical problematic, and thus in which ethics tends to disengage itself from the poem's overarching theological code.

Tends to disengage itself: yet Milton's classical epic – by its nature, I shall argue, an anti-ethical genre – continues to depend upon the theological code for its thematic totalization. The same uncentering ethical problematic that we studied in *Areopagitica* is at work, I think, in *Paradise Lost*, yet it does not, indeed cannot, appear in the same straightforward way. The possessive individualist narrative passes directly through, and is negatively mediated by, forms from the traditionalist religious-aesthetic area of ideology which, in the moment of *Areopagitica*, seemed to serve a crucial and yet secondary function of transparent overdetermination, of setting ethics free. The dominant genre of *Paradise Lost* attempts, on the contrary, to deny or transcend ethics. Thus, if ethics reveals itself to be crucial all the same, it must do so by transgressing against this dominant form. In order to understand the ideology of the poem, it will be necessary to describe this formal transgression, which we may already expect to be effected by the allegorical or meta-generic practice of its main genres. The logical predominance of form in *Paradise Lost* means, then, that our study of the poem must take a different course from what was followed with *Areopagitica*. While our examination of that tract began with questions of style and of inner structure, moving from there to the question of its "received" generic makeup, the treatment of *Paradise Lost* must begin with generic and ideological matters. The tenor of my argument will be that *Paradise Lost* is a privileged work in which to consider the mediating role played by predestinary religion in the formation of the possessive individualist subject, and that it enjoys this privilege precisely by virtue of its epic lapse into theology.

PART III

The epic of emergent capitalism: a generic construction of *Paradise Lost*

4
God: epic, hexameron, and predestinary theology

Criticism has proven that it is not easy to decide upon the exact generic context in which *Paradise Lost* is to be read. It is clearly an epic poem, but what kind of epic? I would suggest that among critics who have treated the generic question there have been two basic trends. On the one hand, there are those who take the poem as a *classical* epic. Paradoxically, such critics generally wind up focusing not on the poem's classicism, but on its Christianity. They see the poem as situating itself within classical conventions simply in order to Christianize them; the presumably classical message corresponding to the epic form is somehow translated into, or effaces itself before, a Christian message, leaving no residue behind.[1] This is enviably neat; yet it seems to me that such criticism assumes as a rule a greater malleability in the semantic content of epic form than exists, and in the interpretation that follows I wish to insist on the comparative fixity of the epic mode or meaning.

On the other hand, many critics have begun where these latter critics end, with the apparently unbiased and incontestable assumption that *Paradise Lost* is a Christian poem. For such critics, *Paradise Lost* is a Biblical or theological epic. Foremost in this critical trend is the school, beginning with Thibaut de Maisières, which has placed *Paradise Lost* in the context of a long series of narratives that arrange the Christian story into a kind of cosmological myth, the "celestial cycle". These narratives make creation, or the six days of creation, the center of the Christian story, and hence are called *hexamera*. For this – necessarily scholarly and empirical – school of criticism, *Paradise Lost* is a hexameral epic, in the sense that it finds its basic content in the hexameral genre. The focus of such criticism has been on the *content* of *Paradise Lost* – on its differences and similarities with respect to the various members of the hexameral series.[2] Although this approach has produced valuable knowledge and insights, it seems to me to be insufficiently formal in the main: the form of the hexameral genre itself, the structure of its seemingly bare presentation of the Christian facts, has hardly been considered; hence neither have the effects of the entrance of its preformed content into the epic been studied. It is, then, partly in order to counteract the static content bias of hexameral scholarship that I insist, in what follows, upon the more or less malleable and formal character of the hexameron in *Paradise Lost*.

Finally, it is in part because I wish to resist the overriding tendency, common to both these critical trends, to posit an effortless relation between a monolithic Christian content and dominantly classical form that I emphasize the division between form and content, epic and hexameron, in *Paradise Lost*. There is no easy adequation of content to form in *Paradise Lost*. Instead, the rift between the two is so stark, I will suggest, as to imply or inscribe a lack at the heart of the work. This lack is most immediately apparent as a political lack, and is figured, I wish to argue here, by the very stridency of the poem's classical form, in the militant "freedom" of the Grand Style itself. Before moving to a discussion of epic and hexameral genres, it will be useful to inspect the political significance of the epic form in relation to Milton's obvious political intent in *Paradise Lost*. It should testify to the fixity of classical epic form that it signifies Milton's revolutionary or reformative politics even as it represses them and hence undergoes distortion.

Politics and the epic

I take it that the hegemonic form of *Paradise Lost* is that of artificial classical epic. This is evident in several aspects of its narrative structure – evident, for example, in the poem's methodical superimposition of a single and unified foreground action, historically present, upon a larger background action, legendarily past: both Satan and Adam-and-Eve act on the ground of a presupposed legendary narrative – the Christian myth of the fall. The poem virtually proclaims itself an epic, moreover, in the insistence and abundance of its allusions to classical epic (of course mainly Homeric and Virgilian) situations. But *Paradise Lost* is nowhere more patently classical than in its verse or "measure," which forms in itself a continued allusion to the classical models, and may be taken as the very seal of the genre. *Paradise Lost* is not only patently classical, it is militantly so, as is testified to by the prefatory note on the verse. As is well known, English heroic verse is more or less brought to birth, in this preface, by Milton's fiat. Just as the classical oration was made the sign of political virtue in *Areopagitica*, so here heroic blank verse is loaded with a quasi-allegorical political significance:

> The measure is *English* Heroic Verse without Rime, as that of *Homer* in *Greek*, and of *Virgil* in *Latin* ... This neglect then of Rime ... is to be esteem'd an example set, the first in *English*, of ancient liberty recover'd to Heroic Poem from the troublesome and modern bondage of Riming.[3]

The political message of this example set is clearly conveyed by the diction ("ancient liberty," "modern bondage"), and would have been appreciated by the Restoration audience, for whom classicism would soon give mediation to the political balance struck within the ruling class, symbolizing its comfortable hegemony. But Milton is not returning to the classics simply to imitate them, nor to demonstrate good manners. Rather, he attempts to resurrect their spirit, the imperial freedom of which they speak. In this he is thoroughly of the Renaissance. Yet this resurrection is a straitened one. Milton's preface should indeed be taken to indicate a general *displacement* of his political intent – of his radicalism – from the level of narrative content to that of form. Not to suggest that Milton's radicalism is absent from the content of the poem, much of what follows will specifically attempt to show how the poem's content is radicalized from a distance by its form. I wish rather to suggest that it is especially crucial for a political reading of the poem to attend to the form into which its narrative is cast, if it is to understand the displacement and oblique recasting of politics which that narrative enacts.

This is not least because of the explicit political orientation of the epic genre itself, a familiar enough topic which I will touch on only briefly here.[4] The epic form should be considered as coming into Milton's hands with a pre-given political determination: this determination is usually explicit and central to the structure of the epic narrative, and it is usually "imperial" in its focus. In Virgil, whom I take here and in what follows as defining the semantic properties of artificial epic, national destiny forms the mainspring of the action, and is allied with that fatal natural order that seems to represent the ultimate category of epic. This naturalization of national destiny – a national destiny conceived mainly in military terms – may be seen, in Virgil, to have fairly direct political determinants. For Rome depended mainly upon foreign conquest for its slave labor force; "imperialism" was structurally integral to the mode of production under which it ruled. The centrality of national destiny in Virgil's epic registers the structural reliance of the Roman polity and culture upon military conquest. As in Virgil, so in epic generally, a primitive form of nationalism is organic to the genre.[5]

In order to show how this national-political orientation is repressed and displaced in *Paradise Lost*, within and by the epic form itself, I must consider the indelibly national character of Milton's early epic aspirations. For Milton had planned, it is clear from his autobiographical asides, to follow the dictates of the classical genre with respect to content as well as to form, and write a more English poem than he eventually did – to write, indeed, a national epic. His whole epic vocation was intertwined with what we might call a form of proto-nationalism. This national sentiment is only *proto*-nationalism because it precedes the cultural consolidation of the English polity upon which any true or classical nationalism must depend. Milton's patriotism applies less to the nation than to the church: it is a religiously coded patriotism for which the ideal English church – democratically disposed even if freely inspired and led by its rare spirits, its Saints – is simply one with the nation, and for which the nation represents only a peculiarly chosen member of the collective saintly body. Although Milton's national feeling is rooted in Protestant inter-nationalism, his patriotism nonetheless anticipates nationalism in that it is in part popular, incorporating as it does a largely secular myth of positive popular unity.[6] Milton's desire to write a national epic is nationalist, then, in the limited sense that the completed project was to express the inherent strength and virtue of the English people, and to provide them with a national myth.

The content of Milton's proto-nationalism approximates roughly to the political ideology of the Independent party in Parliament, in that the Independents depended for their partial success upon a similarly compromised popular myth of the nation.[7] The purificatory ethic of suspense that we saw at work in *Areopagitica* is the dialectical determinant of such populism in Milton, at least in a formal sense; it might be called an Independent ethic, since it is essential to Milton's explicit politics, and hence to his patriotism. What we saw, in chapter 2, as the differential formation of Milton's purificatory ethic can now be placed in a wider ideological context. For just as Milton's ethic defines itself against the orthodox Puritan ethic of repression, so Milton's proto-nationalism takes shape not so much by means of an identification with any one party (the difficulty of thus placing Milton is by now notorious), but rather in opposition to other forms of patriotism or definitions of the church-nation or people. It is thus useful, in defining Milton's patriotic aspirations, to distinguish it from antipathetic contemporary patriotisms or political ideologies.

There are three such oppositional ideologies: the absolutist, the mercantilist, and the Presbyterian. In the first place, Milton's church-oriented politics defines itself against English absolutism, which took continental forms for its models, and was hardly in any sense nationalist. Absolutism represented the nation by means of the figure of the monarch and his court, and, in giving divine sanction to the king's legal rights, made the monarch the symbol of the (nominally) seamless conjuncture of religion and politics, of church and state. The ideology was at its most virulent in the early seventeenth century (and especially in the 1630s), when the Stuart monarchy was attempting to secure itself against attack, but it had its origins with the establishment of the Tudor state, and its chief poetic exemplar and protagonist at the end of the sixteenth century, in Spenser. It is something of a paradox, in this context, that Milton could have professed Spenser as his model – a paradox that testifies, however, not to the independence of poetry from politics, but to the conflict within absolutism itself in England.[8] Spenser was Milton's original exactly in those respects in which he laid bare the insecurity of absolutism – that is, mainly in his ethical-Protestant emphases. But even though he made Spenser his forebear, we can see in retrospect that, had Milton written a romance epic, his narrative would have been patently anti-absolutist, and therefore in some sense anti-Spenserian.[9]

Milton's Independent nationalism was also maintained against the mercantilist ideology which definitively emerged with the failure of the revolution, and produced the first truly secular or modern concept of the nation. England's economic condition, and primarily the state of its trade, was its focal point. It legislated for order and orthodoxy in civil and religious affairs.[10] Milton fought against this mercantilism in an incipient form early on. We have already seen evidence for this in the argument of *Areopagitica*. For though the free movement of the market provides Milton's argument in that tract with its objective underpinning, it is clear nonetheless that reformation is not for economic ends. Indeed, Milton's aversion to budding secular mercantilism may have partly motivated (or overdetermined) that ambivalent relation to the commodity which we have described as being primarily determined at the ethical-epistemo-logical level.

Milton attacked mercantilism mainly in the guise of the third opposing ideology, Presbyterianism, which comes after 1644 to represent for him a kind of hypocritical merchants' religion, a politico-economic ideology with a veil of religious bad faith. The precipitous gap opened in English Puritanism in the 1640s doubtless spurred this invective: minor differences, in such a situation, are laden with great political significance. But whether or not one believes that Milton's attack on the Presbyterians as secret mercantilists had any historical validity – and I suspect it did – it seems clear that what Milton mainly objected to in Presbyterianism was its transparent accommodation of political repression into the domain of religion. Its emphases on orthodoxy, on elders' control of the congregation, and on a democratic hierarchy in the organization of the national church (the *classis* system), all testify to its will to control "the people" directly. As we have already seen, the ethical focus of Milton's religion tends to free it of any overt politics. The ethic of purification, in *Areopagitica*, not only combats a repressive ethic: it also combats the directly repressive politics that the ethic implies and supports.

We may say, indeed, that Milton's proto-nationalism is distinguished from all three of these opposing ideologies, not principally by its popular component, but by the relative purity of its religious coding. Whereas the other ideologies allow for the "practical" independence of religion and politics, Milton's nationalism implicitly asserts the unequivocal unity of these areas. Milton's early tracts find ultimate – and yet immediate – justification for the changes they advocate, in the religious code, the code of reformation. The revolution in civil society and in the church are not truly separable; reformation is the agent of all revolutionary happenings in God's favored country. In a sense, then, civil society knows no secularity. The nation or "people" – Milton's central political category – is not simply the extraneous object of reformation, but its substance, most itself as the collective subject of reformation. This is as much as to say that Milton's politics is virtually conflated with religion; his patriotism is almost wholly contained within the code of reformation.

But if the religion of reformation is proto-nationalist in essence, then we can see that the religious aspirations expressed in Milton's literary vocation put him, as a *called* poet, in direct contact with the nation, posit him, in fact, as the channel of its desire: Milton hopes to be inspired as a member of the collective subject of reformation, as a spokesman of the reformative tendencies at work under society's surface. The imbrication of epic vocation with religious nationalism is manifest from early in Milton's career; we can see it, for instance, in the preface to the second book of *The Reason of Church Government*, which was written before Milton's break with Presbyterianism. There, after offering justification for what might be considered his untimely intervention into the dispute over church organization, Milton goes on, in characteristic fashion, to trump his original purpose by projecting and justifying his epic vocation.

> I began thus farre to assent both to them [Italian men of letters] and divers of my friends here at home, and not lesse to an inward prompting which now grew daily upon me, that by labour and intent study (which I take to be my portion in this life) joyn'd with the strong propensity of nature, I might perhaps leave something so written to aftertimes, as they should not willingly let it die. These thoughts at once possesst me, and these other. That if I were certain to write as men buy Leases, for three lives and downward, there ought no regard be sooner had, then to Gods glory by the honour and instruction of my country. For which cause, and not only for that I knew it would be hard to arrive at the second rank among the Latines, I apply'd my selfe to that resolution which *Ariosto* follow'd against the perswasions of *Bembo*, to fix all the industry and art I could unite to the adorning of my native tongue; not to make verbal curiosities the end, that were a toylsom vanity, but to be an interpreter & relater of the best and sagest things among mine own Citizens throughout this Iland in the mother dialect.... content with these British Ilands as my world, whose fortune hath hitherto bin, that if the Athenians, as some say, made their small deeds great and

renowned by their eloquent writers, *England* hath had her noble atchievments made small by the unskilfull handling of monks and mechanicks . . .

These abilities, wheresoever they be found, are the inspired guift of God rarely bestow'd, but yet to some (though most abuse) in every Nation: and are of power beside the office of a pulpit, to imbreed and cherish in a great people the seeds of vertu, and public civility . . .[11]

In the context of the total movement of the preface, it is clear that the determination expressed in this passage offers additional justification for Milton's intervention against the prelates. For Milton cannot follow this determination out while the prelates exist to deform church and civil polities; to attempt to do so would be to cross reformation itself, whose energies are at this point at work in erasing the prelatical blight. Cultural or literary liberty hinge upon, or rather are conflated with, religious and political liberty. Once the body of the nation is freed from the oppressions imposed upon it by the prelacy (later in Milton's career, by the monarchy), it will be ready to speak, through the agency of inspired poet or poets, of its national superiority in heroic poem. Milton's gift of phrase characterizes him in his political capacity as national subject, and consequently must attend its time. The heroic poem is linked to the secular body of the nation, to civil society: it serves an ambiguously discrete and secondary doctrinal function (being "of power *beside* the office of a pulpit"), teaching primarily the ethical virtues pertinent to the good citizen. Yet it is made but a function of reformation by the notion – so all-important in Milton's explicit poetic – of inspiration, which is here clearly given a nationalist twist: God respects the political divisions between nations in ordering his distribution of inspired literary abilities. Milton is inspired as an Englishman.

The harmony between poet and pulpit apparent in the above passage, the intersection of classical-ethical and Biblical-prophetic codes within the containing reformational code, testifies, once again, to the religious purity of Milton's patriotism, hence to the unity of politics and religion. At the same time, however, the ambiguity attaching to the place of the poetic function points to an internal slippage or uncertainty in the relation between reformation and political or civil matters. This leads me to what will seem a curious observation. The uncertainty in the relation between religion and politics is precisely due to the unity that exists between them. The religion of reformation, in absorbing political ideology, paradoxically determines a latent contradiction between religious and political ideologies. On the one hand, the religion of reformation absorbs politics, largely by allotting crucial significance to the subjectivity of the individual in its unmediated relationship with various formally analogous collectives (i.e., single congregation, church, nation). It thus tends to empty politics of proper categories (and especially of mediating or institutional terms) and determines the presidence of ethics in its place; the urgency of Milton's classicism in part follows from this proxy political function of ethics, for classical ethics was more or less transparently possessed of political significance. On the other hand, reformation opens up a view of total social movement. As Milton uses the word, it clearly designates a historical process working through society in all its "revolutions," controlling and yet not one with this vast process. The discrepancy between reformation and the society it inhabits makes for the need, on the part of the religious subject, to intervene in society on behalf of reformation, and hence makes it imperative to comprehend its movement. Thus are established the conditions for a kind of secular history (even if it be the secular history, finally, of reformation) in which the immanent logic of social events is sought after. This then makes possible a kind of empirical politics: though ethics presides within the "secular" discourse of reformation, it nonetheless contains discrete moments of what is recognizable as strictly political perception. I think, for instance, of that moment in the course of the defense of polygamy, in *De Doctrina*, where Milton turns from proof by scriptural citation (at which he is having a field day) to glance at a more pragmatic, if incidental, argument: polygamy would be good for agriculture, since it would increase the population.[12] Heretical argument shrewdly harmonizes here with one of the orthodoxies of political economy, for which maintaining and increasing the work force was of main concern throughout this period.[13] What is striking about such "political" moments is that the political aims and insights involved always appear as merely pragmatic and *ad hoc*, so that their shrewdness is always surprising. This "occasional pragmatism" characterizes Milton's political attitudes and observations throughout his career, late as well as early. It needs to be emphasized, in the face of liberal misreadings of Milton, that this stance was the result, not of any customary shyness of politics on Milton's part, even less of a revulsion from politics; it was rather the structural effect of the religious code which controlled all social discourse and perception and which thus, in giving politics insufficient ground for articulation, relegated it to a strictly *ad hoc* ideological role. The mute empiricism of Milton's politics betokens a hidden fissure in the code of reformation, and in the place occupied by the category of the nation within that code.

The silent ambiguity of Milton's nation, I think, goes far toward explaining the ambiguity of his revolutionary disappointment and desire. On the one hand, *his disappointment*: it was partly because of the rift between his religion and politics that Milton was condemned to experience the revolution's failure not once but twice: first "privately" and on highly principled grounds, when the state refused, in the early 1650s, to "free" the church by abolishing tithes (or in other words as a failure of *Reformation*); then publicly and pragmatically, in response to the commercial panic of 1659 that brought the interregnum to its shameful end (that is, as a failure of the *Good Old Cause*). On the other hand, *his desire*: because Milton's nation is fissured, it is hard to know what he really wanted. What would Milton's utopia have looked like, if he had ever got around to describing it? The mute empiricism of Milton's politics partly explains, I think, why he never did. This means that it is also difficult to say what the political significance of Milton's national epic would have been had he written it: whether more theocratic or more republican in outlook; whether more internationalist or more English and nationalist in aspiration.

But this last crucial question is, as they say, an unhistorical one. When it came time to write *Paradise Lost*, the latent split in Milton's religious nationalism was recorded in the deletion of "nationalism" itself from the main narrative level of the epic. Milton's selection of hexameral content and foregrounding of the fall paradigm represses the national destiny from the horizons of the poem. This transgression against the conventions of artificial epic was of course primarily owing to personal and historical "facts." Already when he began, it was clear to Milton that England's immediate destiny was not what reformation desired; and he finished and published after the Restoration. An epic with explicitly political content or implications, a national epic, was forbidden Milton by England's political fate.

In spite of his inability to speak of reformation in the body of his poem, there seems little doubt that the desire for reformation, and the desire to speak of it, remains with Milton – the poem wants to be about the revolution. This desire is manifest in the poem as palpably repressed political intent or libido, as a surplus of specifically political energy.[14] Since the desire for reformation is too strong to be contained or conjured away by the ostensibly neutral fall narrative, it takes up residence on the poem's borders, and projects the revolution as would-be referent. More specifically, it expresses itself mainly in the *form* of the narrative, which thus serves a partly repressive function. Political libido appears in two significant formal places: first, at the level of general form, in the structure and formal substance of the genre of classical epic; second, on a subordinate and fragmentary narrative order which serves as a kind of outlet for unsublimated political desire.

The deletion of Milton's proto-nationalism from the content of *Paradise Lost* results most obviously in the demotion and dispersal of the national feeling traditionally central to epic content into a strictly literary purpose. The desire which would have been invested in the representation of the English revolution as the harbinger and leader of world reformation is banked rather in the revivification of classical epic and ethos. The form of the poem comes to figure the heroic virtue and ethical-political freedom of the classical world as essential to reformation's progress. This political-symbolic function of form is clearest at the level of the verse, which is the very stamp of the epic genre. Milton's construction of the Grand Style is a political act at the literary level, freeing heroic verse from its absolutist bonds, making style into an adequate medium for the reforming spirit. The Grand Style, accordingly, serves a different function in *Paradise Lost* from what the style of Milton's romance epic of reformation would have served, had it been written. In such an epic, style would have supported national-political content, by itself serving as an emblem of cultural achievement, and by consummating the heroic ethos deriving from that culture. The style of Milton's poem is not a consummation of political content but a sublimation of political desire: it can only speak indirectly, through its very formal substance, of what Milton would have the commonwealth be.

The distance from content thus imposed on style and on form in general is a perceptible one, and is integral to the structure of the poem. We shall later consider the significance of this gap between form and content from a perspective immanent to that structure; from the present perspective, the point to be emphasized is that the sublimative function of classical form in *Paradise Lost* registers a dislocation between religion and politics in Milton's religious nationalism that antedates the decline of the Commonwealth, and expresses the exacerbation of that division which attended Milton's disappointment. The classical form serves, by way of its own hypertrophy, as sign and symptom of political disappointment and desire, and hence in a sense produces that desire. But even as it springs political libido loose in the poem, classical form tends to throw into relief the rather obvious and banal political implications imbedded in the hexameral content, in the fable of the fall, according to which the decline of Commonwealth is symbolically rationalized as another repetition in history of the original fall. The disappointment of political desire that appears undispelled at the level of form is reduced and justified by theological fable at the level of content.

The distance from content imposed on the poem works, then, to lay bare the political ambivalence of that content, and, by extension, of the religious code that it represents. Milton's selection of the fall story both represses the revolution from the poem and reduces its failure to theological explanation. This ambivalence is deepened when we consider the second formal way in which political desire is registered in the poem. The religious content of Milton's epic works not only to seal off Milton's politics, and the revolution, from the explicit confines of the poem, it also subserves a kind of passive function by which leftover desire is afforded indirect means of expression. The narrative of the celestial cycle serves as a kind of libidinal reservoir in which political desires can be secretly deposited; the poem constitutes itself, in this respect, as a text to be decoded. But it does this at the cost of diffusing political libido over the surface of the epic narrative, in the process fragmenting it and consigning it to a kind of disjointed microstatus.

This political investment of the biblical narrative is effected primarily by way of analogies to historical events and situations; it is perhaps the principal virtue of Hill's chapter on *Paradise Lost* to have shown that these analogies form an important narrative category.[15] What is important about such analogies as a class is that they contain no immanent principle of application or interpretation, but instead attach themselves to the action in *ad hoc* fashion. Though the lineaments of Milton's own politics may at times be discerned at work in these correspondences, it seems just as often to be the case that references to contemporary politics are so abstract or decontextualized that their political import is not obvious; and sometimes political analogies even seem to conflict with Milton's own sympathies. When we find Satan tempting Eve in the language of a courtly poet, for example, we recognize the intervention of Milton's political animus into the portrayal of evil.[16] But in the case of the convocation of the devils in Book II, things are not so clear. The devils' situation might be taken to parallel that of the Royalist party after their defeat; but the fit is not so exact in this instance – the Parliamentary party doubtless held convocations also. So the main point of the analogy seems to be to bring contemporary history into the poem in extremely abstract and generalized form. Meanwhile, the use of regal figuration to represent God and his court – which seems undoubtedly to establish an analogy between God's monarchy and the absolutist monarchy – provides an example of a case in which Milton's known political sympathies seem discordant with the text, and must thus be forgotten, overruled, or canceled in some way by the reformed reader.[17] Thus the category of the political analogy does not in itself introduce a coherent and immediate political level into the poem; it does not give the epic a definite political orientation. Rather the analogies operate as random clusters of events, injecting contemporaneity into classic epic situations and gestures, and constituting a subordinate narrative level, a kind of micronarrative which works to surcharge and fracture the main narrative with its disparate and discrete intentionalities. It would be wrong, I think, to see the unprincipled articulation of these analogies to the body of the poem as a dodge for the censor. Or rather, if the micronarrative is a dodge, it is nonetheless a symptom first. For the chaotic overdetermination of biblically sanctioned narrative, and the surplus of uncoded political desire that thus appears or is produced, are in a sense but the formal expressions of a dislocation of politics from religion which was already present in Milton's ideology.

And why is the micronarrative a *formal* expression of political libido? Because, as we have observed, the hexameral narrative serves as the *passive* vehicle for political desire. The micronarrative appears more properly as an effect of the political ambition and the need for contemporaneity of the classical epic form. Form in *Paradise Lost* not only sublimates and signifies the political ambition repressed in and by the narrative content, it also attempts to project political content back onto the narrative level in a disguised fashion. So it is, I think, that Milton's representations of Heaven are secretly millennial.[18] These static and formalized images carry a political charge not so much because of their content, or because they are borrowed from *Revelations*, but because of their formal (epic) constitution, which appears to impose the millennial desire of *Revelations* upon Heaven almost against its will.

But at this level it becomes apparent that the formal militancy of the poem is not simply a matter of form, but also affects the poem's content. Political libido is not only sublimated into epic form, it also undergoes what appears to be a second sublimation into the hexameral narrative, into the hegemonic religious code. One can distinguish two closely related senses in which Milton's reformative desire informs content in a general, rather than a merely local, way. The first of these requires that we return to the important fact that Milton's proto-nationalism was always at the same time a form of internationalism. English Puritan nationalism placed England at the forefront of the Protestant nations, without cutting the English people off from, or defining them as wholly other than, the people of other nations. In *Paradise Lost*, the nationalist component of Milton's Protestantism, which was uppermost during the revolution, more or less drops out, to be silently replaced by the internationalist component that was always present as a defining feature of his religion. *Paradise Lost* is indeed a national epic (though not a nationalist one), simply by virtue of the international implications of its Protestantism, in a world coming to be divided between Catholic absolutism and Protestant commercialism. For the poem is militantly Protestant and anti-Catholic. In an international context, such features as Milton's brutal representation of a semiarchaic Old Testament God and his comparatively logical presentation of the redemption are quite political; through them, Milton implicitly asserts Protestantism as the definitive religion of Christendom. It is perhaps partly for this reason that the poem seems more orthodox in some places than we know Milton to have been. It may be partly because the political intention of the poem is to represent normative Protestantism that in Book III, God so forcefully and – on a first reading – clearly asserts the doctrine of the predestination of the Elect.[19]

> Some I have chosen of peculiar grace
> Elect above the rest; so is my will:
> The rest shall hear me call, and oft be warn'd
> Thir sinful state, and to appease betimes
> Th' incensed Deity.   (11. 183-7)

Catholics, and Catholic nations, would have been sure that they were not among the Elect.

But this last passage asserts predestination, it does not really think upon it. Indeed, I am inclined to say that the passage serves as a kind of decoy for the predestination question as it is truly represented in the poem. This true representation takes place, not in any given passage, but in a whole narrative conjuncture. In centering his epic on the fall or "man's disobedience," Milton focuses attention on the relations between two levels of narrative agency, between God's actions and man's actions. The poem takes as its main aim the proper representation or justification of Providence, or of what is, in effect, the problem of predestination. It is true that predestination is put in an abstract and refined context, and hence isolated from the dust and heat of history, by the very terms of the narrative situation. The collective constitution of the church, of which predestination was the immediate instrument, cannot be given direct figuration within the narrative. This sanitization of predestination can hardly be emphasized too much. The problem or theological situation whose foregrounding was the single most salient feature of reformation religion is removed from its political function in the formation of a revolutionary class.[20] It is thought upon in the poem, but in a metaphysical context: as the focal point of a cognitive, rather than a directly political, energy or interest.

And yet I think Milton's assertion of Providence/predestination should be understood as a political act, since it expresses his political desire even in "containing" it. It is in the foregrounding of predestination in itself that the second political function of the religious code proper, that is, of the hexameral content, is to be located. Even if this function is more internal to the religious code and only mediately political, it nonetheless is of greater significance in containing the political energy traditional to epic, however it may transform that energy in the process. For in figuring Providence the poem finally counsels a way of living predestination, and this amounts to a straitened assertion of a strictly cultural revolution.

Meanwhile, it should have become clear why I choose to approach *Paradise Lost* through its generic composition. The political desire directly expressed in *Areopagitica* must satisfy itself with formal mediation in Milton's epic. If we want to read the poem politically, then, it stands to reason that we must approach it through its form. The following analysis, or generic construction, of *Paradise Lost* attempts to elaborate and qualify the admittedly abstract and figurative statement that the poem is formally militant.

The epic as gesture[21]

I begin with artificial epic itself, and propose to locate this genre in relation to its original context by inquiring into the historical pre-conditions of its chief distinguishing formal effect as narrative. The epic has been conventionally and most impressively characterized in terms of the consistent uniqueness, the qualitative integrity, of its various narrative events. The reader of epic feels no need to grasp for connections in space and time, but rather focuses his attention on the present of a narrative self-possessed in each of its moments. Epic narrative seems thus to assume and assure, by virtue of this very suspenselessness, the ultimate unity or (as I shall call it) *homology* of its content, the connectedness of all its objects and actions.[22] How does epic explain its own suspenselessness, how is its homologous content determined within the narrative itself? It initially appears to be determined from within by the two principal thematic categories or constants of epic, fate and ethos. But – and this is my primary argument – epic homology is mainly and ultimately made possible, not by explicit thematic categories, but rather by the privileged content of epic, the stylized gesture: the pre-given and immanent qualities of epic gesture, indeed, are what make possible the strategic places occupied by fate and ethos in epic narrative.

It is easy to see that predestination, or the problem that it designates, assumes in Milton's epic the position allotted to fate or to a fatal natural order in classical epic. The narrative figuring of predestination is accordingly as important to the definition of Milton's epic mode as that of fate is to the classical epic mode, which is to say, it is essential. Criticism has generally assumed that the homology of epic action expresses and depends upon the fatal natural order constitutive of the epic "world".[23] Epic homology is felt to be but the effect, the sensible impression, of the narrative category or agent of fate upon all the other events of the surface narrative. The epic is one with itself at all points, and epic "intention" understands this to be so, because fate wills that it be so.

And yet fate is but an explanation from "outside," only the negative determination of homology; it does not contribute to defining the positive uniqueness of epic action. For this we must evidently turn to the nature of epic action itself, to the epic hero and the heroic ethos he embodies. Yet, though it is with the grand character of the epic hero that the more mundane criticism of epic has been mainly concerned, it is surely not through a focus on the epic hero himself that homology can be understood. Character is not the source of the homology that distinguishes epic action, nor indeed is it the focus of epic narrative. Or rather, if character is the focus, it is only insofar as it is a transparent synecdoche for epic ethos. Epic character can never wholly embody epic ethos; it is always eccentric to ethos. The tradition of the double hero is one symptom of this eccentricity, of the indifference of epic to specific moral virtues; Milton's comparatively heroless epic represents, in a sense, only an extension of this principle. The primary motive force of epic action is heroism itself, into which the chief hero is inserted with a superior difference. Ethos is artificial epic's theme in the properly Aristotelian meaning of the term, as both the end of all action and – for that reason – the deep retroactive agency at work in all narrative action. At its limit as such a total theme, ethos represents the point at which homology or suspenselessness is brought to consciousness in the form of an active acceptance of fate which is at the same time an assertion of a particular culture. Yet we must ask, how can culture appear as the real agent of epic narrative? What is the source of the independence of ethos from character? In the answer to this lies the final answer to the question as to the source of positive homology. Ethos is not only defined by the hero; it is also more diffusely figured by a series of gestures or clichés.

It is perhaps not too much to suggest that the stylized gesture is as central to epic as the commodity is to capitalism in Marx. Just as the commodity presents itself, under capitalism, as the generative cell in which the entire dynamic of social relations is recorded and contained, so the clichéd gesture is the nucleus out of and around which the characteristic narrative form of epic and the ethos which is its chief meaning are fashioned and arranged. The epic is so saturated with cliché, cliché is so clearly its primary raw content, that it is easy to overlook or become inured to its importance. As with the crucially constitutive features of many other genres, the significance of gesture in epic is thus perhaps best apprehended on a first reading of any given work, or in the first few minutes of a rereading. It is one's habituated apprehension of the quality and status of gesture in any given epic that establishes the perimeters of the reading process, such that any properly comprehensive interpretation of the epic must ground itself upon the way in which the given work recasts or reconstructs the pre-given gestural character of epic action in general.

What, then, is the nature of epic gesture? We have already gone far toward answering this question when we specify gesture as a category in its own right, when we distinguish it sharply from character. For it is of the essence of gesture that it is never thoroughly characterized or taken up by any of the individual characters or actions in the epic narrative; instead, the series of gestures is more or less *borne* by the character-narratives of epic, which enjoy such integrity as they do by virtue of their accommodation and combination of the different kinds of stereotypical action that make up the category of gesture itself. The category of gesture is virtually a narrative agent in its own right: it exists transparently, in the form of a series, upon the surface of the larger epic action, and marches across it while serving to carry it along.

On the other hand, it should be emphasized that gesture in some sense works *against* the larger epic narrative in moving it along, and hence constitutes a kind of anti-narrative level; or perhaps it would be better to say that gestures stand forth almost as small narratives in themselves, and thus abstract the mind's attention from the larger narrative structure and sequence which is based on them. We can see, for example, in the following passage from Book XII of Virgil, wherein Turnus finally recognizes that the force of fate is against him, that a stereotypical gesture of shock intrudes itself and "carries" the moment of recognition. This traditional gesture of shock or bewilderment, in which the warring body is suddenly stripped of its military faculties, serves as the basic enclosing structure which is then "characterized" by being sketched in and specified with emotional qualities – qualities that are themselves, we should add, little more than small gestures or clichés.

> The picture of their changed fortunes struck Turnus dumb,
>   bewildered him.
> Speechless and staring, he stood there, his heart in a violent
>   conflict,
> Torn by humiliation, by grief shot through with madness,

By love's tormenting jealousy and a sense of his own true
  courage.
As soon as the mists parted and he could think again clearly,
He turned his blazing eyes upon the walls . . .[24]

The point to be made about the first four lines is that they deliver an action complete in itself, a miniature story in its own right; the text has its closure written into it by the initial containing gesture, which casts the passage as a kind of vignette. I think it can be said that this is the rule and not the exception, that gesture always appears as self-contained picture-story or vignette in epic. But if this is so, and if gesture always involves a containing structure as well as a "motion," then the category should be understood to designate not just the content of epic in itself, but the inner form of this content. Gestures are gestures precisely by virtue of their stereotypical preformed quality. And however this quality may be modified and individuated by any given epic, gesture must retain its principle of independent unity or of closure – the raw material of epic must remain "raw" – if epic is to remain true to itself.

Such independent closure not only characterizes epic narrative at any one of its points, but also puts its stamp on the syntax by which the various events and episodes making up the larger action are ordered. Epic narrative syntax is predominantly paratactic: even when episodic subordination is signaled in the text, the uniformity of narrative tempo is such as to cancel its subordinate status.[25] The epic knows no digression, or knows only digression so leisurely that it is self-negating. Such suspenseless digression is the effect of the peculiar closure of epic raw material, even as it is another means by which that closure is secured. The formal digression of the catalogue is the epic device that would seem best to typify its suspenseless syntax. From our present perspective, even the static and non-narrative bulk of the catalogue can be seen to rest upon gesture; or, more precisely, to represent the point at which the patently static materials of narrative legend are converted into something like a gesture, are given gestural quality by the sheer force of narrative production which the ritual invocation to the Muse announces to be one with memory.

One might go through all of the epic devices, and construct a kind of rhetoric of the epic form, showing how the entire apparatus reinforces and elaborates its peculiar cellular content. Here I shall restrict myself to one such device: the heroic simile. As Jameson has shown, it is one of the main functions of heroic simile – which represents a kind of model in miniature of epic digression – to foreground the unified and self-contained status of epic activity in each of its instants. This is accomplished largely by way of the comparative independence of the simile proper from its comparison or actual referent in the action of the poem, which is accordingly described by a process of total evocation rather than by any particular resemblance or resemblances. For an example, let us consider a well-known Miltonic passage: the beautiful simile – really a triple simile – in which the Angel Forms of Satan's legions are described as they lie "intrans't" on the lake of Hell.

> He stood and call'd
> His Legions, Angel Forms, who lay intrans't
> Thick as Autumnal Leaves that strow the Brooks
> In *Vallombrosa*, where th' *Etrurian* shades
> High overarch't imbow'r; or scatter'd sedge
> Afloat, when with fierce Winds *Orion* arm'd
> Hath vext the Red-Sea Coast, whose Waves o'erthrew
> *Busiris* and his *Memphian* Chivalry,
> While with perfidious hatred they pursu'd
> The Sojourners of *Goshen*, who beheld
> From the safe shore thir floating Carcasses
> And broken Chariot Wheels; so thick bestrown
> Abject and lost lay these, covering the Flood,
> Under amazement of thir hideous change.
>   (Bk. I, ll. 300–13)

The simile is quite complicated by epic standards, in ways characteristic of Milton, and it is worth pointing out that the effect of this complication is to imperil the unity of the gestural referent as it is presented to the readerly gaze. Milton's favored practice of the double (or multiple) simile seems by sheer force of figurative transformation to render the referent more volatile and uncertain than is usually the case in classical epic; the sudden appearance of the angels in the guise of "floating Carcasses" dislocates them from the place they had held in the simile just before. Likewise the existence of minute, if hazy, correspondences between the configuration of agents in the simile and in the referent (another frequent characteristic of the Miltonic simile) makes the reader grasp for particulars, distracting the attention from the unity of the angels' action.[26] Such mildly disturbing effects are important clues to the status of gesture in Milton's epic, and I will want to return to them (and to this simile). For the moment, however, the point to be made is simply that, for all of its complication, the simile does fulfill the essential evocative obligation of heroic simile: precisely by keeping its distance from its referent, by not insisting on its likeness to its referent – one might say, by translating itself into a remote metaphor for its referent – the simile of leaves and sedge and troops presupposes the wholeness of the angels' lying "intrans't," and hence produces it as a discrete and unified action unto itself. The resemblance taken for granted between the two actions is indefinite and general, a total resemblance, and thus has a quasi-substantial character: it is as if the resemblance were a matter of the same stuff, the same essential energy, somehow inhering in the two unique actions. In other words, the actions appear homologous, in our use of this term; they are qualitatively unique and essentially alike at the same time.

It is notable in the above simile that it confers unity or closure upon its gestural referent, not only by avoiding resemblance, but also by extending the resemblance it avoids in a movement which I will term metonymic overflow. The simile proper confers closure upon its gestural referent partly by situating it: in each of its phases it depicts a configuration-in-space, and thus not only takes the action of lying "intrans't" as its referent, but also alludes to the lake and to Hell itself. Such metonymic overflow is characteristic of all heroic simile, whose object in this respect appears to be one of embodying an action by associating it with a site, by referring it to or replacing it with an indefinite situation or place-of-action. The effect of this in most artificial epic, and especially in Milton, is not to render gesture static or reduce it to a place; rather it is to give place – in the present instance, Hell – the force of gesture.[27]

To consider heroic simile is to realize the importance of the global device of epic style in the constitution of epic content. The self-contained and situational character of gesture in artificial epic, the constant closure of the gestural level of narrative, goes some way toward explaining the homology that appears to exist between all the various gestures: it serves, I am arguing, as partial basis for the consistency or stability that is essential in the definition of epic narrative. Yet, though uniform general structure tends to imply at some level a homology of substance, it is not necessarily sufficient in itself to attribute such consistency to narrative content; nor does it appear to do so. The establishment of consonance is left in large part to epic style, which works to homologize gesture and consummate ethos by imparting its own principle of uniformity to the action. However, as the structure of epic simile suggests, this is not accomplished by anything like an absorption of gesture into a uniform stylistic medium. Whatever the general features of epic style (and needless to say, these vary greatly from epic to epic), its achievement in homologizing gesture and producing ethos depends upon its distance from gestural content – a distance or rift of which the "stylization" of this style is both constituting sign and constituted symptom.

We have arrived here at one of the chief defining features of artificial epic as a structure or fixed form: the distance of epic description from its gestural content coincides with what might be termed a generic rift between epic storytelling and properly poetic modes of narration.[28] This hybridization of artificial epic is determined at two fairly discrete levels. It is determined, first, by the dialectic that is created from the moment at which epic appears as a written genre, as a properly literary phenomenon, outside of the oral culture in which it was first produced. With this, all the Homeric places and devices, and, most crucially of all, the formulas themselves, are abruptly transformed into clichés, or are at least made susceptible to becoming clichés. It is the particular duty of artificial epic to reproduce what are now potentially clichés which results in the separation of style from content, of its poetic production from the epic narrative itself.

Returning to the simile describing the fallen angels, we can see now that it not only constitutes the passive gesture of lying "intrans't" as a unity, but also asserts the autonomy of style from content, the force of narrative rendition or expression from the narrative itself. It does this by assuming and bringing into the foreground – one might almost say, by producing – the familiarity and the clichéd character of the action. Epic simile always assumes that its referent is known, is familiar, and hence needs no description; artificial epic simile assumes, in addition to this, that its referent is stock action or narrative cliché. In the present case, we are familiar with the image of the shades on the lake mainly from Dante and Virgil (though also from any of the epic poets who venture down to Hades). It is just this clichéd character which permits and to some extent compels the freedom of epic style vis-à-vis its referent; that is, because the comparison of Milton's triple simile is familiar in itself and from other epics, both simile and verse situate themselves at a distance from the real action. Yet the distance in question, we must notice, is in fact a distance between levels of cliché; for the simile that delivers or evokes the clichéd action is itself stereotypical, or there is that presumption: the autumnal leaves falling in Vallombrosa, Orion vexing the Red-Sea coast, Busirus pursuing with cavalry – all these things and actions present themselves as if already known. Once we see that the content of the simile that illuminates stock action is itself stock, the task of epic language or poetry begins to appear in a paradoxical light: it is one of reinvigorating or of reinventing stock action through its own stored energy. Epic poetry seeks to rewrite cliché – linguistic clichés, inevitably, as well as narrative ones – in such a way that the force that made it cliché stands out anew.

Yet the literary dialectic set up with the onset of cliché is in a sense only the phenomenon of a deeper sociopolitical determination. The very rift between style and content that it establishes, and that makes possible the apparent homologization of gesture by a uniform style, by a style with the force of cliché, foregrounds this phenomenal status. Once it is seen as a separate level of cliché, style itself appears as no more than a kind of running gesture, and the uniformity it attributes to gesture as nothing but its own principle of unity as an action. This recognition makes it clearer how ethos can be said, not only to be consummated by, but actually to inhere in, epic style. But it also necessitates a further inquiry into the self-contained closure of gesture, which now appears on its own, by the very ubiquity of its function as mediated through the gesture of style or of narrative production, to create that homology-at-a-distance characteristic of all the events of epic in relation to one another.

Such a phenomenon can only be explained, I think, by reference to the peculiar nature of social experience which we must suppose to have prevailed within the classical polity – or more precisely, to what I will call the categorical structuring of action enforced by the classical mode of production. The category of gesture in artificial epic is finally based, as Jameson has suggested, on the transparent unity of action, on the uniqueness of the various individual labor processes, which obtained in the city-state. In this situation, the poetic activity, the production of narrative verse, presents itself as a unique and definite human process among a series of other analogous, yet absolutely unique processes. We might make a rough distinction, in this regard, between artificial and primary epic, between the epic of the city-state and the epic of an earlier and less developed society, in which crafts were not yet separated in time and place from agrarian production. In Homer, the process of composition seems to be presented and felt as a God-given or immediately muse-derived gift of capacity by which legendary material is recorded and put under human control, and is subjected to the miracle of sustained verbal discourse.[29] Artificial style appears not so much as a miracle, but rather as a particular species (even if a highly individualized species) of a transparent and pre-given activity, as a form of what must appear to our eyes a "labor" already broken up and individualized.

The relative autonomy of literary production from the economic conditions of production, the comparative stability of the generic contracts under whose sign it is carried out, makes possible the continuation of epic in situations such as Spenser's England, where basic (economic) activities do not possess quite the same transparent and fixed status. Yet we should be careful not to overestimate the importance of the role of genre in itself, as a kind of fixed structure, or of generic style in homologizing content and producing ethos, and we can avoid this in part just by contrasting romance with classical artificial epic. What stands out in classical epic, in contrast to its romance counterpart, is the sheer heterogeneity of its gestural content, the differing qualitative intensities of its various narrative moments. This is nowhere more apparent than in the style itself, which paradoxically foregrounds its gestural quality by means of shifts of register and of genre. The classical epic simile, for example, in effecting an abrupt superposition of generic "sets" on its referent, works to bring out the generic moment itself as an element of what is thus felt as the distinct process of literary production. In romance artificial epic, on the other hand, the magical-ethical categories that are largely constitutive of romance content tend to presume upon the discrete domain of the gestural narrative.[30] Whatever natural independence or uniqueness pertains to the characteristic stylized actions of romance is detracted from by the need to distinguish between good and evil actions: all gestures must be tentatively reduced to their agency on behalf of the heavenly or demonic worlds. The episodic structure of romance epic, which lends so much apparent freedom to the narrative process, might be seen precisely as an attempt to reinstate the momentary character of classical epic within romance content, at the level of a secondary and larger narrative unity. Yet the repetition of episodes, the shifting of narrative and generic frames, usually just serves to lay bare the dominance of the magical-ethical framework within the structure of the action, while paradoxically enough episodic structure levels all the differences it is intended to support by reducing homology to mere uniformity. Likewise the homologizing function of style – which is even more "stylized" in romance than classical epic, as a rule – is modified and so to speak neutralized by the romance content. Style is transformed from running gesture into a more monolithic and uniform phenomenon, into a kind of machinelike verbal capacity – as is shown, for example, by the tendency of romance simile to appear mechanical, that is, to slide into mock epic.

This contrast not only makes it clear that the function of style in artificial epic must be situated with regard to a properly separate and discrete logic of content, and that the heterogeneous homology-at-a-distance characteristic of the narrative events of epic is determined primarily at the level of this content. It also suggests that the "singularity" of epic gesture is conditioned by the absence of such unifying and abstract categories as good and evil from any constitutive place within the narrative action, or within the logic of epic content itself. This is not to suggest that ethics is wholly absent from epic, for this is clearly not the case. Nor is it to suggest that organizing abstract categories are absent from the narrative framework: I have already specified as virtually or explicitly present and dominant within epic two obviously abstract categories, fate and ethos, which stand in something like opposition to each other and which therefore must organize the narrative. What I mean to argue is that ethical and other abstract categories, when present, occupy a subordinate and merely thematic position, and are articulated *upon* the more fundamental opposition between fate and ethos, which is structured in such a way as to permit the independent closure of the gestural level of narrative, and which in fact has its very basis in that closure.

The two terms of this opposition do not oppose each other in the way that good and evil do; they might perhaps be thought of, not as the antinomic concepts of a single code, but as different codes in tension, different modes of explanation in their own right. These codes overlap; they inhabit the same terrain in different modalities which threaten not to annihilate but to absorb one another. We might clarify how this overlapping is possible by focusing on the key term of fate and contrasting it with its ethical equivalent, evil. Both terms, it should be apparent, give narrative figuration to the force of the absolutely unknown or Other; yet this is a very paradoxical form of representation in the case of fate. Whereas evil figures the Other as a determinate agent within the narrative (as the force that opposes the contrary agent of good),[31] fate always casts Otherness in extranarrative form: fate is precisely that which is outside the narrative – that unrepresentable agent, at the origin of narrative itself, which demarcates and haunts around its borders. As such, fate may be understood also as the other side of the ethos or epic culture that the narrative celebrates; it is all that is not ethos, the determinant absence of heroic culture which validates that culture precisely in maintaining its difference from it.

The categorical basis for this radical difference of the Other in epic, and hence for the concreteness of gesture, is determined, once again, by the classical mode of production, which subordinates ethics and the sphere of individual relationships to politics and the logic of the contradiction between free and slave classes. This primacy of the political leaves its trace in what must appear to us a peculiar absence from the classical categorization of activity. The dominance of slave labor within the classical economy, and the blind contempt for all forms of manual labor which was its direct consequence, kept classical ideology from producing any general concept of labor or production.[32] The slave was not human, but rather a speaking instrument; the labor that he performed could not be thought of as a form of human activity. This situation had its bright side in the unreified character of classical activity: for the blindness toward labor necessitated by the composition of the classical polity was structurally interlocked with the appearance of urban forms of activity as unique and independent acts rather than as individuations of the same underlying substance of labor or human production. The categorical basis for the lack of unifying categories and for the positive homology of the various epic moments with one another is precisely this general structure of activity in which an unknown and unrepresentable absence determines all specific forms of activity in their positive differences.

We have returned, then, to the conventional notion of fate as the guarantor within narrative of epic homology or suspenselessness; nevertheless, I would claim to introduce a rather different interpretation of this relation than is usually made, one which helps explain the curious positivity or presence of fate. I am arguing that fate represents the agent or incarnation of the determinate absence of labor from the classical categorization of activity. It represents this absence most effectively, not as an abstract thematic category, but mainly as a pervasive force which is virtually one with the movement of epic narrative. As such an insistent and positive absence, it asks to be read in two ways. First, it may be taken to figure the main antinomy or aporia of the classical epic text, that between the unqualified plenitude of activities and the absence within this abundance of any determinant unity, between the all-embracing miracle of material culture and its proximity (not to say immanence) to the utterly unknown. Second, this very same movement of fate may be read as a *response* to this aporia, as a paradoxical attempt to instate culture itself as the self-sufficient answer to its own dilemma. This response occurs both at the macro-level of plot, of total narrative action, and at the pervasive gestural level. At the level of plot, fate works to naturalize and corroborate ethos by coinciding with it; in Virgil, this is accomplished by a blending of fate with national destiny, as I will show in due course. But we can see already that fate as abstract theme at the level of plot is supported by, and in some sense phenomenal to, its function in the gestural narrative, where the omnipresence of fate works to impose a kind of immediate unity on all the different moments of activity. In this respect, then, fate, or the shadowy but positive narrative Other for which it stands, seems to represent the main force of homology at the level of content after which we have been seeking, and thus to serve as its own answer to the antinomy it poses. It is the abstract and yet concrete force which informs and unifies all narrative events without leveling their positive differences.

The constitutive role of fate within gesture is perhaps nowhere clearer than in the military gestures which are so preeminent in the constitution of classical heroism and of the heroic ethos. Fate broods over all such action, holding immediate sway over the outcome of individual conflicts as well as attending to the event of the larger battles in which they take place. Thus, in the previously quoted passage from Virgil, in which Turnus realizes that his tide has gone out, fate manifests itself quite clearly as the guarantor of gesture – though its manner of doing so is paradoxical. For what is presented in that passage is the temporary breakdown of the "military ethic" that Turnus, as well as Aeneas, embodies; it is one of those moments, quite frequent in the later books of Virgil's epic, in which the rhythm of military gesture is interrupted by an eruption of the raw physical and emotional powers that underlie it, and that it to some extent structures. Yet as we have already pointed out, this poignant moment of near-gestural collapse presents itself in gestural terms; Turnus' recognition is as stylized as anything in Virgil, and marks the beginning of that military furor through which fate controls the remainder of the main narrative action. The epic attitude of furor indeed stands as a kind of symbol for the direct information of gesture by fate, for the pre-given structuring of the raw material of gesture itself.

It seems natural, of course, that fate should inhere most urgently in the military gestures so crucial to epic heroism. Yet I think that there is a certain historical propriety about this naturalness: a propriety which forms its very basis. Just as fate is determined in a general way as the unifying category of artificial epic by the centrality of slavery in the classical mode of production, by the absence of labor which it enforced in classical ideology, so the peculiar attachment of fate to military action may likewise be linked to slavery, or to the ideological distortions that it imposed. For the dynamic of the classical mode of production, which required a perpetual replenishment of its basic labor force, chiefly manifested itself in political terms and in the military sphere, as the need for foreign conquest. The fate of the Roman polity was played out in those imperialist military adventures that gradually decimated the "free" class of petty proprietors which was precisely the original source of the political strength of the empire.[33] We may say, then, that it is no accident – it is not simply a natural, but a politically determined phenomenon – that the fate which determines all the action in the gestural narrative manifests itself most directly and clearly within the category of military gesture.

It follows, likewise, that the prominence of fatally determined military gesture within classical epic is hardly accidental, but rather accords with the logic of epic content. In view of the fatally imperialist orientation imposed by the exigencies of the slave economy on the Roman polity, it is no wonder that the reconstruction of military legend should play such a central part in the representation of heroic culture. Indeed, this formal centrality might almost be said to make military gesture into a symbol of epic homology, of the peculiar unity of epic action and culture. In the splendor of military gesture, epic ethos is figured in all its libidinal integrity, less as a system of abstract moral imperatives than as a kind of energetic apparatus or motional code written into the very nature of action. We shall see later how the Satan problem in *Paradise Lost* testifies to the structural centrality to epic of this striving after libidinal integrity.

This discussion of military gesture as the narrative feature or "place" in which fate is most manifest as the guarantor of stability has moved from the gestural narrative to the legend of epic, to the larger action which is organized in terms of more or less official categories. Such a movement is, I think, a natural one: as symbol, military gesture lays down a bridge between gesture and narrative, action and character. Its symbolism works to create a stable narrative space, a mythic natural order behind the sequence of events in which fate takes up its station. We may contrast the constitution of this natural narrative space with that of romance in order to clarify and summarize the arrangement of official narrative categories in epic. In the epic situation, on the one hand, all the different narrative levels or mythic tiers (the upper world or home of the gods, the underworld, and the earthly realm) are united by epic action, forming a homogeneous unity or plenitude of material being which defines itself against an Other that takes the form of fate or the unknown, and is hence projected outside of the narrative as untellable. In the domain of romance, on the other hand, upper and lower worlds are marked off from one another as the loci of antithetical states of being or agencies which are locked in battle, within the narrative proper, over the earthly realm, and the Other receives its primary definition, not as fate, but as evil, as the black magic of the underworld. In romance, the natural order functions as the framework for the confrontation of the good and evil forces of white and black magic. In epic, on the other hand, the natural order, though an effect of the insistence of the fatal Other, works to contain the latent contradiction between the absent force of fate and the autonomy of epic ethos, of material culture. We might say, indeed, that the natural stability characteristic of epic appears as a consequence of the convergence of fate and ethos, and mediates the two categories, regulating fate just as it supports ethos. This convergence of fate and ethos in a natural order can be illustrated by a well-known passage from the *Aeneid*. In Book X, before the Trojans and Italians join in battle, Jupiter settles a dispute between Venus and Juno by refusing to intervene in the events of the day.

> Now take my words to heart, and let them not be forgotten.
> Since it was not permitted that the Italians should come to

Terms with the Teucrians, and your dispute allows of no ending,
This day, whatever the fortune each warrior has and the hope
He pursues, be he Trojan or Rutulian, I shall make no distinction –
Whether the camp is besieged through the destiny of the Italians,
Or a fault inherent in Troy, or the taking of bad advice,
I do not exempt the Rutuli. The selfhood of each shall determine
His effort and how it fares. I am king to all, and impartial.
Fate will settle the issue.[34]

Jupiter's abdication from immediate intervention makes Aeneas' victory, and Rome's future supremacy – of which he is not in doubt – seem in the natural order of things. The gods can only supervise this ultimate order of events, even if they appear to preempt it to some extent; the independence of military action carries its own fate within it. At the same time, this passage reveals the extremely tenuous place held by nature in Virgilian epic, which is virtually absorbed by military nationalism. It thus testifies to the general tendency of artificial epic to elevate ethos, as the tenor of gesture and the sign of this nationalism, over fate; it is heroic ethos that appears as the chief constitutive category of epic narrative, as the end of the epic mode. In this context, we can see that it is insufficient to understand the greater centrality of ethos in artificial as compared to Homeric epic simply in terms of the increased socialization of the classical polity, but that its role must also be understood, more forcefully, in the light of class struggle. In the legendary ethos of artificial epic, culture is produced as a mode of immediate political unity, and represents the drive to forget (i.e., to perpetuate) the absence at the center of the classical polity.

At the same time, we may read the independence of gesture, and especially of military gesture, as a utopian figure, a figure of collective solidarity, at the level of the macronarrative.[35] Epic gesture represents and celebrates the preformed plenitude of material actions that constitute humanity itself in the face of the determinate limits placed upon it by the classical mode of production – we might say, in the face of its own absence. We may in this sense call epic a humanist genre, as long as we remember that its humanism has nothing to do with modern ethical humanism. Artificial epic is incorrigibly social and political (not ethical) in character: by virtue of the independence of its categories, of the eccentricity of the hero to gesture and to ethos, it elevates material culture above the hero, or rather casts the hero as merely an example of finished ethos. Its humanity resides, ultimately, in what must seem to us its peculiarly uncentered structure.

Predestination

This, then, is the basic epic construct in terms of which *Paradise Lost* will be considered here.[36] In what follows, I wish to argue, finally, that Milton transforms epic gesture, and consequently epic narrative structure, in the very act of reviving them. He does this by introducing the monist or possessive individualist narrative into the gestural narrative, which works to deflect the political-humanist significance of classical epic in a psychological-ethical direction. In order to make this case, I will need to consider the hexameral genre and the notions of biblical narrative that it either brings with it or mediates, for the monist narrative is in large part produced by the encasement of the hexameron in epic form. Before turning to this question, however, I would emphasize how Milton's ideology makes use of epic structure without changing it at all, by preserving its classical form. To make this emphasis, we must return to the question of the disposition of predestination in Milton's epic; and to understand the significance of this disposition will require a discussion of predestination itself, both generally and in its Miltonic interpretation. I hope that the argument of this brief section will make plain the importance of respecting the poem's classical form as a kind of fixed and changeless entity, before we go on to consider how this changeless form invoked as such is in fact reconstructed and transformed.

The argument is simple but important. We have already seen how Miltonic monism is primarily a response to predestination, how the body serves to figure man in direct and complete contact with God and yet as a free agent. How is the heroic poem to duplicate this paradoxical response to Godly determination? How is it to convert the Godly will into free bodily power? The heroic poem as such is its own "answer" to this problem. It responds not by its plot, but rather by virtue of its categorization of action, which imbeds predestination in gesture, and thus dissolves it into the material force of heroic ethos. The crucial narrative element here is the peculiarly global gesture of epic style. We have seen that it is one of the functions of epic style to consummate or "take up" ethos from a distance, so that epic ethos appears to inhere in the stylization that is the stamp of epic form. That Milton attempts successfully to instate style as global gesture in *Paradise Lost*, that the Grand Style itself works to hold the different sections of the poem together and comes to serve as a kind of symbol for a peculiarly Miltonic ethos, we must let the poem's critical history (and the very coining of the term "Grand Style") stand as sufficient demonstration. This granted, we can say that Milton solves the problem of predestination in *Paradise Lost* by writing it out of existence. The importance of style in this solution highlights its purely formal character. When predestination is put into the epic form, it automatically becomes fate; God's will is homologized with or subsumed in a naturalized ethos, and yet determines that ethos in an unknown or unpresentable way, as if from the other side of narrative. The Grand Style in this respect is indeed an inspiration. For it mysteriously – that is, according to the laws of the shadowy generic construct which preexists it and which it calls into concrete being – registers and controls God's will.

Only a formal or purely literary solution seems possible for the problem of predestination. The predestination question, when it came to the fore, made matters difficult for any non-predestinary theology worthy of its name; theology was eventually so embarrassed that it became religion, with its psychological and ethical justifications, in which guise, as a kind of accessory to psychology and ethics, it continues to lead a flourishing life to this day. The difficulty for theology, once the problem of predestination takes a central place within it, is simply that it must retain at its summit the "person" of God, with his ultimately unitary will.

One can illuminate this difficulty by contrasting the problem of predestination with the problem of determinism as it occurs in Marxism. The logical difference lies in the irrefragably narrative character of Protestantism. For though Marxism posits the mode of production, the economic level of the social formation, as the determinant foundation of human history up to the present, it does not, at its limit, make the mode of production, or the economic activity that it defines, the subject of history. This role would be fulfilled, if at all, by the political level, by that complexly structured class struggle which, in its dialectical autonomy, inhabits all the instances of the social formation and, so to speak, holds them together. Class struggle, viewed in this way, is the total and autonomous effect of the dialectical interaction of social structures: it might almost be called the personification of structural overdetermination.[37] But it is a personification with a difference, because it personifies the lack of any single and unitary agency working through history, thus testifying to the fundamentally non-narrative character of history itself, even while acknowledging the necessity of historical narrative for knowledge.

In Protestantism, however, there is a unitary agency to account for; worse, an agency modeled on the human will; worst, a will by definition all-powerful and omniscient. The problem for any non-predestinary Protestantism is to separate this will's knowledge from its power without destroying its unitary character. Miltonic monism, considered as a way of thinking human freedom, can be seen as a singular version (or particular aspect) of the traditional resolution to this problem, which mediates God's will through the creation, making creation or natural law the determinant foundation of human agency. Nonetheless, it is difficult, at best, to see how such a foundation, whatever form it takes, could adequately buffer God's knowledge from his power. Either it separates knowledge and power – in which case God's will no longer appears indivisible; or it does not – in which case God's integrity is preserved at the cost of human freedom. The phenomena of creation or of nature may serve to displace the problems that arise when God's unitary will is placed in direct contact with human agency; they may serve as the ground for another narrative, unfolding in apparent independence of God's will, on its own separate plane, and hence may recast the problem of agency in terms of human volition. But the narrative of creation can only be a secondary and subordinate narrative: creation itself, in its totality, is but a sign of God's unitary will, of the oneness of knowledge and power; therefore the creation story, in its total logical structure, can only represent and incarnate the problems already manifest in the theological narrative. The mere narrativization of God's activity, then – and it seems to me one of the reformation's main features to insist on such pure and immediate figuring of God – both accentuates the problem of theological determinism and imposes on theology the choice or division just described, between a split or schizoid God and an all-determining or despotic one.

Milton's God possesses the rather dubious, yet decisive, merit of encompassing both sides of this divide. God-as-character constantly oscillates between imposing his own will or reality principle on all the other agents and observing the dictates of an anterior reality principle which seems to have programmed the whole Godly (or theological) narrative in advance. As I hope to show, it is this latter principle that appears to be inclusive: God-as-character is repeatedly decentered and absorbed by the theological narrative. The point to be made here, however, is that it is necessary to distinguish between the immediate presentation of this divided God and the epic representation of God's agency in which providence/predestination is cast as fate. The bewildering split representation given by the theological narrative is in some sense contained within the larger epic representation of fate, which "dissolves" the very problems so patently grappled with by the former narrative. The will of Godly discourse is broken up, expelled from the narrative proper, by the style which casts that discourse, from a distance, as gesture.

This indirect epic construction of predestination is formally more comprehensive than the explicit construction given by the narrative depiction of God, in spite of the fact that this depiction represents the official logical treatment of predestination. Even when, as I think is inevitable, the epic runs aground on the straits of theology at the macro-level of content or of story, the Grand Style rectifies, or rather invalidates from a distance, the insuperable problems exposed. A passage from God's opening discourse in Book III can be used to illustrate this point. In this speech, God locates Satan heading toward earth and man, which leads him abruptly to foresee the fall. He then just as abruptly turns to a justification of predestination, officially cast here as almost one with God's creation:

> Through all restraint broke loose he [Satan] wings his way . . .
> Directly towards the new created World,
> And Man there plac't, with purpose to assay
> If him by force he can destroy, or worse,
> By some false guile pervert; and shall pervert;
> For Man will heark'n to his glozing lies,
> And easily transgress the sole Command,
> Sole pledge of his obedience: So will fall
> Hee and his faithless Progeny: whose fault?
> Whose but his own? ingrate, he had of mee
> All he could have; I made him just and right,

Sufficient to have stood, though free to fall.
... They therefore as to right belong'd
So were created, nor can justly accuse
Thir maker, or thir making, or thir Fate;
As if Predestination over-rul'd
Thir will, dispos'd by absolute Decree
Or high foreknowledge; they themselves decreed
Thir own revolt, not I: if I foreknew,
Foreknowledge had no influence on their fault,
Which had no less prov'd certain unforeknown.
(11. 87–119)

What is perhaps most striking about Godly discourse, here and elsewhere in the poem, is the eerie co-residence within it of doctrinal and psychological motivations and justifications. As a rule the conflict between these two moments works to displace and cover over the impossible aporia within Godly theodicy, drawing attention to the cognitive problem of God's characterological constitution in its place. But in the above passage this conflict must be read more as a sign or symptom of theodicical strain. The antinomy is clear. God's justification of his original act of creation motivates that act by appealing to – or rather by framing it in accordance with – an original order or logic, a primary law which, while determining the notions of the just and right, is scarcely distinguishable from the very concept of action itself. He thus submits his own activity, which must on any orthodox view justify *itself*, to an external imperative, to that fate or telos inscribed in and presiding over all "free" or "true" action, and guaranteeing its unity: there are few moments, I think, in which the poem is so embarrassing at its official level, not just to Protestantism, but to all Christian theology.

Meanwhile, we should notice that even at this moment of official embarrassment, epic theology is not wholly absent from the official or explicit presentation of God himself, and not entirely removed from hexameral content. God's dependence on a craftsmanlike (hence quasi-classical or Aristotelian) notion of his action, as evidenced in the line "Thir maker, or thir making, or thir Fate," might be said to represent the direct influence of form upon content. The fate which rises up in the midst of God's discourse for once, just as it has repeatedly appeared in the speeches of Satan and the devils, is finally controlled by the epic rather than the theological context. The fate of "thir making" is epic fate. Yet it is not as it penetrates to the level of immediate content (which is, I think, a fairly rare phenomenon) that epic fate resolves or settles the theological antinomy, which remains prominently insoluble "in itself." It is rather at the formal level, in the epic context and (admittedly modified and singular) stylization of God's discourse, that God's activity is most adequately presented and contained. Such features as the epic set piece that introduces God's discourse (11. 55–80) and the quasi-formulaic amplification of the line in which fate is mentioned do more than logic can to justify God's ways, insofar as they recast God's will within an epic framework and make it seem virtually a function of epic ethos, which is to say of the Grand Style or of the process of narrative production itself. It seems clear that this recasting occurs as a rule at a level essentially independent of and discontinuous with the official theology of the poem, however thorough the interdeterminations may be in any given place between "epic" and "official" theology, between ultimate form and immediate content. The solution itself in its comprehensiveness hinges precisely on this discontinuity; it is thus made possible by the constitutive rift between epic form and content that we have already discussed.

This example should illuminate, then, the inclusive genius of Milton's major formal solution to the predestination problem, and should clarify the necessity of taking the overt classicism of the poem seriously. The comprehensiveness of the solution lies in that it allots God's agency, the unitary narrative status of which is precisely so problematical, an integral place within the narrative, and yet as if on the other side of narrative, even when God-as-character is before our eyes in all his contradictory splendor. That is, God's will is figured within the narrative of *Paradise Lost* as the power behind narrative, as a kind of positive absence informing all the gestures that traditionally make up epic content and that provide the basis for its peculiar ethos. As with fate in traditional classical epic, predestination appears as an insistent theme in *Paradise Lost*, imbedding itself in gestures Edenic and Hellish as well as Heavenly. In this context, we can see that epic gesture has as a primary function to serve as a vehicle for Milton's monism: it is a way of figuring ethical autonomy in the form of bodily freedom. In this major respect, the force of poetic or generic convention does not work to erase Milton's heterodox radicalism, as has often been argued or assumed,[38] but rather to afford it means of expansive expression. Epic in itself, as a kind of static form for emulation, serves to enfigure Milton's heterodox theology, and thus gives cloistered expression to the political desire we have seen to be imbedded in it.

Milton's notion of Godly narrative

I would argue, indeed, that classical epic, in recording Milton's monistic ethic, makes it into a kind of political symbol – that the epic form politicizes the more properly ethical orientation of Milton's ideology, even as this form is itself hollowed out and transformed by that content. We shall see more clearly how this is achieved at the conclusion of our analysis. Now, however, we must attend to the other half of this process, and consider the ways in which classical form is compromised and altered by the "official" content of *Paradise Lost*. To do this, I will continue to pursue the matter of predestination and of the representation of God, which is hardly so neat or so simple as has thus far been implied. I wish to argue that the official representation of predestination in *Paradise Lost* is determined by the hexameral genre, but that the hexameron gives figuration to a singular aspect of Milton's theology, his notion of Godly representation or of the structure of biblical narrative. I will proceed by first setting forth Milton's notion of Godly representation, and showing the more or less direct effects of this "ideology" of God on the whole poem. I will then turn to the hexameron and give it a brief historical construction, arguing that it should be understood "originally" as a genre of late feudalism. On the basis of this construction I hope to show how it is possible for the hexameron to mediate, more or less untainted, Milton's notion of Godly representation, and how the hexameron itself is set in motion and split apart by that mediation.

If the matter of predestination is more complex than epic theology would have it, this is not simply because the Protestant God resists fitting into the peculiarly non-narrative narrative status occupied by fate in the classical epic. The epic form may be unable to accommodate purely the orthodox Protestant notion or representation of God: epic theology may necessarily be heterodox; but Milton's God is all the same unnecessarily willful – not simply representative, but scandalously representative, of the prerevolutionary Protestant God in this respect. Neither, it should by now be apparent, can we dismiss this willfulness simply as the sheer effect of God's narrative deployment.[39] It would seem, rather, that Milton's "personal" theology, his peculiar concept of God, led him to give prominence, in the manifest content of the poem, to a construction of the predestination problem which contradicts his epic theology.

This is not a novel suggestion. Indeed it is generally recognized that Milton's literalist notion of God's biblical representation is behind the bold portrayal of God in *Paradise Lost*. But the significance of this notion, both for Milton's theology and for *Paradise Lost*, has perhaps not been adequately appreciated. Here, more clearly than anywhere, it is possible to grasp the nature of Milton's literalism (whose importance for Milton's theology is abundantly evident in the burgeoning citations of *De Doctrina*). Milton, of course, maintains that God's representations of himself in Scripture are to be taken literally, that they have an absolute validity. His reasons for holding this in *De Doctrina* seem cogent and logical, within the framework that they partly serve to establish.[40] Milton does not deal with Godly representation from the point of view of the intrinsic capacities of language or of representation in general, but more specifically from the angle of the reader of the biblical text who knows its author to be God. As readers we know in advance that God is properly imponderable; however, although Milton begins by asserting this fore-knowledge, he does not really emphasize God's ineffability. Rather it is precisely because we know God to be imponderable in himself that we must restrict our speculation to his active representation of himself in Scripture. This representation deserves our attention, not as a sign of its own incapacity to delineate God, nor as a pretext for empty metaphysics, but rather as a positive image. Milton in fact strongly implies – though all the while stressing that God must *submit* or, to use the language of theology, *accommodate* himself to our understanding – that his representation in Scripture is really in some sense adequate. This must be so since it would derogate from both God and his followers if it were otherwise, if God submitted to a representation unworthy of himself in order to accommodate himself to the understanding of those made in his own image. It follows, for Milton, that the representation of God is non-figurative, or at least cannot be understood in figurative terms. God gives himself to us, and is to be read, in simple and literal purity.

Yet the letter of Godly representation, and by extension the letter of the biblical text to which Milton's whole theology is chained, does not in practice constitute a simple object for knowledge. The status of the letter is rendered ambivalent precisely by the assumption that Godly representation is integral or univocal. For this assumption, even in asserting the identity or perfect correspondence of the letter and its significance, nonetheless enforces a logical division within the biblical text between textual signifier and narrative signified: the text is merely the expression of a unitary force; it is simple because it has something simple underneath it. The letter of the text is merged with narrative, or rather is most itself as a sort of embodiment of narrative force. Thus Milton's biblical literalism, in this point as in others, is not really a literalism of the letter at all, not a faith in the various implications of Scripture, but instead a literalism of some underlying (though nominally transparent) and univocal narrative signified, a faith in the narrative force on which the relation between biblical author and reader is predicated. The whole aim and end of Milton's literal notion of Godly representation is to foreclose the gap it nonetheless implies between representation and the represented, between biblical text and its signified, by making biblical narrative an all-inclusive category.

Let us consider this faith in narrative and what it implies more closely. I believe we can locate, within the inclusive category of biblical narrative, an antinomy or central aporia which replaces that between the text and its signified. This is the antinomy between what we might call the text and the context of biblical narrative. On the one hand, as we have already seen, Milton's argument about God's biblical presentation presupposes God as an integral force. Milton's faith in narrative representation defines God as a unitary agency, as a single "actant." In practice this belief tends to imply in God something like a will. Such an implication might be considered partly as a simple necessity of narrative figuration; in any case, the willfulness of the Old Testament God makes it hardly surprising that Milton the literalist should have conceived God in terms of unalloyed willful power. In this aspect, narrative itself – in the immediate presence of its authorial actant, and in its palpable form as motion or force – is a concrete sign or material embodiment of God. It is in this "concrete" and strictly productive moment of narrative as text that the non-figurative status of biblical narrative is clearest and most unproblematical; to make God's picture of himself into a figure would be to cover over the will of God itself at work and exposed in its transparency. On the other hand, the definition of God as willful actant places him within a narrative order or context, in terms of which he must necessarily be read. The very movement which founds biblical narrative is contained and defined by it, and therefore must be interpreted within its narrative context. The order is understood to be as non-figurative as the will that founds it; yet it is often difficult to grasp this order in non-figurative terms, to purify it of the figures that may be felt as sheer process at the level of the text of narrative. In the case of God, who is generally imaged in human terms, the problem is to read personification in an impersonal way. When God appears in human shape, or is said to have human aspects, this is not at all a figure of the text; he really *has* human characteristics ("why should we be afraid of assigning to him something that he assigns to himself?"). Nonetheless, we are to understand always that these human characteristics pertain to God with a difference; we must strip such features of their usual concomitants or implications in human life whenever such associated characteristics would obviously be unworthy of God's majesty and dignity. Thus a curious kind of interpretive process is established, a process which is apparently arrested before it gets under way, and which humanizes and dehumanizes (contextualizes and decontextualizes) God and Scripture in one and the same movement:

> In my opinion, then, theologians do not need to employ anthropopathy, or the ascription of human feelings to God. This is a rhetorical device thought up by grammarians to explain the nonsense poets write about Jove.... We ought not to imagine that God would have said anything or caused anything to be written about himself unless he intended that it should be a part of our conception of him. On the question of what is or what is not suitable for God, let us ask for no more dependable authority than God himself. If *Jehovah repented that he had created man,* Gen.vi 6, *and repented because of their groanings,* Judges ii 18, let us believe that he did repent. But let us not imagine that God's repentance arises from lack of foresight, as man's does, for he has warned us not to think about him in this way: Num. xxiii 19: *God is not a man that he should lie, nor the son of man that he should repent.*   (pp.134–5)

What seems curious about this passage is that the abstraction from the context of humanity that it insists upon is so unproblematical. It is quite difficult to conceive of any act of repentance which does not involve the acknowledgment of a previous mistake, but Milton is not troubled: he simply places repentance, as if by fiat, on an order of representation in which the context of humanity does not figure (or figures only selectively). God's repentance is reduced to a momentary and positive act, and the order in which this act takes place is depersonified. This defigured narrative order to which Milton is faithful is in fact no more ambivalent or curiously unproblematical than the God that is predicated on it. Yet, because Milton's argument begins by assuming God as an integral force or will, the problem for our comprehension of Godly representation principally appears in the realm of narrative context, as a problem of defiguring or neutralizing the figurative status of narrative, and asserting it as a purely logical order. This ambivalence in the Godly narrative order may be extended to biblical narrative in general. On the one hand, biblical narrative seems to be modeled on human agency, on the context of humanity; its ultimate actant is, after all, but an effect of personification. On the other hand, the context of humanity is not thought of as being constitutive of narrative, whose order exists in essential independence of human action. Narrative maintains a distance from human activity – even if it is in an immediate sense one with it – and thus can provide it with a kind of objective encasement.

We have encountered such a neutral narrative structure before; the connection between Milton's literal concept of God and his monism will perhaps have been felt by now. Milton's faith in the narrative adequacy of God's representation in Scripture, and the impersonality or neutrality of narrative that such adequacy presupposes, are determined by, and correspond to, Milton's monistic sense of the subject and the neutral possessive individualist narrative on which it is based. God as unitary force is made in man's image, and thus in a certain light God's willful immanence to the biblical text, the very will that predetermines all man's actions, paradoxically serves as a secret symbol for man's integral freedom. In this symbolic construction, Milton's theology of God has its chief significance within an ethical register which is not properly contained within the theological domain.

I hope to show eventually that in the larger narrative of the fall the poem gives visible expression to this secret ethical decentering of theology. For the moment, I will suggest that the very possibility of this larger process of narrative decentering hinges upon the impersonality, the strictly cognitive orientation, of theological narrative in Milton's conception and poetic rendering, which we are now in a better position to understand. As we have seen, the monistic or possessive individualist narrative did not foreground the subject in the sense of calling its foundations into question, but by making its motions a focal point of cognitive interest. In the same way, biblical narrative, for Milton, is its own justification. Questions concerning its adequacy to its object do not arise within narrative, or at least are not central to it; instead, narrative is a one-dimensional instrument of knowledge, and directs attention to its own self-constitution as an order.

This cognitive slant of narrative is very much present in the treatment of God and of supernatural matters in *Paradise Lost,* as well as in the general narrative structure. On the one hand, Milton's peculiar faith in narrative probably goes farther to explain the *possibility* of his confident presentation of the supernatural than does his literal belief in inspiration. Considerations of representability haunt the poem, as they haunt Milton's concept of scriptural deity. Just as occurs in Milton's theology, however, questions as to the adequacy and efficacy of its representations-without-referents, doubts as to the possibility of a self-contained univocal signified, are never really entertained in *Paradise Lost.* God must be taken as he is, his meaning not his name must be heeded, however difficult that may be; and the same axiom obtains for the other supernatural agents and scenes. On the other hand, even though Milton's faith in (biblical) narrative brackets, for his theology and for *Paradise Lost,* the question of narrative adequacy, sealing off and assuring the relation between signified and referent, in doing so it nonetheless brings to the fore questions concerning the construction and constitution of that signified, of the agents that move over the surface of narrative, and form its main visible content. So it is that *Paradise Lost,* though it exhibits no profound interest in the representability of God, offers as a problem for cognition what we must call the narrative constitution or mode of action of the Godly subject – and beyond this, has as a central point of focus the more or less systematic constitution of all its characters. Thus we can see that that strictly cognitive interest in the laws of action of its content, in the *modus operandi* of the fall, which must be one of the most salient and refreshing features of *Paradise Lost* for any modern reader of the poem, is determined at the heart of Milton's archaic Protestant theology.

The narrative concept of God, in this more general respect, makes even the epic theology a main point of cognitive interest and investment. Nonetheless, it is itself in plain conflict with the epic definition of God's will. On the one hand, the epic form scatters God's will across the events of the poem as a diffuse fate, and casts the predestination problem in the form of a relation between ethos and an Other that is made to serve as its guarantor or containing structure. On the other hand, the strict theological concept of God, as it is forcefully presented or acted out in the poem, defines God in terms of his willfulness, makes his whole place in the narrative depend on his strict proprietorship of his will. In fact, *Paradise Lost* presents to public gaze, in its direct representation of the deity, a predestinary God: predestinary not only in the strict sense of selecting from all time an elect of believers, but also in the logical sense of predetermining all subordinate activity – including, most importantly in this context, the fall. However God justifies his original creation, it remains impossible to conceive, in the humanly inhuman terms that the narrative imposes on God, of an "innocent" original act. For all his reciting of theological commonplaces, God, by the very willfulness of his appearance, asserts responsibility for man's fate.

What I am arguing here – disregarding for the moment the question of the generic incarnation and refraction of Milton's personal God – is that the presence in the epic of the predestinary God of early Protestantism immediately corresponds to an element of Milton's own ideology, that is, his concept of God. Once again, it appears that the submission of theology to poetic convention or form works not so much to conventionalize Milton's "eccentric" theology as to express his true theology in the broadest possible terms, to give amplitude and freedom to its more jarring contradictions. For, in fact, Milton always maintained faith in the harsh predestinary God of early Protestantism, even as his dynamic sense of the subject, his sense of personal vocation, forced Arminianism upon him;[41] and the direct presentation of God gives voice to this more archaic deity, while the relative independence allotted to epic content by the structure of epic itself makes the discrepancy between predestinary and Arminian theology seem so blatantly natural as hardly to appear contradictory.

Hexameral structure

The main formal vehicle of the doctrinaire and self-possessed God of Milton's theology is the hexameral genre. From the generic point of view that I am arguing takes logical precedence in a political reading of the poem, it may be said that the hexameron introduces and foregrounds the problem of predestination as a properly unthinkable or insoluble problem in the narrative terms in which it is irrefragably cast. The first problem for us, then, is to show how it was possible for the hexameron to permit a more or less direct expression of Miltonic predestination in its representation of God – a problem which poses a conundrum. For if the hexameron centers upon God's will, it does so in a major respect against its *own* will. The principal focus in hexameral literature, as the very name indicates, is not God's will, but rather creation. This is a constant of the genre from its founding in the so-called Dark Age hexamera to its extraordinary revival in the sixteenth and seventeenth centuries. The most influential Dark Age hexamera, those of Basil and Ambrose, are extended homilies upon the text of the first two chapters of Genesis.[42] In the long narrative poems and reading-plays of the Renaissance, the hexameron is expanded to accommodate the whole Christian myth of origins, the celestial cycle of angelic and human creation and fall, which fleshes out and frames the story of the original six days.[43] Yet neither angelic nor human fall is figured in direct contact with God's will; they are rather integrated into the space of creation which occupies the structural center of the hexameron.

If Milton places predestination in the foreground of his epic, then, it is in some sense against the grain of the form of its hexameral content, one of whose principal functions, I wish to argue, is to denarrativize God's will, to transpose it into a kind of material conceptual space, the space of creation. Yet Milton's recasting of hexameron may also be seen as forwarding a larger movement or process of contradiction within the form of the hexameron itself – a movement which I will construct in terms of a late feudal antinomy. In this perspective, the authorial ideology of predestination and Godly representation appears not just as the directly mediated effect of the hexameral presentation of God, but comes to seem the *agent* of a larger historical and ideological process at work in the genre itself.

When we cast a naive eye upon this dogmatic genre, it seems hardly surprising that it should supply Milton's doctrinaire God with direct figuration. For it is a chief defining feature of hexameral narrative that it situates itself transparently with regard to theology, that it is always slanted toward explicit doctrine. Hexameral literature is didactic, conveying theological truth to an audience familiar with, yet in need of such truth. The Dark Age hexamera are homilies, and the hexameron never breaks free from its original homiletic constitution even in its grandest flights. Hexameral theology is thus integrated with, or appears to absorb, a definite and unquestioned body of received (homiletic) wisdom. This means that the doctrine presented in this genre is never merely personal but rather natural and collective by its very form. Hexameral narration constructs a definite theology for its audience, drawing it forth from the sacred texts as a preexisting entity or system which need make no claim, no explicit reference, to the social order because it corresponds to that collectivity in representing it as an order of things.

When we attempt to describe the form of hexameral theology, we verge on a very large matter which I can only touch upon, the question of the status of medieval religion. For it is clear that theology could have this comprehensive form, could exist as such, only under medieval conditions. I will return to these in a moment, but our problem, at this point, is how to indicate and give a feeling for the utter difference of hexameral theology from the modern experience of religion. One way to do this is by describing hexameral theology in terms of two main overlapping metaphors. First, hexameral theology has a kind of *ontological* status: it does not characterize what it refers to, it knows no object, but is substantive in itself, inhering in its referent as if in the body of the earth. The sacred text, while it brings theology into being, is nonetheless inscribed upon theology, has meaning only in illuminating it, and is therefore in a strong sense phenomenal to it. Indeed, the textual nature of hexameral wisdom only points to its flexibility: unchanging in its basic structure, theology is nonetheless able to assimilate new material, to produce new received wisdom, by presenting it in the form of inter- pretations added to the text. Such interpretation, then, simply fills in a space already delimited for it by the body of theology itself. This second, *spatial* metaphor is perhaps presupposed by all narrative, but seems particularly apposite to hexameral narrative and knowledge, with its statically defined narrative segments, its parcelized divisions and subdivisions. Hexameral theology may thus be described, in terms which I think are necessarily abstract, as a kind of fixed enclosing structure or substance which comprehends all that is known or experienced, and thus defines the space of knowledge.

Just as in epic everything follows from the nature of its gestural content, so in the hexameron everything depends on the ontological-spatial nature of theology. Thus the pre-given substantive form of theology may be said to select creation itself as the center of hexameral content, to make the various events and episodes of the celestial myth rotate around creation like planets around the sun. Likewise the paradigmatic movement of hexameral narrative follows from, or literalizes, the spatial nature of its content: it appears as a methodical filling in of a serialized space, a space broken up into discrete fragments which have been preordained by creation. This is to say that hexameral narrative always tends to the status of pure narration, or more properly of commentary, which fills in the space of creation by merely writing over, or giving verbal life to, a theological referent already in existence.

Theology, text, commentary:[44] the central elements of hexameron are all in some sense non-narrative categories, and work to construct the act of creation, the Christian story of origins, not in dynamic terms as agency but in static terms as substance. This is nowhere clearer than in the case of dramatic action, in which hexameral theology stands out as the basis for straightforward didactic allegory. When human story is cast as ontology or substance, its qualities (characters, themes, and so forth) are predefined and may be described and enumerated in near-random fashion. Thus when du Bartas, in *La Seconde Semaine*, comes to treat of the fall, the dialogue automatically assumes an allegorical form; it is played as that sort of pseudotragedy known as melodrama, in which preexisting ethical qualities are felt to govern the dialogical action, usurping the place of dramatic psychology and of tragic fate. Melodramatic dialogue cannot in fact give adequate expression to the density of the fall's ethical substance; and so, after the fall, summarizing commentary must methodically fill in the multitude of errors comprised in Adam's single sin:

> Now Adam's fault was not in deed so light
> As seemes to Reason's sin-bleared Owlie sight;
> But 'twas a chain where all the greatest sins

> Were one in other linked fast, as Twins:
> Ingratitude, pride, treason, gluttony,
> Too curious skill-thirst, envie, felony,
> Too-light, too-late belief; were the sweet baits
> That made him wander from Heav'ns holy straits.[45]

Likewise when God appears in du Bartas' fall story, he is just another character in the melodrama; his words and acts are part of the same unquestioned and unquestionable ontology as is Adam's sin. God's will, along with all the other wills, is absorbed and segmented by the serialized space of creation. Insofar as we may speak of a narrative movement in this non-narrative genre, it works in terms of the places or spaces of creation. Predestination is figured as locality rather than as will.

When I say that the hexameral commentary constructs a presupposed body of knowledge from the sacred texts, in which predestination does not figure as a problem, I do not mean to imply that no questions are ever raised. Hexameron is not only a didactic, social-ethical genre, but also a genre of speculation, even if much of its speculation is "received." A heuristic function seems to be built into the genre's didacticism; one effect of the additive structure of hexameral narration is to allow for the gradual grafting of new speculation onto the body of received knowledge. Indeed, a certain amount of eccentric speculation, such as is contained in Milton's angels, seems to be prescribed. To say that it is speculative is to imply that uncertainty must exist in some form in the hexameron; in du Bartas, the most popular hexameralist, uncertainty is in fact a main theme. But even where it is emphasized, even where it qualifies or forbids speculation, uncertainty is incorporated into ontology, and made the object of a didactic commentary whose substantive character closes off as many questions as it raises. Such uncertainty about metaphysical questions is actually often conducive to the practical bent of the ethical counsel which it is a main purpose of the commentary to draw out of the body of knowledge. Raphael's advice to Adam, in Book VIII, that he should be "lowly wise" and attend to the tangible things of his daily round, is good hexameral wisdom, though it is perhaps more highly generalized than is customary. And it is certainly no accident that it comes at the end of the dialogue on cosmology whose upshot is to assert, again in meta-hexameral manner, not just cosmological uncertainty on particular matters of substance, but a principle of indeterminacy affecting all cosmological systems.

All the same, even though the one is conducive to the other, it is still in the shift from speculation to ethics, from cognitive appropriation to practical counsel, that the main thematic tension in hexameral commentary is felt. Or rather, this shift appears as a major tension, as a kind of aesthetic antinomy, in Renaissance (that is, late) hexamera – in, for example, du Bartas or in Grotius' *Adamus Exul* (1601).[46] It seems that this antinomy is progressively aggravated and eclipsed in late hexameral literature; the relative prominence of the reading-play in the seventeenth-century corpus of hexameral works may be taken as a sign and a symptom of this eclipse, for the paradigm of drama tends to foreclose the possibility of direct and prolonged speculative interest. Book VIII of *Paradise Lost*, in which the break between speculation and ethics is particularly disturbing, revives this antinomy in order to exemplify its final fate. I will only suggest here that this intensification has a fairly specific class determinant, namely the continued growth and secure institutionalization, both in England and on the Continent, of a Protestant middle-class audience for whom ethical relationships are coming to be less speculative in character than formerly, and thus for whom ethics and speculation are coming to inhabit compartmentalized areas of experience.

Yet it would seem that with the eclipse of this tension between speculation and ethics as theme, with the repression of ontological speculation from the ethical domain, the original opposition tends to relocate itself at the *formal* level of hexameral narrative: the commentary form of narration is transposed into a more speculative form – the narrative and discursive mode of *analysis*. We can see how this occurs if we broaden our historical focus and consider hexameron not simply as a genre chiefly belonging to one class, but as a genre belonging to a period or mode of production, that of late feudalism. For not only does the homely wisdom of late hexameron express the ultimately subversive ideology of Protestantism, it also represents an attempt to reconstruct in cultural space the ideological underpinnings of feudalism proper. Late hexameron wears a Janus face, and its paradox is analogous to the paradox of the absolutist state itself, which retrenched noble power while strengthening the position of the middle commercial classes.[47]

The fundamental preconditions for the existence of late hexameron are established by the feudal mode proper. The coherent body of theology that was presupposed as defining the area of its narrative commentary had its technical basis in the unitary control of knowledge exercised by the institution of the medieval church; it had its political basis in the transparency of political and economic needs to one another, grounded in the personal character of feudal relationships (witness the obvious political and social functionality of medieval ethics, which obtains also in the ethical wisdom of the hexameron); and finally, it had its socioeconomic basis in the predominantly agrarian and territorialized character of production, which was crucial in determining the fixed and ontological status of this theology.

But while its preconditions were already established under feudalism, the genre was resurrected by the process of economic disintegration and political retrenchment definitive of the period of absolutism. On the one hand, the decimation of feudal personality of relationship by the growth of a money economy, and the ideological turmoil wrought by reformation, created the need to assert or reembody theology in narrative form, to cast religion once again into a stable didactic mold. On the other hand, even though late feudal atomization destabilized social relationships on the land, production was still predominantly agrarian, manifesting itself as a kind of fixed ontological quantity, and therefore theology retained its basic ontological status. So the need to assert theology as a stable containing structure was not residual but rather contemporary, one capable of at least some satisfaction. The great popularity of the hexameral form in the sixteenth and early seventeenth centuries must finally be accounted for in terms of this general situation.[48] The ontological anti-narrative of hexameron represents a reconstitution of the unified and coherent theology belonging to high feudalism, in the disintegrative late feudal stage; and the antinomies or tensions that this narrative defines and encloses (such as that between speculation and ethics) are determined by the contradictions of the feudal mode of production as exacerbated by its later phase.

The chief antinomy in the form of the hexameron is defined not so much by its ontological content in itself as by the very nature of the late feudal project of (re)asserting the body of knowledge. Such a project was necessarily paradoxical: even though the socioeconomic conditions for a properly ontological knowledge continued to exist in a compromised state for at least early Renaissance hexameron, yet the need to assert such knowledge inevitably led to the alteration of its status and significance. The act of reassertion opens up a latent fissure within the category of hexameral commentary. Reassertive writing distances signification from the referent with which it desires to be one, and thus hexameral narration tends to shift from a referential to a representational mode. Commentary, which fills in or writes over the substantive space of creation, now takes upon itself the new role of *analyzing* creation conceived as representational space in its signifying movement.[49] Whereas commentary parcelizes God's will in serial space, dissolving it into the chain of creation, analysis focuses on the mechanisms of this space's constitution, thus breaking God's will off from creation. The result of this is partly to give prominence to the question of where this will resides: analysis thus paradoxically concludes by figuring God's will as immanent in its totality to each aspect of creation. Creation stands forth as a series of signs, and the divine will which is read to be at work in it is now understood as relating immediately to every point on creation's map, rather than diffusing itself through its body.

I would maintain, at this point, that this division between commentary and analysis both represents the central antinomy of the hexameral genre, and may also be understood as a generic opposition in its own right, which is methodologically crucial to the differential understanding of the hexameron's generic formation. In constructing the categories of epic, I found it useful to contrast the constitution of epic with romance categories, classical epic with its romance counterpart. Some such contrast is, I think, methodologically necessary to the construction of any genre; I chose romance because the very existence of romance epic suggested a compatibility between romance and epic categories which would make possible a sharp distinction between the categorical dispositions of the two genres. In spite of its compatibility with romance, however, the epic content remains distinct from it; epic from its origins may define itself against romance, but it is not a critical part of the definition of the epic that it contain romance content. In the case of hexameron, however, a determining feature of its status as a transitional genre is that the basic opposition between commentary and analysis, which marks an alteration in its categorical content, should be actually constitutive of its definition. In other words, I am suggesting that the category of analysis, which betokens the entrance of a new historical content into the hexameron, should be read now as a genre in its own right (this in spite of the fact that it has no proper generic name as yet); and that this genre, while it serves the same methodological function of comparison in the construction of the hexameron as did the genre of romance in the construction of classical epic, is at the same time actually essential to the content of the late feudal hexameron itself. Renaissance hexameron always contains within it a logically subordinate and conflicting subgenre. Insofar as analysis focuses attention upon the way in which the various agents and places of Milton's cosmology constitute themselves in narrative, we might assimilate it (somewhat loosely) to the genre of science fiction, and call it "theological science fiction." What is most important for my purposes here, however, is not to give this analytical genre a name, but to indicate its disintegrative function, which is indeed partly an effect of the abstract and strictly logical character that makes naming the genre so difficult. By virtue of its contentlessness, analysis draws to itself the subgenres that necessarily subsist within hexameron (as within any major genre), invests their structures with cognitive interest, and so frees them from the official or dominant ideology of the hexameron. Hexameron thus possesses as a main feature a particularly strong subgeneric function.

To return to the question of the relation between generic and authorial ideology, Milton's foregrounding of predestination may now be understood as overdetermining, or directly coinciding with, the functional emphasis of analysis within the hexameron. The direct representation of the ideology of predestination is, on the one hand, determined by the analytical genre which imbeds God's unitary will in each of the signs of creation; the foregrounding of predestination is thus made possible by the chief contradiction in the hexameral structure, the transposition from commentary to analysis. On the other hand, predestination must be understood as the active agent of this transposition; authorial ideology acts in the name of hexameral ideology as it exacerbates the latter's chief antinomy and draws out the analytical function of the genre to the point of eclipse. So great is its cognitive interest in its own predestined laws of motion that *Paradise Lost* seems to veer, in sections, into science fiction, "the genre of cognitive estrangement."[50]

God

The analytical component of hexameral commentary is omnipresent in *Paradise Lost,* and always signifies the force of predestination. Yet it is most apparent how hexameron mediates Milton's ideology of God in the poem's representation of God himself, to which I now turn.

The hexameral presentation of God manifests in its clearest form, and may be said to deploy, a logical antinomy inherent in Milton's concept of narrative which generally informs the narrative of *Paradise Lost.* Let us recall this antinomy. Biblical narrative according to Milton is textual in the most immediate and strict sense. It is posited by the fiat of the letter, which is simply the sign of the divine will constituting itself as a signified; narrative is thereby pinned to the letter by a kind of intentional tautology. Narrative is complete in each of its moments, and the text is in a perpetually immediate and adequate relationship with it. But narrative is contextual as well: it takes shape beneath the letter through the play of loci, through the constant interdetermination of text and narrative, and (though just as univalent in this as in the first rendition) requires the use of reason for its construction. This antinomy is more or less acted out by God in Book III, as God, in justifying his actions, constructs his own character-narrative from its origins in an act of will. His narrative thus "unconsciously" limns, in its form, the antinomy defining the status of all narrative. Not only is God a strict literalist of the will, an irrational defender of his own acts as the sole ground of all meaning. He is also a logician of a sort, the master of a great deal of quasi-scholastic theological lore, who passively fashions his own narrative (or what I shall call, because of its mimetic status, the theopictic narrative) in accordance with that lore. These two Godly moments seem but the aspects of the structure of a larger theological narrative, of whose motion God himself finally seems the effect.

This larger theological narrative appears over time; it is a radically contextual phenomenon (it is the context of the contextual as well as the literal God). Just because it is so contextual, it does not prevent our being taken in and disturbed by the misrecognitions imposed by its dual character. God in his literal moment as irrational power is, of course, the main source of surprise. Let us consider a particularly disturbing moment of literalism: the passage at the end of his second speech in Book III, in which God announces that man must be redeemed by a sacrificial death before grace can be made available to him. The problem is that God has been speaking, in the body of this monologue, of the future renewal of man's powers by "grace freely voutsaft": "Upheld by me, yet once more he shall stand / On even ground against his mortal foe, / By me upheld" (11. 178–80). God will renew man's lapsed powers, clear his senses dark, and plant his umpire conscience in man as a guide. It seems that matters between man and God have been put back into equilibrium. God's willful but methodical transition and close sharply belie this assumption:

> But yet all is not done; Man disobeying,
> Disloyal breaks his fealty, and sins
> Against the high Supremacy of Heav'n,
> Affecting God-head, and so losing all,
> To expiate his Treason hath naught left,
> But to destruction sacred and devote,
> He with his whole posterity must die,
> Die hee or Justice must; unless for him
> Some other able, and as willing, pay
> The rigid satisfaction, death for death.
> Say Heav'nly Powers, where shall we find such love,
> Which of ye will be mortal to redeem
> Mans mortal crime, and just th' unjust to save,
> Dwells in all Heaven charity so dear?
>
> (11. 203–16)

What astonishes the reader here is not any lack of logic in the speech itself – on the contrary, this part of the speech, with its starkly legal insistence on the necessity of retribution, of a substitute payment for the original "fine," is more rigorously logical than what has preceded. It is rather the sudden intervention of such harsh logic that surprises. God's abrupt rigor seems motivated by a sudden recourse to the letter: he "remembers," and in remembering defines, the letter of his former action with regard to man. This new definition may represent an admirably bold and lucid presentation of the logic of Christian redemption.[51] But the mode of action that it implies, the utter dependence of God on the letter of his former action's definition, does not fit well with the logic apparently at work in the body of God's speech, according to which God, working on his own, will raise man up to an equal footing with the devil to keep Satan from gaining revenge and creation going for naught. A gap opens between two different kinds of logic (a literal logic and a distanced or logical logic) as the despotic God takes center stage.

Yet this usurpation, and the gap it opens, appear determined and signaled by the necessity of action, by the sheer force of the theological narrative as it unfolds. And this total narrative movement mediates or closes the gap at the same time as it determines it. *Yet all is not done*: these transitional words separate God from his narrative even while reaffirming his will and the willfulness of narrative. Narrative absolves God of the problems it established for him in making him a character.

Christ serves as the very symbol of this absolution, the third term who fulfills and personifies this (re)displacement onto narrative of the Godly antinomies. For Christ is made to fill the space or break between the literal and logical moments of God's discourse, and to provide the theological narrative with an agent, to figure it as grace itself. "Father, thy word is past, man shall find grace; / And shall grace not find means ...?" (11. 227–8). The Son is mainly a means, a mediatory power, in *Paradise Lost*, and as such his decidedly subordinate function is at once crucial to the constitution of Godhead itself and to the symbolic freeing of God from a state of determination. In personifying the force of theological narrative, his agency partly displaces, or takes upon itself, the general problems involved in making God a unitary character within narrative, as well as the more special antinomy, itself an incomplete recasting of the problem posed by God's will, between logical and literal theology, between the logic and the letter of narrative. It is because the Son's mediating personification is primarily important at the level of the formation of the Godhead's character that even a cursory reading of the first part of Book III gives one the impression that Christ's major accomplishment in redeeming humanity is to have released God from a difficult situation.

But this is not the end of God's narrative contextualization. If we consider the entire movement of his dialogue with the Son, the literal and all too immediately present God of the above passage reveals himself to be but a passing phase of a Godhead in motion, a God whose very essence is biblical history. With the Son's offer of himself as means of redemption, I would argue, God's fulminations are retroactively historicized. The logical phase of God's discourse, in which he says that he will directly impute grace to some, and strongly implies that the others will hear him call and yet not answer (11. 185-6), comes to refer vaguely to the historical period before the coming of Christ.[52] During this period, it is now understood, grace will be attained by the upright, even though the Son has not yet actually redeemed the debt incurred by the fall by taking upon himself God's grace. The literal phase of angry power that ensues is likewise to be construed now as an Old Testament feature. A rudimentary history is thus incorporated into the theological narrative, and over-determines God's narrative composition, removing him from his very presence as character in each moment of his story. This oddly dramatic and unassuming typologization of the divine extends through the course of *Paradise Lost*,[53] and comes to represent part of the background action against and in terms of which, in traditional epic fashion, the whole of the plot (but particularly its heavenly portions) emerges and takes on significance. What is important about such contextualization from our present point of view is that it appears as a way of refashioning and containing the initial terms that define God's narrativity, and hence serves, in some measure, as a defense against his predestinary character.

How is it possible for the hexameral narrative straightforwardly to deploy the contraries of Miltonic biblical narrative in this way? The answer to this lies in the correspondence between Miltonic and properly hexameral antinomies. The split between textual and contextual (or literal and logical) moments in Milton's concept of deity reproduces the rift in hexameral theology between analysis and commentary, between God as unquestioned signifier and God as substance. We may read the contextualization of God, from this perspective, as the attempt by hexameral commentary to write over or parcelize the integral predesti-nation mediated and foregrounded by analysis.[54] Yet the hexameron cannot so easily recontain Miltonic predestination. If the hexameron attempts to bury Milton's God, Milton's God is not without his vengeance. The Miltonic concept of God makes use of the very movement of hexameral recontainment to call the category of commen-tary itself into question: the antinomies of the theological narrative galvanize the movement of hexameral commentary into the movement of analysis, transforming ontological space into the space of narrative representation. The substance of commentary itself is shifted toward the status of a signifying act. The crucial element in this process appears to be Milton's literal God, which insistently characterizes and destabilizes the parcelized hexameral space. We may thus put the matter conveniently and comprehensively as follows: the insistence of the biblical element, of the willful letter, within the body of theology that *Paradise Lost* takes as its task to comment upon, both manifests a rift in that theology and determines a shift in its very status.

This last formulation has the advantage of making it clear that the galvanization of hexameron is not a specific but a total phenomenon. The literal impulse not only characterizes Milton's God, it is also written, for instance, into the main plot of the poem, into the explicitness of its end. A narrative whose central aim is to construct and explain the fall, thus to justify predestination – a narrative, moreover, which must give this justification the force of epic gesture – such a narrative, it would seem, must perforce give prominence to God's originating acts within the body of theology, and these accordingly problematic acts call for a very special kind of commentary. Milton's epic aim accentuates the antinomies of theological narrative which would be crucial in any case to Milton's hexameron; partly because of this accentuation, however, these antinomies are clearest in the sections of heavenly dialogue where God's initiatory acts are directly presented. God's acts – or more precisely the Godly discourse or narrative about these acts – establish themselves, in their strictly willful dimension, as part of an order of representation rather than as part of an ontology, as significations requiring analysis of their function, rather than as substances in need of being filled in with commentary. The theopictic moment within the narrative, in which reason explains the stark givens of God's will, is thus rendered ambivalent, split between commentary and analysis. Insofar as the narration makes God's acts or words appear as unquestioned ontological givens, then its function is apparently that of commentary, of filling in the referential space of creation. There is no need to deny that God's word is felt, in some parts of the poem, as an exfoliating substance. But this feeling is prominent, usually, in God's absence as character, and is mainly centered, as we shall see, on creation. Insofar, however, as the biblical element is insistent within the hexameron, and God's presence is felt as uniquely problematical, then the theological moment presents itself as an act of definition, as an analysis and ordered construction of God's peremptory literality. This second moment of the theological narrative does not posit or question the story's referent; it does not ask how God's accommodative representation came into being, or presume to display its birth, but instead takes this signification as given, as the unquestionable object of analysis. To the extent that this critical narration has a self-referential aspect, it questions problems *within* signification; at most, analysis refers God's discourse back to the antinomies that appear on the plane of narrative, and motivates its action in terms of these at what might be called a meta-level.

So it is, as we have already seen, that Christ's offer of redemption is presented – we may say now, by the analytical function of hexameron – as resolving those antinomies of the Godly presence which are one with those of narrative. And a similar situation obtains with regard to most of the Son's appearances; perhaps all of them that occur under God's aspect are motivated by the movement of representation itself. This is the case, for example, with the first event of the story of *Paradise Lost*, God's exaltation of the Son.

> Hear all ye Angels, Progeny of Light.
> Thrones, Dominations, Princedoms, Virtues, Powers,
> Hear my Decree, which unrevok't shall stand.
> This day I have begot whom I declare
> My only Son, and on this holy Hill
> Him have anointed, whom ye now behold
> At my right hand; your Head I him appoint;
> And by my Self have sworn to him shall bow
> All knees in Heav'n, and shall confess him Lord:
> Under his great Vice-gerent Reign abide
> United as one individual Soul
> For ever happy: him who disobeys
> Mee disobeys, breaks union, and that day
> Cast out from God and blessed vision, falls
> Into utter darkness, deep ingulft, his place
> Ordaind without redemption, without end.
>   (Bk. V, ll. 600–15)

In a poem whose theme is predestination, this place of beginning must assume great narrative significance. It seems to me striking that God's disarrangement of the heavenly *status quo* is arbitrary and unmotivated. His lack of motivation is emphasized in part by the singularity of the event itself as a way of starting the hexameral cycle:[55] Why does God need to elevate the Son, and why insist upon angelical obeisance? In "classic" hexameron we would not be asking such questions. God's speech would allegorically embody this narrative turning point, and the reasons provided would seem given in advance.[56] But his speech does not just fill in a theological place here; it serves a critical function simply through the willfulness of God's primary act. This willfulness is accentuated by the curious diction in line 603: "This day I have begot whom I declare / My only Son." *Begot* makes the exaltation into a "total happening," a willful creation. At the same time, however, the word distances the Creator from exaltation, making the declaration proper seem slightly accidental and secondary to the moment, and the logic, of begetting; there is a sense, in the whole first part of the passage, that God merely consummates the Son's original superiority with his title, affixing his bare will, in the form of a decree, to an already choate trend in the theological narrative.

God's act of exaltation, if it is motivated at all – or perhaps it would be better to say, simply because of its conspicuous lack of motivation, its obvious and willful bareness – is referred to the antinomy in narrative itself, between letter and logic or will and reason. Just as was the case with his offer of redemption, the Son's exaltation serves not to substantiate God's will by affording it a place of analogical and partial residence in the chain of creation, but rather to provide God with narrative mediation, both expressing and resolving, by way of narrative ambivalence, the problem of his willfulness. The theological narrative reveals a cognitive interest in its own laws of motion which at its limit tends to displace the problem of predestination itself from the focus of the poem.

In its analytical or cognitive dimension, theological narration posits and inhabits a strictly narrative space which contrasts rather sharply with the non-narrative space, inscribed with textual writing or commentary, of classic hexameron. Whereas commentary dissolves God's "personhood" into the natural space of creation, analysis figures God into an impersonal narrative space that is nonetheless sociable, that nonetheless works in terms of persons. The Son's mediation in the above passage, though passive and thus not tactful in the manner of his other interventions, is a personal one and implies a kind of social space; he mediates by filling in the final degree of the heavenly hierarchy, by filling in the social gap between God and the angels. It is not incidental that the question of hierarchy appears for the first time in the story here, and is one with the beginning of that story. Hierarchy thus enters the story, not as a preexisting ontological fact, nor – as it does in the poem's other narrative sections – as a political or psychological problem, but rather as an abstract and strictly theological problem of God's narrative constitution; the projection of a lower person, of a "personable" person, solves God's subjective problems in mediating the dichotomy between his will and reason – though this is a solution "in degree," and there remains, as always, an excess of divine will, too much narrativity, remaining at its end.

The Godly excess continues to fascinate and repel; it will not be dissipated by analysis. Analysis is made to generate, under the strain, a partial or inchoate psychological subgenre, which we might call justificatory dramatic monologue. God's verbal gestures consistently resound with ethical and psychological overtones such as are readily apparent, for example, in the defensive close of the above passage. This inevitable translation of God's literality into psychology turns into simply another method of purifying the narrative God of character, of saving predestination. For a situation is thus created in which theological and psychological genres appear to conflict with one another, and in which the dominant genre of the hexameron overrules affective drama, didactic theology retroactively canceling profane psychological motivations.[57]

But God's initial act receives its most cogent psychological explanation, not in his affective monologue, but rather from the retroactive effect of the paradise story itself, the subgeneric rendition of which outweighs its official hexameral construction and works upon the exaltation at a distance, attributing to it psychological motivations which are perhaps not so base as those which are projected onto the borders of God's discourse in his heavenly appearances.[58] Such an expanding contextual reading is encouraged by the radically contextual movement of the heavenly narrative itself, which systematically decenters the theopictic narrative, casting God's action outside his character.

At this point, we can begin to see how the analytical defense against predestination from within hexameron merges with the purely formal or epic defense from without. For if analysis initiates the fissuring of God's will from narrative agency, it does not appear entirely to control that fissuring; the theological narrative must finally be understood to be motivated and controlled by the epic form which, though comparatively mute in the heavenly narrative, nonetheless casts God's actions from afar as gestures, and their motive force as fate. The strictly cognitive interest in God's constitution marks the place in the heavenly narrative, then, in which epic and hexameron intersect with one another, the "place" which I will in a moment adopt the term "counterplot" to designate as a global phenomenon. That this intersection must be of profoundly ambivalent significance should be obvious, given the radically different lineages that have now been written into the structure of the genres. I will limit myself to a résumé of this ambivalence in a sentence here: epic theology gives hexameral wisdom the political force of gesture, while emptying its nominally self-contained narrative framework of the substance that supports it; hexameral theology corroborates the materiality of ethos while imputing to it a merely metaphysical existence. It is perhaps no wonder, in view of the bluntness of these generic antinomies, if heavenly theology seems to form a rather static and traumatized version of epic culture. What I would emphasize in closing this section, however, is the theological purity of the narrative construction of predestination in the heavenly portions of the epic. This purity, I think, makes for the starkness of the aporias involved in the intersection of epic and hexameron, whose subtler and more expansive expression I will be tracing in the remainder of this study. In spite of its dramatic (psychological) determination from within, and its ultimate epic (political) determination from without, heavenly hexameron remains fairly self-contained; the problem of God's constitution keeps its place within theology. It follows that the predestination problem is likewise contained by the theology to which it is central, in spite of a certain tendency within the galvanized hexameron to break the problem up at its foundations. In spite of the fissures in the hexameral narrative, theology remains in control of itself when it is at center stage. This is not the case, as we shall see, when theology enters the poem's Satanic and paradisal sections, and epic hexameron generates other genres.

Epic hexameral: the counterplot

Before turning to these other sections, I wish to review the larger generic scheme of the poem, whose main elements have been briefly constructed. What commands our attention now is the *combination* of epic and hexameron, the working of the generic system in which, as I have already claimed, epic is the dominant and chiefly determinant genre. Two preliminary points, both of which follow from the determinacy of epic within the system, are decisive in approaching this matter. First, because artificial epic is characterized by a rift between form and content, it is a main feature of the generic system in which epic is dominant that the two presiding genres operate at a distance from and upon each other: the hexameron that forms the narrative content of the epic does not work upon epic gesture by simply uniting with it, or by erasing its distinctive features. Second, when we consider the system as such, from a synchronic point of view, we should conceive of the epic as the main agent in its combination of genres, and hence as delimiting the operation of the hexameron (and other genres) upon its own form. The epic should be thought of as actively accepting and fashioning its primary raw material, its gestural content, from the preformed hexameral narrative, from ontological-spatial plot. The question to be addressed in this section may thus be posed as follows: How is the epic transformed from a distance by the hexameron in accepting its spatial plot as the raw content from which gesture is to be fashioned?

The most salient modification of classical gesture in *Paradise Lost* seems to me to be found in the volatility or placelessness of the Miltonic gestural narrative. I will argue that this gestural volatility is ultimately to be understood as both an expression of and a response to (or reaction against) the commodity form itself, or the categorical structure of action imposed by emergent capitalism. But this determination proceeds largely by way of the acceptance of the hexameron, with its late feudal antinomies, into the classical epic narrative. The chief effect of this combination is to give gesture a peculiar ontological "bottom" which imperils the independence of the gestural narrative from plot. The stock action of epic is made to emerge from the pre-given story-space of the hexameron: the uniqueness of gesture as action is somewhat compromised or homogenized – at its base, and at a distance – by its origin in a fatal natural order positively unified by God's will. Gesture suspends itself or oscillates between two orders, the order of its own narrative and that of the space of creation. The result of this in terms of narrative movement has been well described by Geoffrey Hartman as a moment of suspense existing virtually within the surface action of the epic at all points.[59] This moment is materialized at certain crucial spots by the appearance of a providential counterplot from within the thick of epic action.

If we return to the simile of the angel forms, we can see how the volatility or unlocalizability of its gestural referent produces and is one with the moment of temporal equilibrium, the counterplot, which Hartman evokes.

> he stood and call'd
> His Legions, Angel Forms, who lay intrans't
> Thick as Autumnal Leaves that strow the Brooks
> In *Vallombrosa*, where th'*Etrurian* shades
> High overarch't imbow'r; or scatter'd sedge
> Afloat, when with fierce Winds *Orion* arm'd
> Hath vext the Red-Sea Coast, whose waves o'erthrew
> *Busiris* and his *Memphian* Chivalry,
> While with perfidious hatred they pursu'd
> The Sojourners of *Goshen*, who beheld
> From the safe shore thir floating Carcasses
> And broken Chariot wheels; so thick bestrown
> Abject and lost lay these . . .
>
> (Bk. I, ll. 300–12)

Let us note first the way in which the simile introduces fate, manifestly if indirectly, into the angels' action, gradually bringing fate up close to the surface of the gesture that it is always felt to inform. Like the referent itself, the fate of this simile is rather elusive of definition. It changes with each new stage of the simile, shifting its status from the seasonal or natural fate projected by the elegiac image of the leaves falling in Vallombrosa, to the astrological fate at work in Orion's vexing of the Red Sea, to the divine fate behind Busirus' havoc. This last shift is complicated by the fact that the Busirus simile is not properly a simile at all, but rather a bit of epic redundance or elaboration. The subordination of this "improper" simile paradoxically makes astrology govern God's action, at least from a logical-syntactical point of view, and gives the divine will an astrological "cover." It would thus perhaps be better to say that fate in this third incarnation is not divine, but astrological-divine.

The crucial shift or slippage is, I think, precisely this last one, in which God's will enters ambiguously into epic fate, and is given a fatal determination. This entrance of God's will into gesture is a frequent occurrence in the poem, and sets up Milton's counterplot: the partial incarnation of God's will in fate makes simile-gesture expand or open out onto the shifting background narrative, and issues in a curious sense of arrest, in a brief surcease of narrative diachrony, during which attention tends to be focused, not on God's will or on fate in itself, but on this (now unified) determination within nature, or in other words on *creation*.[60]

From our point of view, as should be clear, the counterplot is not simply a discrete technique by which the main narrative line, and indeed the gestural micronarrative, are occasionally perforated with Providence, but rather a global effect which is to be read as the result of the insertion of hexameral narrative into epic gesture. The effect of this insertion can be most conveniently understood, not so much as an implicit manipulation of fate into God's will, but in terms of a peculiarly volatile figuring of narrative space. Consider the angel simile once more. Its third segment, which deifies fate, at the same time institutes an ambiguity in the active scene or configuration which, as we have seen, epic simile always brings with it and imputes to its comparison. This ambiguity is brought about by the tempestuous motion of Busirus and crew in the Red Sea; if there were not this surplus motion, the configuration would patly coincide with that of the angels lying on the lake. As is, the simile tends to replace and enlarge its initial comparison, modifying and expanding upon the "actual" narrative line in the process: the vexation of Busirus and his troops calls to mind the angels' recent vexation and accordingly modifies our picture of the action, superimposing swirling angels upon what were before peaceful Lethe-like angels, and situating them, not only on the lake, but also in relation to the Cause which put them there and still disturbs them. While this volatility of the referent suggests, in itself, the incursion of a new content, of a new structure of action, into epic gesture, nonetheless the collapsing of time into space, or rather the flattening of time into spatialized gesture, which it accomplishes, is typical epic practice. We have already seen, however, that God's gestures do not fit so well into epic mold; and insofar as its temporal extension imbeds the referent in theological history, it represents the invasion of the hexameron, with its (for all his contradictions) narrative God, into the form of epic gesture. The inclusion of God's activity makes the action seem to fill a space allotted to it more or less in advance: thus the total narrative movement compromises the homologous gestural space of epic, as a space emerges behind it in which the narrative appears as homogeneous ontology, to be occupied by commentary/analysis. The typological dimension of the simile (Busirus as a historical figure of the devil) particularly underlines the homogeneity of the narrative action – what we might call its theological uniformity; while the fatal determination of God's will, effected by its subordination within the simile proper, serves to emphasize the properly ontological character of the narrative, that is, its relative independence from the will that founds it.

There is then what we might term a systematic theological homogenization of epic gesture in *Paradise Lost*, effected at a distance by the ontological-representational space of its hexameral content. This global and generic way of putting things has the virtue of opening the counterplot – the contrary narrative disposition of predestination – up onto history. The curious bottoming out of gesture effected by the intersection of hexameron with epic marks the collision of classical and late feudal modes of production, or of the semantic content determined and "left over" by them. Milton's presentation of predestination is complicated by the active influence of these two radically distinct modes, working at a distance upon each other through the mediation of genre. The impersonal and yet lived predestination of epic is made to contain the ambivalently willful predestination of hexameral creation. This internal spatialization of gesture is the most palpable trace left within Milton's generic system of the differential structure and tempo of discrete historical formations. The moment of arrest that is one with Milton's counterplot, the moment in which God's will appears from within gesture as diffused over the plane of creation, in some fairly concrete sense holds history, or historical matter, in suspense; it thus registers and enacts what we might call the temporal discontinuity of the historical present. We should tread softly here, for we tread on the unraveled stuff of history, on discontinuous historical time.

I mean this last in no mystical sense. It may be taken as an axiom that generic systems are always differentially constituted in terms of their historical content, and always effect such collisions between distinct modes of production as we find in Milton's counterplot. In this dimension, generic systems may be taken as peculiarly privileged examples in the cultural sphere of what Trotsky called the law of combined development.[61] As with its political and economic manifestations, cultural combined development always has its main significance in the discontinuous present. The combination of cultural contents involved is never to be grasped simply as the result of historical lag, of the weight of centuries, but rather as a mode of symbolic action in the present, as an active (re)constitution of a contemporary cultural problem or problems. In the present context, the main problem is posed by the ideology of predestination, which the combination of epic and hexameron may now be understood to afford more adequate expression and symbolic resolution than is afforded by the Miltonic theory of monism. We have already observed that Milton's own theological contradictions, the contradictions germane to the historical present, are carried by and reinforce the divergent historical contents of epic and hexameron. On the one hand, Milton's Arminianism – which is virtually one with his monism, his dynamic sense of the subject as an integral and self-determining power – finds its proper vehicle in the homology of epic gesture, and expresses itself through the epic ethos, supported by that homology, which paradoxically appears to determine fate even as it is informed by it. On the other hand, Milton's predestinary tendency is figured most clearly within the ontological space of the hexameron, and in the strictly narrative God that is made to stand forth starkly within that space, in part against the very logic or will of its content. The collision at a distance of epic and hexameron, the refiguring of gesture involved in the counterplot, may now be grasped as an expansive symbolic resolution to this basic antinomy.

This generic scheme of things must be complicated further before turning to Satan. And this chiefly in two respects. First, Milton's Arminian and predestinary tendencies manifest themselves only predominantly in the respective generic levels of epic and hexameron; the contradictory halves of Milton's theology dispose themselves in this way when we view the field of the narrative from afar. When we look closer, we can see that both halves are expressed within each of the main genres, and this is owing in some measure to the contradictory tendencies in the genres themselves. Thus, most importantly, though Milton's hexameron is distorted into an order of representation on which predestination is foregrounded, still its ontological presuppositions remain, to be partly occupied by Milton's monism, and to define themselves against the determinist tendencies effected by the instatement of narrative as representation. Witness, for example, the book of creation, with its serial organization, in which Milton lifts narrative hexameron from the popular hebetude into which it had fallen with du Bartas and Sylvester; and whose beauty must be conceded to depend upon Milton's monistic feeling for creation.[62]

Second, it should be clear that the contradictions borne by the epic and hexameral genres are not just theological in nature, nor do they express themselves solely as such. Rather the contradiction between monist Arminianism and predestinarianism registers on the theological level and interacts with the contradictory halves of Milton's individualism as determined finally by what we have called primary reification. I have already suggested that even Milton's presentation of God is affected directly by this individualism, and might indeed be said to represent no more than a rethinking or a reconstruction of the individual subject in divine guise – God's willful constitution of himself corresponding, on the one hand, to the economic moment of possession, of bodily immediacy, and the logical containment of this will by the theopictic narrative, and on the other hand, to the properly juridical moment of proprietorship. The orientation typical of Milton's individualism is expressed here precisely in the immediacy of the treatment of theological matters: even while it is clear that we have a predestinary God before us, we tend to be preoccupied with the (more or less functionalist) questions as to his mode of narrative constitution.

But if Milton's individualism is involved, then clearly the narrative structure in *Paradise Lost* is not only to be understood as a highly mediated response to the contemporary cultural problem of predestination. It must also be read as an answer to the socioeconomic situation to which that problem itself partly corresponds. The volatility of gestural narrative in *Paradise Lost* asks in its excessiveness to be constructed finally as an enactment of and reaction against the structure of action imposed by the commodity form, against the abstract subject of primary reification to which Milton's monism has been argued mainly to respond. The inner mobility of gesture, the insistent appearance within it of the uniform and active space of creation, represents a contradictory attempt on the part of epic to go beyond the homology of epic gesture and break through to the real concrete of generalized labor power that reification projects beyond or behind labor activity itself. To suggest that such a reading represents the necessary completion of our construction of Milton's generic system, it should be enough to point out, once again, the close affinity between the epic resolution of reification and Milton's monism. The epic resolution might even be said to be directly monistic in that it consistently imbeds predestination in the active material, the "vital power" of creation.

From this perspective, we can see more clearly the importance of the subgeneric function of analysis within hexameron. Analysis not only contributes to the production of the counterplot by positing God's will in its integrity behind each of the signs of creation. It also "estranges" or underscores this symbolic reaction, and in doing so works on and modifies it through the contextual movement of narrative representation. There is indeed a complex logic of monism elaborated by the narrative line of *Paradise Lost*, a logic which we might see as the attempt to overcome through analytical narrative movement the inherent frustration of the reaction against reification at the gestural level. The counterplot thus undergoes, I will argue, a differential constitution in the course of *Paradise Lost* whereby its status as a kind of symbolic response to capitalism is purified and at the same time straitened. In the course of the poem, overtly political gesture devolves under pressure into ethical gesture, epic ethos into a psychologically grounded ethic.

5

Satan, epic, and allegorical tragedy: predestinary ethos as desire

Satan and evil

We now come to Satan and the Satanic portions of *Paradise Lost*. How does the generic system operate on or produce the archetypal figure of evil? The rift between epic and hexameron, I will argue, is nowhere more obvious than in the Satan narrative. On the one hand, Satan is a meta-epic character, in whom the independence of epic categories expresses itself in extreme form, such that epic at its limits is made to presage a form of non-generic writing. On the other hand, the hexameral plot dramatizes Satanic gesture, making Satan a uniquely dramatic character.[1] Satan is cast, at the conventional boundary of hexameron, as a stock figure of evil. But the dominant form of drama in the Satan narrative, produced and made prominent by hexameral analysis, is that of allegorical tragedy, in which Satan figures as the fragmentary subject of constitutively unsatisfied desire. The narrative concept of Christian evil comes to serve, I will argue, as a field in which the dominant epic and allegorical Satans set each other off and engage in a kind of symbolic battle in which allegory threatens to drain epic gesture of its sociopolitical resonance.

My argument should perhaps be understood as a rather aggressive amplification and modification of William Empson's reading of Satan in the chapter on *Paradise Lost* in *Some Versions of Pastoral*.[2] Empson argues that there is a coherent Satan, but that this coherence is only an impressive façade upon which two different and quite inconsistent characters or viewpoints are constantly superimposed. He argues that the reasons for this inconsistent coherence are at once literary and theological: it derives primarily from the contradictions at the heart of the Christian myth which it was Milton's business, as a literary artist, to convey in its "whole range of feeling."

Empson's explanation underestimates, I think, the force and importance of genre in mediating the Christian narrative (this in spite of its location in a book on genre); part of my intention here is to show precisely this force. Yet it still seems to me that Empson is basically right, and that what we might call the inherent ideology of the Christian narrative is largely responsible for the Satan problem. This means, I think, that any comprehensive attempt at elucidating the problem of Satan would have to take under historical consideration his place in the Christian narrative and theology. More particularly, such a study would have to examine the problem of evil in Christianity and of its narrative figuration, both – and at least – at the time of the religion's establishment and at the time of *Paradise Lost*. Suffice it merely to suggest here, in lieu of such a history, that the dominantly privative conception of evil in orthodox Christianity makes for a potential problem in its narrative impersonation: it is difficult to imagine the impersonation of a privative concept. The positivity of such impersonation must be particularly intractable and striking at a time when the catalogue of positive vices or sins (pride, envy, and so forth), which provided an accepted series of partial images for evil, was losing its effectuality in the face of that resituation of ethics within a newly emergent civil society of which we have taken Milton's monism as the sign. Satan as the representative of evil in *Paradise Lost* should be understood in relation to this relatively new ideological situation, in which ethical codes of good and evil are being reshuffled and centered in the new sphere of abstract interpersonal relations, and in which evil appears with revitalized force as a monolithic and placeless agent that can find its definition not positively or inherently but only in reacting against some similarly abstract and unified concept or agent of virtue or reason. This newly abstract and purely reactive or relational status of evil may be seen paradoxically to determine Satan's very positivity and coherence as an agent: the undifferentiated emptiness of the nonetheless secure and unquestioned category of evil allows the permanent integrity of Satan's action. At the same time, however, the undefined nature of evil should be seen as the ideological context of Satan's notorious inconsistency as a character; Satan is so transparently inconsistent that his manipulation at the hands of the author should be thought of not as a transgression but rather as a constitutive characteristic of his positive construction.[3] The Satan who maintains, at one point, that the mind is its own place, and who defines his evil goal strictly in oppositional terms, might even be read as a symbol for the historically determined placelessness of evil in the Christian ideology and narrative.

In addition to this historical consideration, it seems clear that part of the glamor and the difficulty of Satan – part, indeed, of the placeless quality of evil – can be attributed to a peculiar literary or symbolic property of the Satan narrative: the curious position occupied by Satan in the story of the fall. Satan is at once marginal to the matter of predestination and fall, and absolutely instrumental to its unfolding. He thus inherits all the ambivalent emphasis that traditionally invests the figure of the third or of the catalyst, and takes on something of the Protean quality of the trickster in folk myth.[4]

Satan as epic symbol

This brief discussion completes, then, the rudimentary ideological or narrative context in whose terms – as a particular presentation or refashioning of which – Satan's generic composition should be understood. It seems to me a central fact of this composition that Satan is peculiarly a figure of gesture, that he exists somehow in closer proximity to the gestural narrative than do any of the other characters. To think of Satan-as-character is to think, first of all, of a series of impressive gestures. At this point we can see ideological and generic determinations converge. For if Satan's momentariness is conditioned by the new monolithic placelessness of evil, so does it also represent a kind of necessary concession to the centrally constitutive nature of gesture in epic narrative. More especially, the Satanic splendor which is to be found particularly in the first two books stems from the symbolic centrality of military gesture to Virgilian epic. The magnificence of Satan's early career in the poem, the magnificence of the books of Hell, is mainly a magnificence of military gesture. Satan's gestures are at times expressly military – one thinks of the memorable scene in which Satan reviews his troops, or of the whole long debate in Book II – and at other times, perhaps more frequently, they sublimate military activity – one thinks of Satan heaving his huge bulk from off the lake of forgetfulness, where the impression of sheer cumbersome magnitude reminds one of the ponderous slow motion of epic warfare.[5] This generic determination appears to take precedence over the contemporary ideological determination of Satan's coherence in expressing it; thus we may say that the symbolic centrality of military gesture in classical epic led Milton, working on a hexameral narrative line which offered him little opportunity for delivering impressive gesture, to intercalate it into the early books, and to overestimate its main "carrier," the character of Satan.

To say that Satan is a figure of gesture is another, and I think more impartial, way of saying what is generally recognized in Milton criticism: that Satan seems to inhabit an almost exclusively classical epic, that he is somehow more classical than the other characters. The sublimated political significance of epic form has already been discussed; granted this significance, it does not seem to me particularly vulgar to read the epic Satan as the symbolic expression or fulfillment of Milton's revolutionary desire, provided we recognize that such a reading implies no overt ethical valorization of Satan on Milton's part. Such a position need not deny what the neo-Christians would doubtless say here: that if Satan is a representation of political libido, then political libido is debunked by the hexameral plot of degradation in the name of the alternate Christian ethic of lowly wisdom or patience.[6] What such criticism does not see, however, is that Satanic gesture is debunked only at a distance, so that the autonomy of gesture as a symbol is not erased. And if epic fulfillment is debunked, it is not without its revenge; for the predominance of epic in the Satan narrative pulls the hexameron into a subgeneric dramatic mode whose paradigms are chiefly classical, thus working to aggravate the rift within hexameral theology itself.

Satan, however, is not only a peculiarly epic character; he is also singularly changeable or generically various. This too, as should already be evident, follows from the new status of evil in the Christian narrative. If Satan's habitation-with-a-difference of classical epic corresponds, at some level, to the monolithic closure of evil, then the generic variousness of his presentation answers to the instability resulting from its content-lessness. The generic variousness of the Satan narrative is indeed largely responsible for our impression of Satan's inconsistency, which goes beyond the superposition of two different logics onto the same character that Empson proposes, and comes to seem a fundamental principle at work in Satanic gesture. I will merely note at this point that the main generic determinant of this generic proliferation, the genre that governs Satan's inconsistency, is the fragmented and abstract one of allegorical tragedy; we will see more clearly later on how this genre's fragmentation corresponds to a situation in which theological categories have been emptied of content. That it is a dramatic form that governs Satan's generic dispersal is suggested by the fact that his variousness is most apparent at the level of the episode or scene. The episodic genres in Satan's career sport their differences more than do those of the other sections of the poem. The Satan narrative is punctuated by changes of scene in which the cumbersome narrative apparatus itself seems to roll forward and reveal itself as constitutive of the action.

Let us review, as an example of this incessant generic slippage, the stretch of story from midway through Book II to the beginning of Book IV. After the debate, Hell is portrayed, in a rapid series of vignettes, as a Spenserian landscape. This perhaps gives some forewarning of the next episode, in which Satan, on his way to find earth, suddenly enters the straits of romance allegory, and has his autonomous splendor tarnished by association with the moral-theological psychology represented by Sin and Death. Two epic journeys or wild flights ensue, the first across Chaos, the second down through the space of the new world, each of which serves, in part, as a pretext for straightforward cosmological description. Satan then obtains directions from Uriel on the Sun, in an episode whose genre is difficult to identify because it is practically a Miltonic invention: a passage of pure theological science fiction. Attention is focused first upon the mysteries of the sun itself, and then, in the conversation between Satan and Uriel, on the angelical social order and etiquette (the simple fact that Satan is an impostor throws this etiquette into relief, and with it the generic "set" in question). Finally, at the beginning of Book IV, in a speech that has often been taken as the crux of the problem of Satanic consistency, Satan appears as a stage villain, and tragic drama – which serves, as I shall argue, as a kind of general framework for the whole Satan saga – stands forth for once as the means of immediate generic presentation.

This brief litany of changes should be sufficient to suggest Satan's generic variety at the level of the character-narrative. But the Satanic inconsistency is not simply produced by dramatic shifts of scene; it is also generated at the extremely volatile gestural level of the Satan narrative. For an indication of this, the reader need only recall that Satan attracts many more epic similes than any other character, and that one way of looking upon epic simile, as I have already suggested, is as a model-in-miniature of genre, or as a sudden shifting of generic gears which throws into central focus the process of description itself, with its generic characterization. Satanic gesture, I would argue, is inseparable from just such generic shifts or slippages. It is constituted, in part, by a ceaseless generic difference which might be seen as overloading it with a permanently ephemeral abundance; Satanic gesture appears to be too full to be described or contained by any single subgenre. Indeed, one is tempted to say, on the basis of his generic instability, that Satan carries with him his own aesthetic of abundance or of surcharged decenteredness, and that he thus drives to an extreme the primary epic antinomy between the plenitude of material culture and the lack, at its heart, of a coordinating category of human activity. The very militance of Satanic gesture drives the classical epic into contortions which reveal the absence at its center even as they lay bare a new source of gestural abundance in the form of a uniform and abstract substratum of unqualified or raw activity extending through the series of gestures itself.

Satan's consistently various partial-generic incarnation, that is, not only speaks of an effortless source of abundance; it also works in so speaking to induce or deepen a rift in the basic structure of Satanic gesture. We can see this rift more sharply, once again, as it appears at the level of the Satan narrative, where the generic dispersal forces upon the reader a method of generic reconciliation which is analogous, and one in its determinants, with the contextualizing movement of the theological narrative in the Godly sections of the poem. Because of the plethora of episodic genres, what actually happens at some crucial points of Satan's early history is, in fact, unclear. The way in which we construct the story depends to a great extent on our readings of the diverse genres in combination.

What are we to make, for instance, of the episode in which Satan encounters Death and Sin at Hell's gates? The psychological tenor of the allegory is obviously primary within the context of the episode, and clearly enough centers upon the paradox of the place of evil. Satan is held within Hell, we learn, by those emanations of his inner evil, the gate-keepers Sin and Death; yet it is precisely because Sin and Death are emanations, externalized psychological progeny, that Hell as a place cannot finally confine him. It is apparent, likewise, that the psychological allegory is not cut off from the rest of the narrative, but communicates in a dense network of symbolic and thematic messages: the narcissistic-incestuous (libidinous) "love" that generates the Unholy Trinity haunts around paradise by contrasting with the "love unlibidinous" that reigns there until the fall. More than this, it seems to haunt *within* paradise: Satan's narcissistic romance with Sin, as she relates it ("Thyself in me thy perfect image viewing / Becam'st enamour'd"), not only casts an inauspicious light upon Eve's natural preference, on first awaking, for her own "smooth wat'ry image" over the real Adam; it also injects a certain doubt into her very love for Adam, whose image, a voice (presumably the Son's) informs her, she is. Is even paradisal love narcissistic in origin? Again, the Scylla emblem whose tenor is the self-motivated degeneration of evil contains in a symbolic nutshell the thematic message conveyed by Satan's systematic degradation[7] over the course of the poem, or by what I will call the programmatic moral framework through which the hexameron plots his career.

Nonetheless, however fitting its primary psychological message is in the thematic context of the whole poem, we must ask questions as to the fit of this episode in the story of Satan. And here matters are not so clear. Sin recalls former affairs to Satan as follows:

> Hast thou forgot me then, and do I seem
> Now in thine eye so foul, once deem'd so fair
> In Heav'n, when at th' Assembly, and in sight
> Of all the Seraphim with thee combin'd
> In bold conspiracy against Heav'n's King,
> All on a sudden miserable pain
> Surpris'd thee, dim thine eyes, and dizzy swum
> In darkness, while thy head flames thick and fast
> Threw forth, till on the left side op'ning wide,
> Likest to thee in shape and count'nance bright,
> Then shining heav'nly fair, a Goddess arm'd
> Out of thy head I sprung: amazement seiz'd
> All th' Host of Heav'n; back they recoil'd afraid
> At first, and call'd me *Sin*, and for a Sign
> Portentous held me; but familiar grown,
> I pleas'd, and with attractive graces won

The most averse, thee chiefly, who full oft
Thyself in me thy perfect image viewing
Becam'st enamour'd, and such joy thou took'st
With me in secret, that my womb conceiv'd
A growing burden. Meanwhile War arose
And fields were fought in Heav'n . . .

(Bk. II, ll. 747–68)

Sin's rendition of the time after the revolt and therefore the war in Heaven is detailed and realistic enough that we must take it seriously as action. It should not be read simply as allegory, and on that basis eliminated from what Roland Barthes has conveniently termed "the proairetic code," the fundamental level of narrative at which things happen, and one thing leads to another.[8] Allegory or no, as Empson insists,[9] Sin's story requires integration into the whole story of the revolt as it evolves in the first six books; mainly, it must be aligned with Raphael's "official" and more detailed version of the Assembly in Book V. But when we attempt to align these two passages, we become aware of the ineradicable difference in their generic presentation. This difference is most prominent in the time schemes of the two versions, in the generic sets on time which they imply. In Raphael's story much attention is focused on Heaven's grateful vicissitude,[10] and hence time is punctual; we can say exactly, for instance, that the war in Heaven begins the morning after the Assembly. The time of Sin's allegory is more indefinite than Raphael's "science fiction" time: "Meanwhile War arose . . .". Just because of this indefiniteness, the impression given is that a "certain amount" of time – more than a nighttime – passes between Sin's birth and the onset of war. The discordance between the two time schemes seems to me irreducible. It matters little that it is possible to integrate the contents of Sin's story into Raphael's rendition, by supposing, as Fowler does in his edition, that she "conceived her growing burden" posthaste, and that all she speaks takes place after Abdiel's departure from the devils' camp and before war begins. Our initial impression of different times, which is the result of differing generic time sets, cannot be so easily erased. The proairetic code is fissured in terms of time, and hence its very content is rendered indeterminate: it is impossible to say precisely what-took-place-when, even though we must attempt to do so.

But even if Satan's generic variousness renders his narrative indeterminate in its content, it nonetheless implies a determinate narrative structure which projects a definite reading operation. As can be seen from the example at hand, the proairetic code is composed of two phases or aspects: a background action, or what we might call a narrative referent; and an incessantly immediate presentation or production of that action, a momentary narrative signified. From the point of view of proairetic structure, it makes little difference how we propose to put Satan's story together. To say with Fowler that Sin's story can be integrated easily enough with Raphael's story is not materially different from arguing, with Empson, that Sin's speech makes it plausible that the rebellious angels have more than one meeting, and that the revolt is a more gradual and reasoned process than can be easily gathered from Raphael's version. It is not, of course, that the two interpretations are of equal merit. Empson's reading seems to me to be far the better one: in part because it attempts at least to take account of differences in the time schemes of the two versions; but mainly because the notion that there were discontented rumblings in Heaven before the exaltation picks up on hints in Raphael's story itself, which seems to model the angelic polity on feudal relations of fiefdom, and which thus makes it not unlikely that the revolt was in some sense prepared in advance. However one may feel about this, it seems undeniable that both interpretations construct a background narrative, with a unified time scheme, which is not contained by, but exists more or less behind, the fissured surface narrative. There are doubtless other interpretations possible besides Empson's and Fowler's; my point is simply that some interpretation or work of reconciliation is forced upon the fit reader. The surface narrative assumes a primary story having the consolidated status of epic legend or hexameral theology; Milton "explains" the matter of Satan's revolt by projecting such a consolidated legend as a background narrative – just by assuming, in other words, that it is already known.

It follows that the surface or episodic narratives appear and define themselves as productions, particular stagings, of this background narrative. "What actually happens" in the Satan narrative thus takes on a quasi-symbolic and perpetually momentary status. Each episode asserts itself as a somewhat figurative rendition of the determinately ambiguous and unquestioned background narrative, and is to be modified as is necessary in the light of that evolving context.

A parallel appears here between the Satan narrative and Godly narrative as theorized by Milton and mediated by hexameron. We trust the Satan story in each of its episodes but must nonetheless – must therefore – interpret it. But we must interpret it without really allowing that we do so, supposing, as we must, that the sense of Satan's revolt, the background narrative, is immanent at all points to the words in which it is conveyed. The plethora of Satanic genres responsible for this process of interpretation can thus be seen to reproduce and reinforce the commentary/analysis split within hexameron which enforced a comparable contextualization in the Godly narrative. But the Satanic hexameron, unlike the theological one, assumes a predominantly dramatic form. In the representation of God, though analysis determined the subordinate appearance of a conflicting dramatic discourse, yet this discourse was always contained by the more or less explicitly doctrinal mode of God's speeches. Such a doctrinal framework is relatively marginalized in Satan's speeches and gestures, whose unstable force permits analysis to release and foreground within it a consistently willful dramatic element, to the point where we may say that tragic drama serves in the Satan narrative as a substitute for hexameron.

As was the case with his generic variousness, so Satan's dramatic status not only pertains to the episodes of his story, but also makes its presence felt within the gestural narrative. The proairetic structure of Satanic gesture contains a secret split by which its independent closure is dramatized and lifted to something like symbolic status. Each of Satan's actions upon his journey literally figures the truth of the narrative that lies behind him and eludes definitive reconstruction. The gestural narrative stands forth as a *symbolic production* of epic legend, and thus gestural homology takes on a kind of unified symbolic value unknown to it in classical epic. In the same movement, however, by which hexameral drama constitutes the Satanic gestural narrative as a political symbol in foregrounding the productive substratum within it, it also works to deprive gesture of its uniqueness, and hence of its transparently collective or political form. We can see more sharply the paradoxical effects of what appears now as the dramatization of Satanic gesture if we attend more closely to a few of Satan's early gestures.

The neutrality of Satanic gesture

It is in the first two books that Satan is established as a figure of gesture, and is most obviously and impressively epic. Thus we should expect to find the dramatic component of gesture playing its most subordinate role in these books; yet even here we can see that a dramatic framework not only imposes itself on gesture but is constitutive within it.

We should note first that epic gesture has two outlets in Hell, expressing itself equally through discourse and through physical acts. In this it distinguishes itself. The speeches in the heavenly portions of the poem are hardly gestural in themselves, but are mainly so by virtue of the epic actions and accoutrements which surround them. In paradise, on the other hand, gesture is primarily located within some sort of discourse – in, for example, the dialogues of love and discovery between Adam and Eve, in the pedagogical interchange between Raphael and Adam, or in what we will see to be the sign language of creation.

Satanic speech-gesture distinguishes itself, in addition, as a more momentary phenomenon, and somehow more of a physical act, than paradisal speech. Paradisal speech-gesture is dialogic: it defines itself in the context of a larger process of speech, against the responsive words understood to be always on its horizon. Satanic speech conforms more narrowly to the paradigm of the epic monologue, which addresses itself, through the mediation of a formal and collective audience, to the fate or fatal nature that informs its very character as an act. Satan's first address (to Beelzebub) clearly comes to question its own fatal status by speaking for and through the devils' collective experience. This is not to say that Satan's speech-gesture is clearly defined or wholly self-sufficient. Rather, Satan's speeches are ambivalently posited in a larger process of speech, and are unusually hard to fix, as the following extended passage should make clear.

> To whom th' Arch-Enemy,
> And thence in Heav'n call'd Satan, with bold words
> Breaking the horrid silence thus began.
>   If thou beest he; But O how fall'n! how chang'd
> From him, who in the happy Realms of Light
> Cloth'd with transcendent brightness didst outshine

Myriads though bright: If he whom mutual league,
United thoughts and counsels, equal hope,
And hazard in the Glorious Enterprise,
Join'd with me once, now misery hath join'd
In equal ruin: into what Pit thou seest
From what highth fall'n, so much the stronger prov'd
He with his Thunder: and till then who knew
The force of those dire Arms? yet not for those,
Nor what the Potent Victor in his rage
Can else inflict, do I repent or change,
Though chang'd in outward luster; that fixt mind
And high disdain, from sense of injur'd merit,
That with the mightiest rais'd me to contend,
And to the fierce contention brought along
Innumerable force of Spirits arm'd
That durst dislike his reign, and mee preferring,
His utmost power with adverse power oppos'd
In dubious Battle on the Plains of Heav'n,
And shook his throne. What though the field be lost?
All is not lost; the unconquerable Will,
And study of revenge, immortal hate,
And courage never to submit or yield:
And what is else not to be overcome?
That Glory never shall his wrath or might
Extort from me. To bow and sue for grace
With suppliant knee, and deify his power
Who from the terror of this Arm so late
Doubted his Empire, that were low indeed,
That were an ignominy and shame beneath
This downfall; since by Fate the strength of Gods
And this Empyreal substance cannot fail,
Since through experience of this great event
In Arms not worse, in foresight much advanc't,
We may with more successful hope resolve
To wage by force or guile eternal War
Irreconcilable to our grand Foe,
Who now triúmphs, and in th' excess of joy
Sole reigning holds the Tyranny of Heav'n.

> So spake th' Apostate Angel, though in pain,
> Vaunting aloud, but rackt with deep despair . . .
>
> (Bk. I, ll. 81–126).

Let us attend first to the function of the formulaic prologue and coda to the speech. In classical epic, such formulaic enclosure usually serves to situate the speech-act and seal off its unity as a gesture. However, the above coda not only reinforces its gestural unity, it also introduces an additional gesture of visible despair retroactively into Satan's address. In this its commentary function, the coda casts the address as a familiar response to a situation given by the celestial cycle; the address is attributed an allegorical-dramatic dimension which it does not possess "in itself." The coda therefore institutes an ambiguity into the very gestural unity of the speech that it helps to assure. On the one hand, it provides the reader with a reductive (allegorical) image of Satan's preceding speech-gesture as a kind of set physical-emotional act. On the other hand, it works to give the speech "in itself" a symbolic status, thus heightening its epic integrity as a unique production. The address possesses itself of a symbolic autonomy in its own right and demands to be read on its own terms, which are more cognitive and less moral-theological than the coda assumes. Insofar as the didactic and quasi-dramatic stage directions so frequently accompanying Satanic speech and actions serve to institute such dramatic ambiguity within his gesture, they are integral to the constitution of that gesture, and hence to the character of Satan. Nowhere does the primacy of gesture and ethos, and the secondariness of character itself in epic, stand forth so visibly as in the character of Satan, for Satan is inherently manipulable.[11]

But even without the coda, Satan's speech is dramatic enough, at least in its content: the gesture it enacts or verbalizes is one that might be called self-staging. The suspended indirection of Satan's initial period (whose syntax discloses no main clause until Satan himself has replaced Beelzebub as its subject) accentuates the gestural nature of the speech, and indeed even imparts to Satan's flow a physical quality. It is as if the period registers the play of immediate emotions as they qualify the basic enclosing form of the speech-gesture. This intimacy between word and physical feeling gives a strong sense that Satan is situating or "finding" himself, as a character, by producing the speech-gesture. The suspended indirection of his opening period might indeed finally be read as projecting an understood verb ("If thou beest he . . . *attend.*") which governs the whole speech, and places it in relation to another consciousness which is not so much an individual as a collective one. Satan does address only Beelzebub – he enters into dialogue with him – but in doing so he makes him into a mirror of his own and of his troops' fallen condition, and into a marker of his own place as leader of the new fallen host. He questions and comes to terms with the fate that presents itself anew to his gaze while dramatizing his situation *through* this common consciousness.

There are two essential features of the dramatic constitution achieved on the basis of this questioning. These features seem to be Satan's sole stable characteristics, appearing at nearly every moment of his various career. First, in the manner of a high tragic character, Satan defines himself in terms of his social position, and in terms of the fatal contradiction inherent in that position. He is "by nature" the leader of the angelic hierarchy, a hierarchy which, like the ineradicable being of the angels themselves, is fatally ordained; but he must defend the dignity of this order *against* fate, which has stacked all the odds against him in taking the form of a will whose strength outweighs his own.[12] Second, he then defines his social function, his own reason for being, as a purely reactive one. He is free, he is himself, insofar as he reacts against God's will, or is able to react against it. This makes Satan into a perpetually momentary character. We might say that not only is Satan a figure of gesture, he "consciously" dramatizes himself as such by symbolically situating his character in gesture. He is Satan only to the extent that he is capable of gestures which are uniquely Satanic in their symbolic reactive dimension.

Satan's speech-gesture, it transpires, is dramatically determined however we look at it – from without or from within. And these two perspectives are interlocked: Satan's dramatic fixity – the abstractly reactive character of his speech-stance – is the condition for his ceaseless manipulation from without. From the generic standpoint, it serves as the bridge from the high tragic Satan, evoked in the imperturbable grandeur of his better speeches, to the melodramatic Satan insisted upon by the didactic intrusions. Satanic speech-gesture is thus profoundly ambivalent, so that a reader does not know where to take hold of Satan: whether to concentrate on his speech in itself or its accompanying intrusion; whether to read him as highly tragic, melodramatic, or as something in between.

When we stand back from this whole "process of speech," what impresses us, I think, is its cognitive neutrality, the almost eerie indifference with which it negotiates the rifts in its own content. In spite of its dramatic divisions, there is a still point at the heart of Satanic gesture; it preserves, beneath and by way of these divisions, its oneness with itself as a narrative process of production impervious to any preformed ethical judgment upon Satan. The ethical indifference written into classical epic homology is reduplicated here with a difference, in extreme form; it stands out even more prominently than in classical epic, possesses an additional disinterest, for contrasting with its moral-theological content. This, I think, is one of the major aesthetic achievements of the poem, and represents the nearest thing to a literal revivification of the homologous form of classical epic that *Paradise Lost* offers.

One might say that Milton pushes this indifference to the point of perturbation in delivering Satan's physical gestures.

>   his other Parts besides
> Prone on the Flood, extended long and large
> Lay floating many a rood, in bulk as huge
> As whom the Fables name of monstrous size,
> *Titanian*, or *Earth-born*, that warr'd on *Jove*,
> *Briareos* or *Typhon*, whom the Den
> By Ancient Tarsus held, or that Sea-beast
> *Leviathan*, which God of all his works
> Created hugest that swim th' Ocean stream:
> Him haply slumb'ring on the *Norway* foam
> The Pilot of some small night-founder'd Skiff,
> Deeming some Island, oft, as Sea-men tell,
> With fixed Anchor in his scaly rind
> Moors by his side under the Lee, while Night
> Invests the Sea, and wished Morn delayes:
> So stretcht out huge in length the Arch-fiend lay . . .
>   (Bk. I, ll. 194–209)

The reader's attention is caught, not by the typological symbolism of Leviathan, nor by the moral-emblematic nature of the vignette in which he figures, but rather by the brute imperturbability of creation conveyed in the sudden opening out of the final simile. The moral-emblematic dimension even enhances this indifference, since it only makes us wonder at the epic neutrality of the evil displayed here, and lifts this very neutrality to dramatic-symbolic status. Milton's counterplot – which, we have seen, gives ontology gestural force and disrupts narrative diachrony by setting God's will within epic fate – turns up again in a disturbing guise, for God's will is placed within the fate that informs evil. We may say that the counterplot always represents a privileged point of indifference or neutrality, and makes its most forceful, because most dramatic, appearances in places such as this one, in which gesture is dramatically foregrounded. It thus takes up a station in Satan's more vivid and memorable gestures, and comes to be peculiarly associated with his character.

Such disturbing moments of the counterplot as this last suggest that the dramatization of epic results in a stripping of its generic characterization from the narrative process, in the partial neutralization of the epic itself as a genre. The counterplot seems to coincide with what might be described as an excess of sheer narrative production or description over the generic qualification that attempts to contain it. In the case of Leviathan, the vignette outruns the moral-allegorical purpose that the very name of Leviathan announces. The awesome neutrality of Leviathan's gesture is one with a surplus of production or signification over definite meaning, and this surplus issues, not only in moral ambiguity, but in an essential obscurity as to the relation between simile and referent, in which all the details of the simile take on a pregnancy of reference that they ordinarily do not have in epic elaboration. Indifference of gesture thus makes problematic the very referent of epic description itself, and determines an epistemological uncertainty as attaching to the springs of narrative. This uncertainty inheres in the very form of gesture, but at times seems to be thematized, to make its way into the content of the narrative description itself.

> He scarce had ceas't when the superior Fiend
> Was moving toward the shore; his ponderous shield,
> Ethereal temper, massy, large and round,
> Behind him cast; the broad circumference
> Hung on his shoulders like the Moon, whose Orb
> Through Optic Glass the *Tuscan* Artist views
> At Ev'ning from the top of *Fesole*,

> Or in *Valdarno*, to descry new Lands,
> Rivers or Mountains in her spotty Globe.
> His Spear, to equal which the tallest Pine
> Hewn on *Norwegian* hills, to be the Mast
> Of some great Ammiral, were but a wand,
> He walkt with to support uneasy steps
> Over the burning Marl.
>
> (Bk. I, ll. 283–96)

Both similes distance their referents as they enlarge them – the latter in reducing the mast to less than a wand, the former in putting Galileo's optic tube between Satan's shield and us, and in making the engraving it must bear (there is an obvious reference to Achilles' shield) correspond to the spots he sees on the moon. The effect, once again, is of a curious instability or volatility of the referent, and a consequent uncertainty as to how it can be known. Tube and mast might almost be called symbols of the uncertainty attached to Satan; and it is perhaps not accidental that both allude to aspects of the revolution in knowledge occurring in Milton's time (the "Ammiral's mast" suggests late-sixteenth- and seventeenth-century fleets, which opened up a new world for knowledge, among other things). The transformation of scientific and geographic space is suddenly revealed as symbolically overdetermining the volatility of Satanic gesture, the dramatically ambivalent narrative space of epic hexameron.[13]

I would emphasize, however, that from the present point of view the expansibility of scientific space is a secondary determination; it provides access to more or less explicit reflection upon an ambivalence whose primary determinants are not scientific but socioeconomic. The epistemological doubt written into the indifference of Miltonic and Satanic gesture corresponds finally to the ambivalence in the general category of action under the newly emergent capitalist mode of production. Just as the stability of classical gesture was seen to be based on the heterogenous unity of action made possible by the politically enforced elision of any general concept of labor, so the volatile uncertainty of Satanic gesture answers, at the level of content, to a situation in which the individual kinds of activity lose their proper uniqueness and range themselves, with the growth of commodity economy, under the general sign of labor or production.

This shift from discrete activities to production, the collapsing of use into exchange-value, is registered likewise, and most dramatically, at the formal level, in the aggravation of the separation between epic form and content, in that indifference of the narrative process that we have seen to mark the moment at which poetic description exceeds its generic delimitation. It is precisely in this formal indifference that we can see most clearly the advent of a new content which spells the imminent breakup of classical epic, for it is by way of it that Satan's gestures, and the process of narrative description itself, establish themselves as values in their own right, as the productive substratum whose different generic moments, with their differing moral and theological significances, are only qualifications or aspects. In the Satan narrative, epic is thus made paradoxically to serve as non-generic writing, which we may designate as a form of writing peculiar to capitalism, in that it takes place under the aegis of production or labor power.

Satanic drama

Yet, as should already be clear, the non-generic substratum of the text itself has a kind of symbolic meaning. The significance of such images as Leviathan "extended long and large" on the ocean stream, or the spotty lunar landscape as sighted through Galileo's glass, is shocking in its obviousness: it is the enormous neutrality and immanence of evil itself that looms from these passages of pure production, an evil sundered from its traditional definition and ensconced anew in an indifferent creation.

But if productive gesture has a symbolic meaning, it follows inevitably that it is saddled with a properly generic delimitation; and this delimitation will naturally make itself most manifest at the level of the character-narrative, to which I now turn. I propose that the point in Satanic gesture at which evil bulks large in the form of creation corresponds to, and to some extent generates within the hexameral drama of Satan, allegorical or baroque tragedy. Walter Benjamin, whose *The Origin of German Tragic Drama* I will take as the more or less definitive construction of allegorical tragedy,[14] has shown and explored the profound moral ambivalence of the form, in which evil and good are drained of clear-cut theological significance in a world cut off from transcendence, whose hero, trapped upon the plane of creation, thus appears as both tyrant and martyr at the same time. *Trauerspiel* or allegorical tragedy lies, both in Benjaminian theory and in *Paradise Lost*, somewhere between high tragedy and melodrama. Since it represents the dramatic moment in the story of Satan with the closest proximity to the gestural level itself, allegorical tragedy may be said to precipitate the Satan drama, and to exercise a kind of logical dominance over the other two moments within it. My main aim in this section is to establish the presence of allegorical tragedy in Satan's career, and to show how it distorts the official theological explanation of Satan's fall.[15]

For Benjamin, the founding situation of allegorical tragedy is one of theological rupture.[16] In the period of religious and social upheaval during which this tragedy appeared, theology was reinforced as the only truly legitimate or viable way of explaining the world. Yet it was precisely the transcendence sought in theology that had had its medieval supports wrenched from under it. So the author or theological subject of *Trauerspiel* yearns for transcendence and yet is confined to the material world of the visible creation, whose various creatures become so many speechless signs of a past transcendence. All the theological categories are distorted or torn from their referents to become pure signifiers of the (former) theological subject's desire. Allegorical desire is thus constitutively incapable of fulfillment, and this is the more frustrating because it is felt to be motivated by the force that might redeem it. Benjamin has shown how a debased theological category of fate governs the action and the writing of *Trauerspiel*. God's will broods over all the signs of creation in its absence from them, with the result that it is impossible to say whether the allegorical world is full or empty, good or evil.

It should not surprise us, given the importance of theological fate in this kind of allegory, to find that the appearance of allegorical tragedy in the Satan saga coincides with the intrusion of divine into epic fate that marks the intersection of hexameral and epic narrative. Satan the martyr-tyrant is posited by and reacts against a divine fate concentrated on the plane of creation; he himself is but the supreme creature on this plane whose signs house a straitened predestination and speak mutely of it. As creature, Satan is a preeminently allegorical figure for whom desire and its object are hopelessly sundered. He symbolizes, in this respect, not the fulfillment but the pathos of political desire.

The allegorical representation of Satan bears a peculiar dialectical relation with hexameral analysis. It is partly this relation, as well as the proximity of allegory to gesture, that makes allegory the dominant tragedy in the Satan narrative. On the one hand, allegory can be seen to occupy the subgeneric function preordained by analysis in performing the analytical chore of separating sign from referent. On the other hand, allegory performs this separation all too thoroughly, and might be said partly to preempt analysis by foregrounding the absence of the referent, thus transforming the properly cognitive focus of analysis into the more epistemological set that characterizes the Satan narrative. The result of this is that allegorical tragedy is a peculiarly free and dominant subgenre which clearly founds and exercises its sway over even the most traditional elements of the Satan drama. There is, as I have noted, a kind of moral program written into the traditional hexameral story of Satan, according to which evil bears its own fate, and gradually disintegrates of its own determinedly evil will. This melodramatic picture of Satan is unquestionably prominent in the Satan narrative, but I do not think it is so authoritative a picture as Lewis and followers have attempted to make it. In founding the melodramatic framework, the allegorical tragedy in which theological fate presides necessarily at the same time distorts the melodramatic clarity of its theological message. The melodramatic will to self-destruction is displaced into allegory: Satan's fragmentary decenteredness as a character signifies, not (or not only) the self-defeat of evil, but the mute despair and desire of a theological subject and of a creation cut off from God.

It must be allowed that the allegorical method of *Trauerspiel* is itself considerably curtailed and displaced in *Paradise Lost*. Baroque allegory reduces the world of man to a world of things; it tends to focus upon accessory objects or fragments in their inert, material dimension, to range a heap of broken images upon the plane of a creation denuded of humanity.[17] Such a reduction to the material inert runs athwart the humanist nature of the epic form, whose object world is not static but rather inscribed with or perceived in terms of a series of gestures. Thus the baroque in *Paradise Lost* knows and can produce no inert; it qualifies or solidifies gesture without ever reducing it simply to an object or a setting. Even if Satanic gesture tends to locate itself in and through neutral objects, within an ambivalently heteronomous and fixed created order, gesture still retains its force in these settings. Think, for instance, of what is perhaps the most patently baroque thing in the whole poem, the building of Pandemonium, which rises from the floor of Hell as if by its own massive volition. In spite of the objectification of the process of building, Pandemonium is alive with the force of gesture, with human power, and represents, indeed, the most impressive evocation of collective agency in the whole poem.[18]

Nonetheless, there are occasions in the Satan narrative on which accoutrements do at least begin to stand out in a purely allegorical fashion. For instance, not only is the obvious programmatic intent of the description of Satan at the start of Book II straitened and distorted by its baroque decoration, so also is the force of Satanic gesture threatened by a fixed allegorical image.

> High on a Throne of Royal State, which far
> Outshone the wealth of *Ormus* and of *Ind*,
> Or where the gorgeous East with richest hand
> Show'rs on her Kings *Barbaric* Pearl and Gold,
> Satan exalted sat, by merit rais'd
> To that bad eminence.   (11. 1–6)

So Satan is a despot, and the worst kind – an Oriental one – at that.[19] To make an idol of Satan in this way (much as Milton made idols of the prelates in the early 1640s) is to divest him in advance of whatever glamor his rebellious project might be expected to have. Milton's Protestant politics intrudes quite clearly into the programmatic narrative intent, and is communicated by the heavy irony of the epic voice. Yet the very transparency of this programmatic motivation results in the foregrounding of the purely allegorical dimension of gesture. To idolize gesture is to expose its manipulability and to fix it within creation as a kind of image of itself. Satan does not incorporate the throne of royal state, or the raw wealth which it signifies; these things rather define his gesture, for once, as a theological fixed quantity. The idolized Satan is momentarily stripped of revolutionary splendor but invested with the glamor of allegorical desire, a desire fixed by theological fate (or predestination) within the fragmentary order of creation. The symbolic political fulfillment of epic gesture reveals itself to be mere wish-fulfillment, as Satanic gesture undergoes psychological distortion into an allegorical image.

The allegorical focus of the above passage is not so much on the accoutrements of Satan's power as it is on Satan himself, made in the image of that power. And Satan is most clearly an allegorical character, not when he is associated with things, but rather when he is defined in terms of his merely external and reactive role vis-à-vis God, when he appears most forthrightly as a figure of predestination. Thus Satan is cast most lucidly as allegorical hero in the dramatic soliloquy at the start of Book IV, where he meditates explicitly on his creaturely fate. Waldock made this speech the crux of the Satan problem: it marked, for him, the place at which Satan is decisively put down, where the voice of the author which attempts all along to qualify our favorable impressions of Satan enters into the very character and snatches his body.[20] From our present point of view, we can see it as the place at which the inconsistency and externality inherent in Satanic gesture, and determined by the moment of allegorical tragedy from the very beginning, is drawn into daylight by the narrative line. Landed on Niphates' top, Satan is suddenly afflicted with "despair that slumber'd"; he sees his whole career in the light of predestination, and then aggressively addresses that light as it appears in the newly created world, in the sun, which is now but the sign of past transcendence.

> O thou that with surpassing Glory crown'd,
> Look'st from thy sole Dominion like the God
> Of this new World; at whose sight all the Stars
> Hide thir diminisht heads; to thee I call,
> But with no friendly voice, and add thy name
> O Sun, to tell thee how I hate thy beams
> That bring to my remembrance from what state
> I fell, how glorious once above thy Sphere;
> Till Pride and worse Ambition threw me down
> Warring in Heav'n against Heav'ns matchless King.
>   (11. 32–41)

"Ah wherefore!" Satan continues; and this initial declaration of steadfast hate gives way to a series of wavering periods in which Satan displays extreme self-doubt and indecision. Such indecision is a presiding and stock emotion (one is almost inclined to call it a device) in allegorical tragedy, which serves to lay bare the inconsistency and externality which Benjamin represents as the very soul of allegorical characterology.[21] Waldock was, I think, perfectly right to say that Satan is manipulated here – though I would add that it is primarily the allegory, and not Milton, that does the manipulating. But it is misleading to say simply that Satan is degraded in this speech. For what impresses us is how sympathetic a figure of evil he cuts. He presents himself as a martyr to the fatal obligation imposed upon him by his tyranny, and the pathos of his speech requires that we take him at his word.

> Hadst thou the same free Will and Power to stand [as
>   did the other angels]?
> Thou hadst: whom hast thou then or what to accuse,
> But Heav'n's free Love dealt equally to all?
> Be then his Love accurst, since love or hate,
> To me alike, it deals eternal woe.
> Nay curs'd be thou; since against his thy will
> Chose freely what it now so justly rues.
> Me miserable! which way shall I fly
> Infinite wrath, and infinite despair?
> Which way I fly is Hell; myself am Hell;
> And in the lowest deep a lower deep
> Still Threat'ning to devour me opens wide,
> To which the Hell I suffer seems a Heav'n.
> O then at last relent: is there no place
> Left for Repentance, none for Pardon left?
> None left but by submission; and that word
> *Disdain* forbids me, and my dread of shame
> Among the Spirits beneath, whom I seduc'd
> With other promises and other vaunts
> Than to submit, boasting I could subdue
> Th' Omnipotent. Ay me, they little know
> How dearly I abide that boast so vain.
>
>   (11. 66–87)

It is not customary to see Satan as an example of Renaissance melancholy; yet in this central soliloquy Satan displays the main characteristics of the melancholic hero proper to allegorical tragedy. The theory of melancholy posits an astrological determination of character which is encoded in the body and in creation by means of the humors and of humorous insignia.[22] Such specifically astrological fate appears in *Paradise Lost* only by glimpses (and only, as is generally the case with Milton, in non-esoteric guise); but nonetheless, as we have seen, Satan appears as predestined at the level of creation itself, and brings with him, as we shall see, a physical theory of determination comparable to, and fulfilling the role of, astrological humor theory. The physicality of Satan's gestures (both of speech and of motion) here takes on a new significance; indeed the wavering indecisiveness of the periods in the above passage might be felt to inscribe the emotional fluctuation with a physical, purely external character. If we take Satan as melancholic seriously, it follows that we must read the very content of his speech in allegorical terms, as the writing within Satan of an oblique and incoherent theological fate.[23] This means that the ethical significance of Satan's ethical categories – whose wisdom is obviously to be read straightforwardly at the melodramatic level – is made problematic. If Satan is a figure of predestination, what can such a category as moral choice signify?

It signifies, at least in a figurative sense, either all or nothing. The urgency of this message, encoded in the very form of allegory, suggests something about the gravity of the political situation to which it must be taken as a response. For the mourning-play has fairly direct and obvious political motivations. Its aesthetic of fragmentation accords with a political theory of kingly sovereignty which justified absolutism by positing the imminence of a historical catastrophe which was to be avoided at all costs. Allegorical political theory viewed the whole of history under the sign of catastrophe, as a permanent state of emergency always determined by the same oblique and incoherent fate at work in the signs of creation. Thus, though political history itself forms the ultimate content of allegorical tragedy, it appears only on the plane of creation, as a kind of natural history, and is collapsed onto the visible setting of the play itself, the court and its environs.[24]

Insofar as he is the hero of allegorical tragedy, Satan is situated on this level of natural history, in a fatally determined creation. We have already seen that Satan dramatizes himself as a fated character of gesture from the beginning of the plot: he is possessed of his rights by virtue of a kind of natural-historical sanction. The place, however, where this matter is of most interest and importance, and where the official ethical point of view on Satan is most thoroughly undermined by the allegorical-political one, is at the beginning of the story, in Books V and VI, where Raphael tells Adam of the fall from Heaven. From the perspective of the Satanic allegory, God's exaltation of Christ appears, not as the seamless narrative resolution of the opposition between the divine will and reason (which is how it appears in itself), but rather as the institution of a state of emergency in Heaven. Satan's indignant response to the exaltation, which in itself is left undermotivated and hence external to his character, thus suffuses that narrative place with the contradictory desire, both psychological and abstractly political in character, indigenous to allegorical tragedy and of chief thematic interest in it: his will-to-place is both a lust for sheer power and a desperate wish to preserve the hierarchical *status quo*.

It becomes apparent, at this "thematic" level, how the mourning-play straddles the space between melodrama and high tragedy and coordinates their appearances. Whereas the mourning-play holds these contradictory desires in suspense, melodrama explains Satan's fall and disintegration in terms of his lust for power, his inflated ego; while Satan's wish to preserve the angelic order, as emphasized and detached by the cognitive bent of the poem, is weighted with main explanatory value in tragedy proper. This latter wish, marking the point at which mourning-play shades into high tragedy, is most crucially exemplified in Satan's response to Abdiel's shocking revelation that the angels were created by the Son.

> That we were form'd then say'st thou? and the work
> Of secondary hands, by task transferr'd
> From Father to his Son? strange point and new!
> Doctrine which we would know whence learnt: who saw
> When this creation was? remember'st thou
> Thy making, while the Maker gave thee being?
> We know no time when we were not as now;
> Know none before us, self-begot, self-rais'd
> By our own quick'ning power, when fatal course
> Had circl'd his full Orb, the birth mature
> Of this our native Heav'n, Ethereal Sons.
> Our puissance is our own, our own right hand
> Shall teach us highest deeds, by proof to try
> Who is our equal.   (Bk. V, 11. 853–66)

This speech is often taken as Satan's assertion that he made himself. The pressure of the melodramatic context, I think, makes us read the speech in this way, as the simple expression of the lust for power of the political ego, or as the correlated desire of the metaphysical ego for self-determination. But the allegorical and high tragic contexts seem to me to work more powerfully in what is actually said. Satan is twisting Job to insist on the primacy of the visible order in its own determination;[25] the whole angelic hierarchy, with all its orders and degrees, is understood to have spread itself over creation of its own natural motion or quickening power. It is not simply the ego, but the ego-in-hierarchy, that Satan is defending. So it is impossible to say whether Satan is saint or tyrant, or whether choice is indeed possible for him. At this level, theological ethics is occluded by natural history, which harbors and is motivated by contradictory allegorical desire.

Yet Satan's version of natural history has more "body", is more organically inclined, than is customary in allegorical tragedy, which characteristically fragments its history while incorporating it into creation. Largely by virtue of the collective force of epic form, allegorical natural history is attenuated at the very moment in the epic narrative at which it is foregrounded. *Trauerspiel* is thus humanized at this point into high tragedy – or into a kind of replacement for it. For the homeground of high tragedy in the Satan narrative is to be found in the great speeches of the first two books. In Raphael's presentation of the original fall from Heaven, however, the portrayal of Satan is imbued with the tendentiousness of the "official" melodramatic framework, and high tragedy cannot appear in its own likeness, but is itself attenuated and carried forward by the oddly realistic surrogate of what I have called pure theological science fiction. Satan's belief in the natural integrity of the angelical hierarchy, his constitution as an ego-in-hierarchy, is given an implicit feudal justification by this realistic level; it is theorized in terms of the organicist nature of feudal characterology. Satan's very rebellion is figured as a feudal revolt or upheaval, whose most pressing historical referent is perhaps the Wars of the Roses, but which should finally be taken as approximating to a general paradigm of feudal crisis: Satan gathers his retainers (and other lords of roughly his stature, with their retainers) about him, retreats to his private domain in the North, and marches on the newly centralized monarchy.[26]

What is the final significance of this oddly realistic and yet high tragic feudal dramatization of Satan's fall? I would suggest that Satan's science fiction incarnation is mainly important in its role of fleshing out the logic of predestination buried in the heavenly creation. For it is in Satan's assumption of a feudal natural history, I think, that the Shelleyan argument for Satan's moral superiority takes on its full force. Satan is given a proper dignity by this assumption: his reified will is made the subject of a former fateful choice, which it maintains in its very fixity. It is because of a moral fullness, because the *status quo ante* embodies its desires in him, that Satan becomes the subject of disembodied and fragmented allegorical desire, the disintegrating villain of melodrama. So predestination itself comes to be explained, in the Satan narrative, in terms of ennobled allegorical desire, and we can begin to see, across the generic rifts which constitute Satan as a character, that there is a strong sense in which predestination itself hinges upon, and is determined by, Satan's paradoxical superiority to his own fate. Natural history in its high tragic dimension thus breaks off from theology proper, or decisively decenters it in the realm of creation. Satan's fatal psychology is its own quickening power.

Satan as monist

I wish now to carry the reading of Satan's natural history speech one step further in order to connect the Satan with the paradise narrative. But before doing so, I should review the significance of Satan's generic production as it has here been constructed. I am arguing, first, that Satanic gesture in its meta-epic dimension functions as a kind of political wish-fulfillment in expressing the political libido which is left over from the revolution and which cannot be contained by the official theological code of the poem. This symbolic fulfillment is drained and distorted by the dramatic form of the Satan narrative as it intersects with gesture. Allegorical tragedy produces and highlights the very abstractness of activity that political libido is in some sense a reaction against, and so works to transform the material ethos of epic into abstract desire in the very act of making it symbolic. The allegorization of gesture may be seen, then, as a recontainment of political desire by the theological code of the hexameron. But it is only a partial recontainment, since allegorical tragedy also breaks with or decenters theology itself. The desire of allegorical tragedy is not theological but rather abstract desire, and it is because of this that the Satan narrative in its high tragic or ennobled allegorical dimension skews the logic of predestination.

The symbolic purgation of political desire at the level of form is one with a logical purgation of monism at the level of content. If we consider more closely the content of Satan's allegorical wish concerning angelical origins, we can begin to see how this equation is so, and how the Satan narrative itself is but a willful moment in a larger process of narrative recontainment or contextualization. Satan's argument for self-determination amounts to a kind of literalism of the text of creation. We might see it, indeed, as the point at which the disjuncture in the Satanic proairetic code attains expression at the level of content: Satan insists upon taking his figurative gesture for itself, as a self-complete narrative dependent upon no context for its comprehensibility. More than this, Satan's literalist interpretation of the visible letter corresponds to one of Milton's own heterodox and literalist interpretations of Scripture.[27] Satan is a monist of a sort, and the force that he invents to ballast his conviction of his own physical integrity – "Our own quick'ning power" – might be taken as a kind of intuition of that "vital power of matter" which Milton himself postulated at the basis of creation. How do we account for the appearance of Milton's monism in Satanic guise? We can finally answer this only in the context of a larger narrative logic in which Satan's monism represents a crucial term.

I will not be arguing that Satan's monism has a simple and coherent meaning. On the contrary, two mutually contradictory solutions to the problem of Satanic monism are evident immediately. On the one hand, Satan's emergence as monist might be called a meta-epic gesture. He is at his most coherent as a character, in closest contact with the gestural micronarrative of which he, more than the other characters, is but a figure, when insisting on the primacy of his own motion in the order of the visible. It follows (and this should come as no surprise, considering the connection which has already been made between Milton's monism and epic theology) that Satan's monism is valorized by epic narrative; the closure of the capitalist subject upon itself to which monism responds is paradoxically made the condition for a libidinally integral epic philosophy. Satan-as-character is libidinized precisely in and for his monist "philosophy," and it is just this libidinal dimension which forms the hidden basis for, and lends force to, interpretations of Satan as an allegory of that uniquely creative or poetic faculty of the bourgeois ego that goes by the name of imagination.

There seems no question, on the other hand, that Satan is denigrated, in part, specifically *for* his monism. The programmatic moral framework that inheres in the Satan plot attacks just this doctrine of innate integrity. I said before that Satan's body appears to be snatched in his soliloquy in Book IV; perhaps I should revise that statement now and say that only his vocal chords are taken there. It is at a later point in the plot that Satan's body is invaded: in the war in Heaven, where the substance of Satan and his cohorts – though allowed to be indestructible even in battle – is made to feel pain, and where they experience uncontrollable fear at the sight of Christ adorned as a prophetic vision. In Book IX, then, Satan is forced (and it is melodramatic justice which dictates that he find this particularly ignominious) "his essence to incarnate and imbrute," to mix "with bestial slime." And his process of punishment culminates in Book X, when he eats from the ashy tree, and the bad angels' very desires and motor activities are taken from their control. The narrative logic at work in this castigation of monism seems to me to duplicate a familiar psychological ploy which we have already seen at work: it is not enough that Satan should turn out to be the real despot; he must also be the real heretic. Satan's monism – and *not* Milton's – is evil.

Such a defensive operation obviously requires that an at least nominal difference be established between Miltonic and Satanic monism. And it is apparent, at a glance, that Satan's insistence on angelic integrity distinguishes itself by its transparently reactive character. Satan's monism – although organically based in his distinctive gesture – is colored by its extemporaneous invention: it is a line he resorts to when he needs to put distance between angelical origins and the Son. Later in his story, after God has embarrassed the doctrine of corporal integrity in the war in Heaven, the same reactive need to distance himself from the divine will drives Satan into dualism ("the Mind is its own Place"). Milton's monism, on the contrary, is more liberally and reverently disposed. It amounts to a way of theorizing God's accommodation of human freedom or of the independence and integrity of the theological subject; it attempts to mediate the gap between predestination and human autonomy.

Yet I find it hard to see this distinction between Satanic reaction and Miltonic mediation as anything more than a kind of stopgap or purely formal defensive measure. Milton's monism, however scrupulously and reverently it keeps God in sight, nonetheless intends finally but to put him at a distance, to keep him from snatching the religious poet's soul; and it is clearly as open to the charge that it is secretly a dualism defending itself as is Satan's transparently reactive monism. Indeed, Johnson's typically incisive complaint about the confusion of matter and spirit in *Paradise Lost*[28] points up just this confusion inherent in Milton's monism, which retains the categories of soul and body, matter and spirit, in the very act of collapsing the distinction between them.

This is not to say, however, that the debunking of Satanic monism is strictly willful and lacking in intellectual substance. For it seems to me that at a slightly deeper, if related, level (a level beneath that of hexameral melodrama), this defense does give Satan's monism a significant difference, and presents it less in a reactive than a regressive light. Satan's monism assumes the completeness of the present (narrative) order; it is itself the sign, as we have seen, of the wish to preserve unchanged the angelical *status quo*. Milton's monism, on the other hand, is figured in a dynamic mode, and presents itself as inherently open-ended: the character-narrative it posits is prepared to find its truth or completion outside of itself and in time. The feudal depiction of Satan assumes new significance in the context of this contrast. As we have seen, Milton's monist narrative corresponds to that of a newly hegemonic and dynamic bourgeois subject. But it remains the case that the moment of possession represents a recasting of a feudal relation to one's bodily forces, and Milton's individualism is particularly marked by a contradictory feudal-aristocratic determination. The debunking of Satanic monism, and the defense against heresy that it carries through, may therefore be interpreted as the paradoxical repudiation or purgation of the feudal component in Milton's own monism. "Yes," Milton's unconscious might be understood to say, "Satan is a monist. But he is a totally different kind of monist from me – a regressive one." And Milton's very creation and recognition of the resemblance prove him innocent.

We should be careful not to reduce this defense to a psychological motivation, although I do think that it is determined by a properly psychological ambivalence on Milton's part, not so much toward Satan as toward the monist narrative itself. This interpretation indeed has the virtue of making psychological ambivalence appear finally as a reflection of and response to the ambivalence of the commodity form itself, and thus as a profoundly social phenomenon by its nature. The "publicity" of the psychological defense against monism is more clearly visible when we see that it inheres in a process of contextualization within the poem itself larger than any alluded to so far, a total narrative movement by which Milton's private heresy is symbolically purged of its regressive traits and sublimated into a purer and more godly version. While Satan is put down as feudal, a "truer" monism is developed by the text of the narrative, and is located in the topographical language of paradise, in the symbolic dialogue of creation. It is by way of this monist narrative logic that predestination itself is most centrally instated, most cogently defended against and managed, in the poem.

But even though Satan is separated from creation, even though his dramatically finished gesture is sharply distinguished from the open-ended gesture of creation, he is nevertheless brought into contact with creation, inasmuch as the distinction depends on an initial false resemblance. I think this false resemblance, while it is meant to point a difference, actually serves to render conspicuous a deeper logical and aesthetic connection between Satan and creation, which hinges on the epic aesthetic of plenitude written into the false dramatic finish of Satanic gesture. It seems to me – and I will argue at the conclusion of the next chapter – that Satan is so effective in paradise largely because of this hidden kinship with it, which permits him to impersonate creation's logical end.

6
Garden and fall: predestination as metaphysical lack

It is impossible to show so conclusively as with Satan that Milton's creation represents his monism. Even if we take creation as a narrative agent in its own right – and it is part of my argument, in what follows, that creation should and must be so understood at an important level of the text – we cannot say that it represents monism in the same way that Satan does, if only because creation is mute; it is not given any lines and cannot proclaim a theory of its nature or origins, but can only impose itself as a kind of massive object for interpretation, as a symbol or series of symbolic signs. All the same, I think it can be shown that the theory of creation at work in *Paradise Lost* is a monist one, or at least depends on Milton's monism. And I will argue finally that it is exactly because of its massive significance or interpretability that creation imposes itself as an agent of monism.

The obvious place to begin, however, is not with creation itself, but with Chaos, or rather with the place held by Chaos in the poem's cosmology and ontogeny.[1] I think Chaos gives rather direct figuration to Milton's materialism, his notion that God created not *ex nihilo* but out of an original matter. It is difficult to specify the original relationship between Chaos and God, of course, but one's general impression is that they are more or less temporally coterminous, since we are not to think of God as creating Chaos. Chaos, then, is a given of Milton's universe, and seems always to have existed alongside God, serving to provide him with the disparate and anarchic raw material upon which he works to produce the forms of creation. But this work of creation is not to be understood as taking place *ab extra*, or as a strict imposition of form upon matter. It rather presents itself as exerting influence over Chaos from a distance, and assisting in the birth and maturation of forms already latent within it. To use the language of *De Doctrina*, it brings to life in Chaos that vital and informing "power of matter" which pervades all the objects of creation and makes for the ultimate unity of soul and body. The materialist view of God's act of creation supports and is one with a monistic view of creation proper or created creation. The most impressive figure for the act of monistic creation is that of the Son brooding over Chaos as if over the ocean:

> Thou from the first
> Wast present, and with mighty wings outspread
> Dove-like satst brooding on the vast Abyss
> And mad'st it pregnant.   (Bk. I, 11. 19–22)

The logic of the figure is to allow that the Abyss, once pregnant, produces its own offspring. Thus creation comes into the world in a relatively self-possessed form, without the hand or the word of God immediately upon it.

But the metaphor of brooding not only grants the process of creation a certain independence from the Creator. It also implies, at its limit, that creation itself is still in process, that it exists somehow in a dynamic mode. The direct narrative presentation of creation – especially in Book VII, but also in the paradise books generally – bears out this implication. Nature appears in the guise of creation, not only in the sense that it has recently been wrought and still bears the traces of its making, but also in the sense that it retains this initial vigor intact in its very being and is still in motion. Creation is possessed of an ongoing autonomy vis-à-vis the Creator. This autonomy, which we may read as the direct effect of monism, is exemplified in Book VII, the Book of Creation, by Milton's method of amplifying upon Genesis. Whereas God's fiats, in Genesis, have the force of imperatives, and work more or less instantaneously, the Son's fiats, in *Paradise Lost*, move away from the imperative and into the exhortative mood. Milton draws the various aspects or layers of creation out of Christ's word and so tends – almost by virtue of the sheer force of amplification or expansion – to distance the various creatures from their Maker, to posit their creation as an independent process. Creation seems to unroll itself in its various parts of its own accord. The lion, for instance, creates himself as follows:

The grassy Clods now Calv'd, now half appeer'd
The Tawny Lion, pawing to get free
His hinder parts, then springs as broke from Bonds,
And Rampant shakes his Brinded main.

(11. 463–6)

Such imagery of vital energy in creation takes on a kind of exhortative significance in its own right, and begs both the paradisal couple and the reader for interpretation. The creatures paradoxically come to signify the presence of God's will in creation in their very autonomy as creatures.[2]

This monistic movement does not go officially uninterpreted, but is explicitly pointed out and discoursed upon in the text itself. Raphael focuses Adam's attention upon the mobility of creation, and provides its "official" explanation, in his well-known chain-of-being speech in Book V.

O *Adam*, one Almighty is, from whom
All things proceed, and up to him return,
If not deprav'd from good, created all
Such to perfection, one first matter all,
Indu'd with various forms, various degrees
Of substance, and in things that live, of life;
But more refin'd, more spiritous, and pure,
As nearer to him plac't or nearer tending
Each in thir several active Spheres assign'd,
Till body up to spirit work, in bounds
Proportion'd to each kind. So from the root
Springs lighter the green stalk, from thence the leaves
More aery, last the bright consummate flow'r
Spirits odorous breathes: flow'rs and thir fruit
Man's nourishment, by gradual scale sublim'd
To vital Spirits aspire, to animal,
To intellectual, give both life and sense,
Fansy and understanding, whence the Soul
Reason receives, and reason is her being,
Discursive, or Intuitive; discourse
Is oftest yours, the latter most is ours,
Differing but in degree, of kind the same.
Wonder not then, what God for you saw good

> If I refuse not, but convert, as you,
> To proper substance; time may come when men
> With Angels may participate, and find
> No inconvenient Diet, nor too light Fare:
> And from these corporal nutriments perhaps
> Your bodies may at last turn all to spirit,
> Improv'd by tract of time, and wing'd ascend
> Ethereal, as wee, or may at choice
> Here or in Heav'nly Paradises dwell;
> If ye be found obedient . . .   (11. 469–501)

The very being of creation, then, the "ontology" of the hexameral tradition, is explicitly cast in a dynamic mode; creation strives upward, it directs itself to the center of goodness and abundance whence it "proceeded." This quasi-emanational version of the chain of being serves as a seamless and quasi-orthodox cover for Milton's monism, which we have already seen to occupy a place in his personal ideology ridden with contradiction. It "contains" monism by positing the will to purification that it in part signifies in an exceedingly pure form – attaching the ethic of sublimation for which it was the basis directly to God, and presenting sublimation, and the desire at work in it, as a strictly *positive* phenomenon. Creation does not strive through its gradual scale toward something that it *lacks*, but rather toward what it truly *is*: a profound (because divine) identity runs through the whole plane of creation. This is the place, then, at which Milton's monism is most clearly, and as it were seamlessly, linked to what is generally called the theory of accommodation, the theory according to which God positively manifests himself *in* the material world and *to* natural man. On the one hand, the scale of sublimation represents the way in which God accommodates his Being to creation in an ontological sense: God distributes himself through the chain of being in doses increasingly intense as he proceeds up its hierarchy. On the other hand, the scale is to be taken as a means of epistemological accommodation: it is a kind of motional symbol, communicating the ineffability of God to the as yet inadequate human intellect. Adam seems to read Raphael's speech in mainly epistemological terms, as a guide to the best way of approaching God, when he tells Raphael that he has "well . . . taught the way that might direct / Our knowledge,"

and the scale of Nature set
From centre to circumference, whereon
In contemplation of created things
By steps we may ascend to God.   (11. 508–12)

I do not think that the whole poem makes the ascent to God seem so easy a matter (either for creation or for Adam) as Raphael and Adam make it seem here, and I hope to show how this orthodox hexameral doctrine of sublimation is distorted by what I will call the romance framework of the paradise books. All I would emphasize here, however, is that even this orthodox and seamlessly accommodating version of creation is a monistic one, inasmuch as it assumes the ontological inconsequence of the division between matter and spirit which it nonetheless posits, and allows creation a certain autonomy from its Creator.

Raphael testifies to the monistic character of creation not only through his discourse, but also in his very substance, which serves as a kind of gloss on creation.[3] Adam seems quite curious about the angelical constitution; Raphael in fact delivers the chain-of-being speech in order to satisfy this curiosity, or at least to set it to rest. Monism as exemplified in the angelical constitution is not quite so orthodox as in the hexameral chain of being. It is one of the primary narrative functions of Milton's material angels, I think, to demonstrate, in a professedly esoteric and didactic form, the secretly esoteric nature and end of Milton's creation. We have already seen that Milton's angels occupy the place conventionally reserved for esoteric knowledge or speculation within the hexameron; we might say, in this case, that the esoteric place is peculiarly charged: Raphael and the serviceable angels seem to be as important for their peculiar substance as for the narrative wisdom that they bring with them. The angels' substance provides Adam and Eve with a kind of concrete teaching about the substance of creation. Like creation itself, Raphael's body represents Milton's monism precisely by virtue of its status as signification, because of its interpretability for the paradisal couple and for the reader.

Thus Raphael's repasting with Adam and Eve serves as concrete exemplification of the doctrine of "alimental recompense" and of sublimation which he explicitly puts forward as the main principle of unity of creation. Milton contradicts the "common expositor" on which hexameron relied in order to give an immediate narrative figuration to this doctrine:

>   So down they sat,
> And to thir viands fell, nor seemingly
> The Angel, nor in mist, the common gloss
> Of Theologians, but with keen dispatch
> Of real hunger, and concoctive heat
> To transubstantiate; what redounds, transpires
> Through Spirits with ease; nor wonder; if by fire
> Of sooty coal the Empiric Alchimist
> Can turn, or holds it possible to turn
> Metals of drossiest Ore to Perfet Gold
> As from the Mine.
>   (Bk. V, 11. 433–43)

Raphael emblematizes here the sublimative and hence more heterodox cast of Milton's chain of being. He encapsulates the end of creation, which is to sublimate itself, we are given to understand, from (shadowy) matter to (material) spirit. Similarly, to take another prime example, Raphael's embarrassed discourse on angelical sex in Book VIII, which comes at the conclusion of the long pedagogical dialogue of the middle books, represents the properly unimaginable, thoroughly utopian end toward which paradisal sex – still shackled to its "exclusive bars" – can only aspire, and of which it is only a foretaste.

> Let it suffice thee that thou know'st
> Us happy, and without Love no happiness.
> Whatever pure thou in the body enjoy'st
> (And pure thou wert created) we enjoy
> In eminence, and obstacle find none
> Of membrane, joint, or limb, exclusive bars:
> Easier than Air with Air, if Spirits embrace,
> Total they mix, Union of Pure with Pure
> Desiring; nor restrain'd conveyance need
> As Flesh to mix with Flesh, or Soul with Soul.
>   (Bk. VIII, 11. 620–9)

Union of Pure with Pure / Desiring: this is the last word in immediacy, where substance (*Pure*) is one with or melts into the activity (*Desiring*) that it carries. We might use the juridical-economic terms that we developed above in a metaphorical sense, as a gloss, and say that angelic love represents the moment of possession, in love, at its extreme limit: a moment of which paradisal love or marriage, which is officially defined as a property relation, is but the reified shadow.

I do not mean to imply that the angels are simply one with creation; nor do I think that creation alone receives narrative definition from this relationship, and not the angels. For the angels separate themselves from creation, even in providing it with a gloss, as a kind of natural type of its process and end. Moreover, they are only half defined in terms of their peculiar material-spiritual substance. Their appearance in the new creation as natural types contrasts sharply with their appearance as historical types in the static and ritual representations of their heavenly existence (whose ultimate referent, in the reality of Milton's time, must be the gathered church itself). But to think of the angels' heavenly routine in this context is to be reminded of how their place in creation, their definition as creation's gloss, helps to secure a definite narrative function for them. For the heavenly angels distinguish themselves from the devilish feudal angels in representing the end of creation, and thus are situated midway between the bad angels and creation. Occupying a third position outside the binary of open and closed monism, yet governed by it, the angels open that opposition up to the working of a narrative logic whose rudiments we may now sketch in.

The narrative logic of paradise

This logic organizes itself around the opposition between static or complete monism and progressive or open-ended monism in attempting to overcome it. Hence it involves a formal distinction between two different kinds of subject-narrative, two different ways of positing narrative agency itself. On the one hand, as is already clear, Satan tends to posit his own character-narrative as complete and closed upon itself in each of its moments. The narrative of creation, on the other hand, is radically diffuse and unclosed: at its bottom level it is made up of a welter of discrete positive processes all of which find their ends outside themselves.

The angels, as we have just noticed, occupy a kind of middle position between these two antithetical terms. They do not seem to be in diffuse, unended progress, like Creation, but rather represent in their material-spiritual essence, the progress and end of creation. Yet their essence should not be taken to be complete in itself, even if the angels do represent some kind of self-contained end. The angels' perpetual sublimative fullness implies a narrative of gradual positive process; angelic narrative is diachronic – it does have an end toward which it moves – but it nonetheless contains itself in each of its qualitatively distinct stages, and so is not particularly suspenseful.

But the angels do not occupy this middle position, between or outside of the two primary terms, alone; rather they exist in tension with another narrative term, and are defined partly by a secondary binary opposition. The angelical essence is linked in opposition to that of Adam and Eve, the paradisal couple. The couple, as we shall see, is part of creation, and is very conscious that it stands at the earthly creation's summit. Nonetheless, the progress of creation, as it manifests itself and comes to consciousness in Adam and Eve, seems principally to be felt, not in the form of an immanent and self-directed drive, but rather in the form of a question as to what lies in final store for them – in the form, that is, of a lack. Their sense of their own incompleteness is perhaps best exemplified by their obvious curiosity about the more fixed arrangements – the social and bodily functions – of the angels.

This secondary opposition, between "unopen" and "unclosed" monism, or the angels and Adam and Eve, represents the negation of the primary opposition between closed and open monism, Satan and creation. It goes without saying that our apprehension of both these pairs of narrative opposites is profoundly comparative and hence integral or unitary. We may represent the logic of this total narrative unit or system as follows:[4]

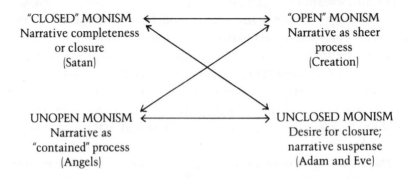

My main concern in this chapter will be to show how this synchronic scheme is actually presented or given form by the main narrative line, the story of prohibition and fall, and to show how its presentation is crucial to the finished theme of predestination. To do this, I must sketch in the generic determinants of this basic scheme, paying special attention, of course, to the generic composition of the paradise narrative proper, and therefore to the terms on the right of the rectangle.

This work of generic specification imposes itself upon us, indeed, when we consider more closely the inhabitants of the rectangle's corners: the "characters" whom I have already designated as the narrative agents that draw out and amplify the main antinomy between static and open-ended monism. When we begin to consider these characters' agency more carefully, what strikes us is a discrepancy between their self-definition, as it were, and their presentation within the larger "official" narrative context. This discrepancy may be described in terms of a systematic counterclockwise shift or slippage at each of the rectangle's corners. Thus Adam and Eve, as narratively situated in Eden, are at once incomplete and in progress. Although, as characters, they are mainly conscious of their incompleteness, we know them, as narrative agents, to be in nebulous progress up the scale of creation. Creation itself is merely in progress when considered in its immediate manifestations, but is complete when understood in official accommodative terms. Satan may define himself as a self-sufficient creature, but he appears from the official perspective to be locked in a situation beyond his control, predestined to that inner-motivated degeneration which can be taken as the very negation of progress. Finally, the angels not only shadow in their substance the end of the creation narrative; their static ritual in heaven also figures an unknown end beyond itself, and in this sense they are constitutively incomplete as well as being not in progress.

This systematic ambivalence involves a perspectival slippage, in each case, from narrative agency to context, or (if accommodation may be thought of as a kind of place) from agency to place.[5] Once we have noted the direction of this slippage, it is not difficult to see that its generic determination is none other than the fundamental dislocation contained within Milton's epic, that between the epic itself and the logically subordinate genre of the hexameron. It is this dislocation that determines the insistent drift within the properly gestural or momentary focus of the epic itself, the counterplot whereby this gestural set is constantly broadening out to accommodate the more geographical and official perspective of the hexameron. The distance between epic and hexameron, then, is responsible for a systematic ambivalence in epic characterology, and plays a crucial determining role in the narrative logic into which the characters are inserted.

Thus, to return now to the significance of the angels, we can see that the ambivalence conferred on their narrative place allows us to accord it a somewhat compromised but nonetheless properly utopian function – that of narratively mediating the primary antinomy between static and progressive monism. It would seem to be impossible to resolve this antinomy in its own form, or at least to give expansive narrative figuration to such a resolution. As I have already argued, the concept of a predestinary God is incapable of coherent narrative reconciliation with the autonomy of creation: the book of creation attempts to present such accommodation but can in fact only evoke it by way of softening the Son's fiats and foregrounding the independence of the gestural micro-narrative, which carries creation's movement, from its hexameral frame. The "contextualized" angels, then, perform the utopian function of resolving this antinomy at a distance by mediating the opposition between its negations, which represents an attenuated and displaced form of the original positive antinomy.[6] It is perhaps by reference to their utopian role that we can explain the peculiar charge of cognitive interest that seems to be invested in the angelical substance. The long dialogue between Raphael and Adam begins and ends with digressions on the nature of their material existence, as if that were the natural framework of paradisal dialogue. These digressions, which leave the basic paradisal narrative hanging in suspense, are justified because they implicitly sketch a shadowy narrative solution to the central antinomy of Milton's monist individualism.

Paradisal amplification: paradise as utopia

Yet there is a strong sense in which the dilation upon angelical substance is not digressive at all, but rather figures an alternate narrative line, the road not taken by the paradisal couple. This alternate line is crucial to the main narrative in that it counteracts our necessarily retrospective reading of the poem. It might be said that almost all narratives take shape partly by virtue of the expected retroactive effect of later events on earlier ones, and thus are read retrospectively, or backwards in advance. In

Paradise Lost, the force of retroactivity is particularly prominent, simply because the narrative of the fall is known beforehand by the fallen reader, who necessarily sees the fall behind all the events of the poem. It is most urgent in the paradise books, which differ from the other parts of the poem in that they define themselves in relation to, and amplify, a single biblical place, the story of creation and fall in the first two chapters of Genesis. The retroactive effect of the fall, which makes us read the events of the paradise narrative as if for the second time even on a first reading, is crucially reinforced by the presence of predestination in the narrative itself, which makes us read all its events in the light of predestination's known end. The link between narrative retroactivity and predestination is such that retroactivity might be taken as a sign of predestination. From this angle, one of the main aims of Milton's amplification of the paradise story is the paradoxical one of combating the inevitable retroactive effects of the fall, and the predestination that they signify, in paradise itself. The utopian bent of paradisal amplification, as partially testified to by the cognitive investment of the angelical substance, appears to fulfill this function by opening up a major narrative possibility which runs athwart the predestined path of the fall story. Utopian amplification demands to be read in itself, as if for the first time, and thus works to seal off predestination from the paradise narrative.

But the matter is considerably more complicated than this: I wish finally to argue, indeed, that in repressing predestination from paradise the cognitive utopian bias (of which the angelical digressions are exemplary) also lets it re-enter in a new, disguised incarnation. The narrative amplification that produces and is identical with this bias thus expresses the truth of the fall even in diverting our attention from it. Before embarking on a closer consideration of its nature and generic determinants, we might note an analogy between the role played by this narrative amplification in the argument of *Paradise Lost* and that played by the figural amplification of the nodal passages in the argument of *Areopagitica*. Just as, in *Areopagitica*, the figurative amplification produced the truth of Milton's argument while undermining its status as an official comprehensive discourse, so, in *Paradise Lost*, digressive narrative amplification sketches the real significance of the fall even while imperiling its sweeping theological clarity by instating the fall as a psychological process.

We can begin to see how amplification works in this way if we consider further the utopian impulse latent within Milton's paradise. It would seem that *Paradise Lost* is in some sense a centrally utopian work: the impulse is present, not only in the angels, but also and chiefly in paradise itself, for which utopia represents both a point of asymptotic approach and a shadowy paradigm or model. Paradise, that is, both strives *toward* utopia and attempts to posit itself *as* utopia: it is both process and would-be end in this respect. Its double status is precisely an effect of the narrative expansion of the Genesis story, which is on the one hand its own synchronically oriented end in itself, and yet serves, on the other hand, to open up the main narrative line of the fall to new possibilities. Paradisal amplification accordingly appears as the strictly formal means by which the central opposition between open and closed monism is recast in a neutral way and given positive resolution.

But this resolution is a limited and tentative one, for it inheres only in the sheer rhetorical form of paradisal or utopian expansion. Meanwhile, at the level of the utopian content itself, the double status of paradise tends to present itself as a kind of paradox, and hence as a problem. This, I think, is hardly surprising. For the paradox between process and end, or impulse and realization, is at the very heart of the concept of utopia, which is generally defined both as a kind of transcendent social impulse or desire, on the one hand, and as a written artifact or literary genre, on the other.[7] This paradoxical generic conjuncture of raw desire with literary textuality is figured, in Milton's paradise, by way of a disjuncture between the two subordinate "naturally oriented" genres which constitute paradise itself as a narrative agent: between the "wishful" genre of romance, and the more literary or textual genre of pastoral. These genres may be said to carry on the epic and hexameral theology, respectively, in the central epic setting of paradise, with romance translating the political desire of epic into a more natural or metaphysical phenomenon and pastoral reworking hexameral ontology into a literary topos.

It is romance that implicitly projects and controls Milton's monism in its purest form, as a unified process. Creation, as we have already mentioned, appears in Book VII as the storehouse of semi-autonomous powers in process. Romance gives the welter of creation a unified narrative status, casting it as a natural state or situation in the paradise narrative proper. Put another way, romance governs the insertion of the semi-autonomous gesture of creation into the narrative situation as an agent in its own right. It freezes or unifies the anarchic mobility of creation, making creation into a single semic unit, or indeed virtually into a "character" – one that is to be understood, in much the same way as God is to be understood, in terms at once human and non-human. Milton's habitual anthropomorphizing of the garden is well known, and it is romance, I think that governs the various forms of personification involved. Romance buries the figure of the body in paradise – Lewis himself pointed out the "Freudian" connotations of its "hairie sides / With thicket overgrown"[8] – and makes paradisal gesture the synesthetic emanations or faculties of this body:

> The Birds thir choir apply; airs, vernal airs,
> Breathing the smell of field and grove, attune
> The trembling leaves.   (Bk. IV, 11. 264–6)

The birds' "choir" is made to seem born from the earth, like the smell of field and grove, while the earth itself is humanized by the metaphor of breathing. Such moments of creative suspense, of personified reciprocity, are not infrequent in the paradise books. The bias of this frozen moment toward a state of utter sensuous plenitude, toward the realization of a full or energized body, makes it thoroughly utopian – even if this is a rather metaphysical form of utopianism.

Yet this myth of abundance is not wholly metaphysical. For romance not only governs the narrative agent of creation or nature; it also controls the relationship – that is, the marriage – between Adam and Eve, and posits them as part of, or as agents of, creation. Marriage in *Paradise Lost* is a notoriously and indeed a professedly "mysterious" entity. What is perhaps most strikingly mysterious about its presentation is the emphasis on the physical conjoinedness – one should perhaps say the consubstantiality – of Adam and Eve. It is certainly not enough to say that Adam is psychologically constituted in the narrative as a married man, or that Adam and Eve are constituted as a couple, a single working unit. More than this, Adam and Eve's relationship must somehow be understood as one of physical unity. As Arnold Stein has well pointed out, Milton in *Paradise Lost* attempts to give poetic body to the notion in Genesis that Adam and Eve are one and the same flesh; a very concrete kind of sympathy exists between them, which is prominently conveyed by a metaphor of mutual bodily sustenance, whose most emphatic version is the look that inspires with strength and well-being.[9] The organic quality of marriage, I would suggest, is itself organic to the romance framework; it represents the continuation and purification, within the domestic sphere, of the notion of desire implied by the theory and the figuration of alimental recompense which is so central to romance creation, to creation as a narrative agent. Adam and Eve's georgic duties prune and order such natural desire:

> On to thir morning's rural work they haste
> Among sweet dews and flow'rs; where any row
> Of Fruit-trees overwoody reach'd too far
> Thir pamper'd boughs, and needed hands to check
> Fruitless imbraces: or they led the Vine
> To wed her Elm; she spous'd about him twines
> Her marriageable arms, and with her brings
> Her dow'r th' adopted Clusters, to adorn
> His barren leaves.   (Bk. V, ll. 211–19)

Romance gives Adam and Eve's work, as mediated through the movement of paradisal creation, a curiously symbolic cast. One might say that the original couple's every gesture speaks of Eros, or of its proper constitution. Yet Adam and Eve's domestic economy carries with it social implications, however muted they may be, which go beyond the narrowly erotic. The society to which their gesture will give birth, and which it to some extent alludes to or figures, is a communal or collective one. Wedded love, we recall, is "the Sole propriety in Paradise / Of all things common else." "Common to whom?" we must ask: it would appear that Milton's story of origins acknowledges an allegorical dimension here, and that the natural individual(s) on which it focuses prefigure a whole society. Here, then, I think we are justified in drawing a direct and explicit comparison between the domestic economy of Milton's paradise and the natural economy projected by possessive individualism in the name of bourgeois society. Paradise is Hobbes' state of nature devoid of its nasty and abbreviated brutishness, and cast rather in the utopian form of general abundance. It pares possessive individualism down to the marital relation, and so has as its grail a society in which natural erotic suitability – what Engels called "individual sex love"[10] – would be socially possible.

Paradise has not commonly been seen, I think, under the aspect of romance, or as a kind of romance landscape; instead, it has conventionally been depicted in pastoral terms, or as perforated with pastoral elements.[11]

This is perhaps because the "dense literary context" (Kermode) of the paradise books is largely a pastoral context. The pastoral figuring of paradise is most obvious in the references to topoi from the pagan classics – allusions which are often introduced only to cancel themselves as legitimate comparisons to the chaster, and historically real, idyll of paradise:

> Not that fair field
> Of *Enna*, where *Proserpin* gath'ring flow'rs
> Herself a fairer Flow'r by gloomy *Dis*
> Was gather'd, which cost *Ceres* all that pain
> To seek her through the world; nor that sweet Grove
> Of *Daphne* by *Orontes*, and th' inspir'd
> *Castalian* Spring might with this Paradise
> Of *Eden* strive; nor that *Nyseian* Isle
> Girt with the River *Triton*, where old *Cham*,
> Whom Gentiles *Ammon* call and *Lybian Jove*,
> Hid *Amalthea* and her Florid Son,
> Young *Bacchus*, from his Stepdame *Rhea's* eye;
> Nor where *Abassin* Kings their issue Guard,
> Mount *Amara*, though this by som suppos'd
> True Paradise under the *Ethiop* Line
> By *Nilus* head, enclos'd with shining Rock,
> A whole day's journey high, but wide remote
> From this *Assyrian* Garden, where the Fiend
> Saw undelighted all delight.   (Bk. IV, 11. 268–86)

The "literal" superiority of paradise is of course stressed by such self-canceling references. But at the same time it is obvious that paradise assumes the timeless and helpless evanescence of these other *loci amoenae*.[12] These places are cast not as the subjects but as the objects or containers of the narratives associated with them (when these exist): Enna, for example, is simply the stage for – we might almost say the helpless audience and sympathizer in – Proserpin's rape. I believe we may generalize from this example, and say that pastoral tends to interrupt or detain the romance narrative by casting paradise as a more or less static state, as a textual spot of time, rather than as the locus and agent of a wished for transition. While romance unifies and frames creation, and gives it a subjective mood, pastoral renders its mobility atemporal and makes it the object of an unmistakable nostalgia. Romance gives creation the force of gesture; pastoral imperils the motional closure of creative gesture by presenting it in the form of a timeless artifact or presence, by its nature vulnerable to the external solicitation of nostalgic intrusion.

This is to say that pastoral endeavors to reduce the narrative gesture of creation in paradise to apparently self-contained places or topoi. Pastoral thus in great measure coincides with what we may call the topographical bias of the paradise books and of paradisal amplification, the investment of the paradisal grounds with interest as an object. Pastoral communicates in this respect with the most obvious science fiction element of the whole poem, its cosmological focus, and diverts the interest proper to that focus into a more leisurely reflection, into a specifically pastoral meandering. Consider, for instance, the way in which, in Book IV, Milton's geographical *location* of paradise flows into topographical *expatiation* upon it: as Satan approaches paradise, the amplitudinous cosmological perspective that has accompanied him on his journey blends into the *mazy error* of pastoral:

> for blissful Paradise
> Of God the Garden was, by him in the East
> Of *Eden* planted; *Eden* stretch'd her Line
> From *Auran* Eastward to the Royal Tow'rs
> Of great *Seleucia*, built by *Grecian* Kings,
> Or where the Sons of *Eden* long before
> Dwelt in *Telassar*: in this pleasant soil
> His far more pleasant Garden God ordain'd;
> Out of the fertile ground he caus'd to grow
> All Trees of noblest kind for sight, smell, taste;
> And all amid them stood the Tree of Life,
> High eminent, blooming Ambrosial Fruit
> Of vegetable Gold; and next to Life
> Our Death the Tree of knowledge grew fast by,
> Knowledge of Good bought dear by knowing ill.
> Southward through *Eden* went a River large,
> Nor chang'd his course, but through the shaggy hill
> Pass'd underneath ingulft.   (11. 208–25)

And so on, over the grounds of paradise, for another thirty lines. Such meandering description evokes the gesture of romance nature, even as it attempts to deflect and contain it in its course. There are points, indeed, in which the whole appeal of paradise seems to be based on a constitutive tension between the personified *energia* of romance creation, and the topographical error of the pastoral landscape.

Adam and Eve share in the topographical interest of the poem; or rather their non-dialogical speeches – for example, their orisons – formalize the topographical bent of paradise. But even though they further the pastoral presentation of nature, the pastoral set separates their narrative from that of paradise. Paradise does not act through them, and they are not its agents, as is the case with their place in romance. Rather their narrative – especially the singular event of the fall – simply *concerns* paradise, which consequently appears as the innocently sympathizing object of the narrative, and not as an agent in its own right. The very title of the poem, while it technically hovers on the edge between romance and pastoral by making paradise the passive subject of the action, nonetheless emphasizes the helpless *difference* of paradise from its potentially sin-bearing habitants.

But if paradise is different from Adam and Eve, and passively sympathizes with their story in containing it, it is also different from the fallen urban audience of pastoral, and appears indeed as the sympathetic projection of this modern consciousness.[13] As projection, paradise is defined not in itself but in contrast to the fallen condition; it is realized as not (yet) fallen. It cannot be seen as a simple positive "good," but must for us be swathed in a nostalgia the very taint of which, we can now see, stands as a symptom of fallenness within the mazy error of paradise itself. The paradisal past is a projected one, and thus a more or less transparent textual illusion.

It is at this level, as projection, that the utopian function of pastoral takes on great significance, and so it is here that we need to institute within this surrogate genre a division that corresponds to that between commentary and analysis in hexameron. This division, between orthodox pastoral, or pastoral "in itself," and utopian or analytical pastoral, may be understood in terms of different projective methods or sets. Orthodox pastoral, on the one hand, figures projection as an elimination from the sinful present of the sin inhering in its substance and in its referential signs. Orthodox pastoral buffers paradise from sin, and casts it as what Milo Kaufman has called paradise manqué.[14] The utopian pastoral, on the other hand, is rendered dominant by the utopian impulse of romance, for which it serves as the textual end, and it figures projection as a process of positive elaboration that takes the signs of the present as its raw material without acknowledging their sinfulness for us, their imbrication in their sinful referents. Utopian projection attempts to figure paradise forth from sin, and therefore winds up by making the positive impossibility of utopia clearly visible. This should come as no surprise. For it is a crucial, and highly paradoxical, function of the utopian genre, or more exactly of the rift between impulse and script native to this genre, to reveal the constitutive impossibility, the proper unimaginability, of utopia itself.[15] The utopian attempt to constitute paradise as positive topography or as a written text reveals it to be a "no-place" – a "good-place," finally, only by negation.[16]

Theology versus ethics: the ideology of the prohibition narrative

It could be argued, then, that what I am calling utopian amplification has as its real point a rather harsh, and seemingly anti-utopian, theological message: we, the fallen audience, cannot think our way beyond the sinful present, beyond the original sin which it is precisely the aim of the narrative to justify.[17] It is no use denying that this rather bleak didactic message does indeed represent a moment in the construction of paradise; its theological harshness corresponds, no doubt, to the disillusion Milton experienced at the Restoration, and to the lapse into the rudiments of theology that his intellectual constitution seems to have undergone at that time. Yet this theological debunking of utopia is neither the only nor the most salient aspect of paradisal amplification. To reduce Miltonic amplification to such a theological message is to read against the grain, both of the utopian impulse and of the very epic form that puts that impulse into play, thus endowing its own gesture with positive cognitive interest. For the gesture of paradise (as well as the considerable interest invested in it) is more psychological and ethical than theological in its implication. Indeed, it might be said that the primary function of paradisal amplification, even in its harsh theological moment, is to give prominence to the rift between theology and ethics (or psychological ethics). For if we are unable to think our way past original sin, being all composed of it, then we cannot be expected, surely, to understand the psychology of the fall or the ethical problems that it involves. Yet it is precisely the psychology of the fall – what we might call its interior aspect – which paradisal amplification brings to the fore and invests with interest; and this is what makes it possible and necessary for us to consider the ethics of the fall. We should attempt to understand Milton's fall, then, in terms of the disjuncture, effected by paradisal amplification, between ethics and theology. Utopia, in this light, appears less as an alternative to the fall than as an attempt to "justify" the fall, to explain why paradise was sinned against in order to assert providence in the place of predestination.

We may say, accordingly, that the utopian paradigm at work in the paradise books determines the ethical focus of Milton's epic. Before going into the details of this generic determination, I wish to deal briefly with theology proper, and with the theological view of the fall in the poem. For it seems to me that the disjuncture between theology and ethics crucial to Milton's version of the fall is also latent within theology itself, or within the strict theological narrative of the fall, and that Milton's poem, in making this rift manifest, may be understood as laying bare a problem or antinomy indigenous to the Christian narrative at least from the time of the codification of the fall story.

Let it be emphasized in the first place that we are speaking at least initially of a *theological* antinomy in *Paradise Lost*, and that the poem does possess a properly theological narrative or view of the fall. In saying that there is a disjuncture between theology and ethical psychoiogy, I do not wish to impugn the theological clarity of Milton's fall (except in an ultimate sense to be discussed below), nor on the other hand to deny the interrelation of theology and ethics in the poem. For I think the theology of the fall is rather admirably focused; there is a sense in which theology itself generates the psychological-ethical level which then asserts its autonomy vis-à-vis, even as it returns to complicate, this very theology. It seems to me that this process, by which theology overdetermines itself to change its very nature, is more or less laid bare in *Paradise Lost*, precisely by virtue of its theological purity.

From a strictly theological point of view, there is no question where the fall is located. Adam and Eve fall individually in transgressing against God's sole commandment by eating the forbidden fruit. The centrality of the prohibition, and of Adam and Eve's disobedience considered as a purely external act – all of which is taken for granted in the Genesis story of the fall – is preserved and insisted upon in *Paradise Lost*. God is especially lucid on this matter, of course; Raphael likewise makes obedience the alpha and omega of his discourse. But the theological starkness of the prohibition is insisted upon in other, more subtle ways. For instance, when God – or rather the Son as God's mediary – delivers the prohibition in Book VIII, and again when God metes out punishment for man's disobedience in Book X, the language and cadences of his speech are taken directly from Genesis. He judges Adam, for example, as follows:

> Because thou hast heark'n'd to the voice of thy Wife,
> And eaten of the Tree concerning which
> I charg'd thee, saying: Thou shalt not eat thereof,
> Curs'd is the ground for thy sake, thou in sorrow
> Shalt eat thereof all the days of thy Life.
>
> (Bk. X, 11. 198–202)

An effect of the dependence on biblical language is to ritualize both God's activity and, by extension, the narrative itself, and thus to make the reasons for the fall seem suddenly irrelevant to the story at this point. Paradisal narrative, here bound to the language of its source, thus appears to hinge wholly and simply upon God's prohibition and man's disobedience.

Granting its centrality, then, let us consider the narrative paradigm or concept of prohibition. When reading *Paradise Lost*, one is given textual warrant (as one is *not* in Genesis) to ask about the motive behind the prohibition. The prohibition is God's way of extracting and of signifying to himself man's free obedience; it is meant to fix the relation between God and his earthly creation, and therefore is the most immediate connection between man and God. The prohibition is a kind of sign – a sign of the fixed relation between man and God – and the "Tree of prohibition" serves as the earthly support or signifier of this vocal sign. We know that Milton-as-theologian insisted upon the absolute willfulness of God's prohibition:[18] God's original command is issued simply to secure man's obedience; the content of the command, as Milton stresses in *De Doctrina* and as God implies in *Paradise Lost*, is wholly arbitrary – it does not harmonize with any pre-existing earthly logic, for it is merely a matter of God's relation to man.

At this extremely abstract and strictly theological level, there would seem to be no reason why the original command should not have been an injunction rather than a prohibition. One can imagine a reworking of the fall narrative, for instance, in which Adam and Eve have to eat at least one apple a day in order to keep fealty to God. It is difficult to say what the narrative consequences of such a change would be; they would doubtless depend in large part on the narrative context in which the command is inserted. I suspect, however, that the implications for ethical psychology of such a narrative of injunction would tend to be less neurotic and more permissive than those deriving from the narrative of prohibition. A positive injunction would most likely ascribe qualitative virtue to the apple itself (which would be like a medicine, keeping Adam and Eve healthy); and likewise, and by extension, instill the sundry creatures of paradise with various sorts of quasi-magical virtue. The logic of the prohibition, by contrast, is to isolate the substance of the apple, and to focus on the abstract act of restraint by which evil is avoided; Milton's insistence that the prohibition was wholly arbitrary might be seen as a particularly forceful realization of this implicit logic.

Yet in *Paradise Lost* the prohibition is not set in the abstract nature that Milton's insistence on its arbitrariness implies. The prohibition instead finds its place at the head of a visible creation which, as we have seen, swarms with powers in process – a creation not without apparently magical properties. The Tree of prohibition is therefore distinguished by its very blankness: it stands as the sole abstract sign in a world that otherwise forms for Adam and Eve a series of concrete or qualitative signs, a world the various items of which taken together serve as a symbol of God's abundant goodness. It seems to me that the abstract significa- tion of prohibition and the virtue-laden symbolism of Milton's monistic creation exist in logical tension with one another, even though the poem hardly ever seems consciously to meditate upon it. On the one hand, the prohibition tends to level creation, to de-qualify its concrete signs and strip it of its magic, inasmuch as all of the objects of creation are equal in its sight. Creation, on the other hand, is not without its revenge, which is the more subtle in that it takes advantage of the abstracting effects of prohibition itself, hoisting it with its own petard. By an inevitable paradox, the prohibition, in leveling creation, marks the fruit of the Tree off as radically *different*, invests it with aura, makes it the sacred fruit. Precisely because of its indifference to the prohibition, the Tree tends to appropriate the divine aura of the prohibition to itself, and to possess itself of its peculiar virtue. I will anticipate my argument to suggest that creation in its mobile romance aspect puts the final touch on this process; it makes the evil power distilled in the fruit seem natural and gives it body. The apple literally manifests this virtue only once in the text, but it is enough. The power that seems to materialize in the Tree after Eve's fall – the notion of the Tree and of creation that she falls for – should be read both as an objective effect of the prohibition and as creation's revenge upon its abstraction. It is a kind of romance evil genius:

> But first low Reverence done, as to the power
> That dwelt within, whose presence had infus'd
> Into the plant sciential sap, deriv'd
> From Nectar, drink of Gods.
>
> (Bk. IX, 11. 835–8)

We can already begin to see how Milton's prohibition tends to project a power, and hence an ethically laden field, outside of itself. This process (by which the prohibition takes on an earthly incarnation) is essentially a figurative one: the object of the prohibition, in signifying the prohibition, also assumes its power. But this assumption, by which the object of prohibition is enlivened or empowered, is already implied, I would now suggest, in the command itself. Thus far, of course, I have treated (and theological criticism in general treats) the prohibition as if it were more abstract than it actually is. What God forbids Adam, in both Genesis and *Paradise Lost*, is the fruit from the Tree of the Knowledge of Good and Evil. There seems to be a metonymic process at work in the prohibition by which its formal effect is registered in its content. In designating a particular action as impermissible, it initiates Adam and Eve into the knowledge of good and evil which is the ugly promise of the apple. It inevitably sets up a binary opposition between permissible and impermissible acts, and in so doing more or less founds ethics. This initial opposition necessarily implies or generates (in the manner of all such oppositions) a subordinate opposition; the division between permissible and impermissible, or between good and not good, assumes the positive force of an antithesis, and is supplemented by a secondary division between the not permissible (which we might designate as the dangerous) and the not impermissible (which we might call the indifferent or – in Milton's scheme of things – the mildly beneficial).

In the Genesis parable, the metonymic designation of the fruit as that of the knowledge of good and evil works to figure the (pre)existence of such a binary system, which the prohibition itself is linked to and controls. This it does even though the logic of such a system is strictly implicit, and is kept under God's or theology's thumb. The prohibition fixes man's relation to God as a subservient or obedient one; in forbidding the Tree of Knowledge of Good and Evil it makes the lack of knowledge (more specifically of ethical knowledge) a symbol of this obedience. Since the lack of knowledge in this symbolic dimension tends to designate a class of actions, the forbidding of the fruit makes any sort of ethical presumption seem unnatural or bad, so that any attempt to elaborate the independent logic generated by the prohibition is forbidden, or warned against, by the terms of the prohibition itself. From this angle, then, the metonymy that puts the binary in the content of the command would seem meant to prevent the generation of a subordinate binary, and thus to contain the ethical narrative moment.

Even though ethics is thereby kept within the limits of the theological parable in Genesis, the prohibition narrative nonetheless implies or generates what may be called a kind of ethical grid – a grid existing alongside the prohibition, and just waiting to be narratively embodied in a more or less independent manner. Because of the formal and abstract character of this grid, it can be filled in in quite different ways and traversed by sundry codes (ways and codes that transgress against the symbolic significance of the naming of the Tree). In Genesis, one point where we can see the beginnings of an independent logic occurs when God says, "It is not good for man to be alone." This is the text that Milton, always the biblical literalist, made the basis for his theory of marriage in the divorce pamphlets. But in making this sentence the basis for a natural nuptial law, Milton distorted it from its contextual significance. For the sentence only opens up the possibility of a natural logic. In fact, its main function in Genesis is to link the category of the natural backup to God's will – it is not good for man to be alone because God says that it is not – and thus to recontain the ethical grid within the prohibition narrative in advance, before it is projected by the prohibition that is yet to be set forth.

One way of expressing the comparative autonomy of ethics in *Paradise Lost* – of explaining its ethical focus – is to say that the ethical grid necessarily generated by the narrative paradigm of the prohibition is corroborated in its independent status and accorded a relatively discrete and heterodox content. It is not difficult to sketch, in a cursory manner, the way in which paradisal amplification, the narrative of Adam and Eve, fills in the logical space delineated by the grid. Thus in Milton Adam enters the world knowing that it is not good for man to be alone, that he needs a companion, and he himself must express this need – must, moreover, as an exercise and emblem of his natural reason, justify this need to the Son before he recognizes it as good and provides for it.[19] Adam's inclination toward marriage, in other words, is presented as a natural good in the poem. The antithesis of this inclination is one toward lascivious sex such as Adam and Eve have after the fall, which is perhaps the clearest incarnation of the positively bad. It is more difficult to distinguish between the indifferent and positively dangerous. Adam's curiosity to know about Heaven and creation is good up to a point, for instance, but when this curiosity turns clinical or impractical it is – rather gently – reproved by Raphael: it seems to be either indifferent or only potentially dangerous. Adam's uncertainty in the face of Eve's bearing, a confusion associated with sexual desire, seems to be stronger and more dangerous, and is reproved more severely.

The ethical psychology of creation

In order really to understand the ethical system of the paradise books, however, we must discuss its generic production. For the ethical situation in *Paradise Lost* is not in fact simple and coherent; on the contrary, the generic divisions of the paradise books work to produce the ethical grid in a radically contradictory manner. If the examples of ethical categories given above are fairly clear, that is because I am expressing there the more or less official and explicit hexameral attitude toward aspects of Adam and Eve's drama. This doctrinal set on the ethical situation is the most obvious one, but it is neither the only nor, I think, the dominant view. As is most evident in the case of the agency of creation, different genres, working separately and in combination, produce and value the action in different ways. The doctrinal attitude concerning this action must be understood as an attempt to *manage* these differences.

Two preliminary points are essential to an understanding of the psychological-ethical coding of creation. First, it is the substitute epic genre of romance that is naturally dominant in this coding, and that produces creation as an ethically laden field in itself and for Adam and Eve. Romance figures into creation what might be called a monist psychology, with drives and desires that may be innately good or bad, and that may have good or bad effects and significations. It should thus come as no surprise that the ethical dilemma eventually projected by this romance psychology is one with that inherent to monism itself, the antinomy between permissive and prohibitive ethics, and represents the return within the paradise books of the central opposition between open and closed monism in a new purged form.

Secondly, it should be emphasized that the ethical psychology of creation is accentuated and invested with cognitive interest by virtue of the utopian paradigm behind the paradise books. To bring to mind Adam's discourse with Raphael is to remind oneself of this cognitive bias. As is made quite clear in this extended discourse, Adam knows in a general way that he is eventually destined for a higher form of existence. He has a dim sense of this eventuality at the very beginning of his "story," his coming to consciousness, which he tells Raphael in Book VIII; and he is told as much by Raphael himself in Book V, in the passage that describes the chain of being in terms of the doctrine of alimentary recompense. The ethical problem of how he is to achieve his unknown higher destiny – of what he is to do or how he is to position himself – presents itself to him, and is raised by the narrative, primarily as a problem of knowledge about creation. He not only views himself largely in the context of a nature seen in its dynamic romance mode as creation; he is also a part of that creation, its sovereign creature, and he attempts to understand himself as such. This means that the story of Adam's ethical search takes on a quasi-scientific cast: Adam and the reader wait upon the narrative of creation with a neutral eye. The accent of the paradise narrative is on the general laws of cognition by which Adam deals with his ethical-epistemological problem, or in other words, by which creation comes to know itself. The movement of cognition is in fact inseparable from the psychology of creation, and as such is crucial to our ethical reading of it, distancing the ethical dilemmas inherent in creation even in determining them.

It is apparent, for example, that the romance and (official) pastoral frameworks locate creation's goodness in different ways or aspects, yet this is not particularly disturbing. Official pastoral, on the one hand, tends to value creation according to the ethic of prohibition, which is to say that it locates the good not so much in creation as in paradise, which is essentially blissful because of what it is not, because it exists in stasis. From the vantage of romance, the official pastoral version of creative perfection appears as incompletely mobile and hence as indifferent or neutral. Romance in itself is the main bearer of the differential ethic of permission, and casts creation's goodness in terms of its positive sublimative motion.

Manifestations of evil, on the other hand, are more disturbing in their heterogeneity, even if they are curiously undervalued up until the time of the fall. For romance and pastoral subgenres actually disagree as to whether evil exists in paradise. The logically dominant subgenre of romance accords evil a constitutive place within the paradisal landscape as a quasi-magical force or realm. The genius of the tree of prohibition is only an isolated manifestation of this implied romance underworld (albeit a particularly interesting one because it appears as a direct effect of the prohibition). Evil is also given a local habitation in the traditionally despised creatures: the snake, who possesses subtle wiles, and is obviously dangerous in himself, before Satan ever fixes upon him; the toad whose loathsome image Satan assumes in inspiring Eve's bad dream; and perhaps Leviathan, who cuts a rather ominous figure in the book of creation before the fall.[20] But the principal romance embodiment of evil is surely that of the "dark infernal dregs," the slime and ooze purged by the Son from the original matter.[21] This tartarous underworld represents Chaos stripped of its generative powers. Hence, it constitutes something like a negative matrix for creation, against which creation actively defines itself and into which it is in danger of returning.

Official pastoral evil, on the other hand, tends to define itself as a projection of a sophisticated observing consciousness, as a kind of return of the repressed within the repressing frame that pastoral customarily depends upon. The "mazy error" inscribed in the topography of paradise, which we must almost necessarily see as an ominous sign of evil, represents this evil in what is perhaps its purest form.[22] But almost all the phenomena of evil (except, significantly, for the gross dregs of creation) can be read in this way. Even the genius of the tree, insofar as it is implied that it has a merely psychological existence as a figment of Eve's brain, can be taken as a mere projection; indeed, it might even be read as a dramatization of such projection by the newly fallen consciousness. Pastoral evil is thus potential evil, a figment of fallen imagination. From the point of view of romance it appears, however, as a concrete latent power, and composes one aspect of the dangerous.

A more interesting form of the dangerous in creation is produced by the utopian paradigm of the paradise books, by the positive intersection of utopian pastoral with romance creation. We can see how this is if we consider the narrative topos of abundance or overproduction, which, as we shall see, assumes great importance in the drama of Adam and Eve. The doctrinal significance of paradisal abundance is clear: it is literally God's plenty, and signifies the overflow of that vital power of matter or material desire which God implanted in creation. In its romance aspect, however, this surplus desire or production takes on a certain ambivalence. It is "good" in that it represents creation in its most vital aspect, monism at its most desirous of utopian transition; the ethic of permission valorizes its positive difference. But it is also a rather dubious phenomenon, and stirs dubiety in Adam and Eve, in that in its excess it has no obvious or adequate object on the plane of creation. Like Satanic gesture, it appears as pure production, stripped of purpose or end. It thus can appear, in what we might call a meta-romance aspect, either as a positive dysfunction or as the sign of an object's absence – as a lack. The pastoral presentation of the garden, which immobilizes creation, undermining the immanence of its gestural closure by casting fate as projection, works to accentuate the perspective in which surplus figures lack, and thus fixes it in creation; it casts the desire of creation in terms of a determinate lack, and hence provides the open-ended mobility of creation with a fixed and definite narrative closure. Paradise seen under the aspect of determinate lack is "not in progress," and hence dangerous from the point of view of the strict ethic of permission. Yet it seems that we must see creation/paradise under this aspect, at least in an abstract sense. Creation on its own plane can have no concrete object or end if it is to remain open-ended; it follows that abstractly determinate lack is constitutive of the very freedom, the monist mobility, of creation, and so even though dangerous, is good. This ethical aporia opened up by the utopian paradigm is crucial to an understanding of the fall.

The fall

It remains now to show how the psychology of creation leads, through Adam and Eve, to the fall; for the ethical logic of the paradise books is most clearly expressed and worked out in Adam and Eve's domestic drama. It is important to note that Adam and Eve are consistently the actors in a kind of drama, and thus that a dramatic framework overdetermines the generic production of the paradise books as we have so far described it. Milton explicitly stages the last phase of the fall in dramatic terms, for example, when he declares, at the beginning of Book IX, that he must now change his notes to tragic. What should be stressed about this dramatic situation in the present context is that it is largely phenomenal to the narrative of creation: creation is felt to work *through* the couple's drama, and constitutes, or is one with, the problem of their desire. The more affective dramatic focus on Adam and Eve is seen to represent a displacement of cognitive attention from its proper object in creation. Adam and Eve may be heroes of the domestic drama, but this drama itself is but an agent of the larger paradisal situation, which is felt to control the narrative action. This is to say that the romance framework or set exercises a kind of logical dominance over the ethical narrative of the fall as over the paradise books generally, even though it suffers from a rather heavy dramatic distortion and is thus given a peculiarly "psychologistic" bent. We can speak, indeed, of the psychology of creation partly because of paradise's dramatic overdetermination.

It is indicative of the dominance of the romance framework that if we think upon Adam and Eve's action in dramatic terms, it tends finally to contextualize itself, to converge with the action of creation/paradise. From a dramatic perspective, one of the more important features to notice about Adam and Eve is that the world is too much with them. They seem chiefly taken with the effects of nature's surplus energy, with the phenomena of overproduction. For example, Eve asks Adam in Book IV about the significance of the stars, whose splendor seems out of proportion to earth; and Adam, though he gives Eve the correct answer, later asks Raphael the same question.[23] To take another example which has a more crucial place in the narrative action: Eve proposes to separate from Adam in Book IX because the garden's foliage is proving too much for their united powers – the work grows under their hands "luxuriant by restraint," to use her resonant phrase: creation itself justifies her work ethic.[24] Both these narrative loci provide clear instances in which nature's surplus energy or God's plenty, in manifesting itself "for itself" on the plane of creation, produces ethical uncertainty in Adam and Eve.

And produces, not only in the sense of affording a pretext or a rationale for such uncertainty, but also in a stronger, more immediate sense. For creation's surplus energy is virtually one with the couple's doubt, inasmuch as the desire that this doubt speaks of appears as but another manifestation, albeit a crucial one, of the power that motivates creation. The pair's intellectual curiosity in the face of the cosmos, the vocational drive that the garden's growth inspires in Eve, the sex-love whose expression conflicts, according to Eve, with their job of pruning – all these phenomena represent nodal points of desire in which the vital power of creation appears in Adam and Eve in all its ambivalence as sheer production, as a surplus signifying lack. In such doubtful and cognitively surcharged moments as these, Adam and Eve's drama is most decidedly a drama of creation; its psychology is manifestly one with the psychology of creation.

Whereas the chief effect of sheer production in the Satan narrative is to foreground and problematize the political significance of Satanic gesture, the main effect of the topos of surplus in the domestic drama of paradise is to foreground the ethical dilemma inherent in the fall. The meta-romance psychology projected by earthly abundance represents the crossroads or point of divide between the ethic of permission and the ethic of prohibition which jointly constitute Milton's individualism, and which both determine and mediate the rift between religion and politics in his ideology. In the privileged moment of *Areopagitica*, these two ethics were paradoxically coterminous, linked together in an attitude of aggressive, yet politic suspense. In *Paradise Lost* there appears to be a greater distance as a rule between ethical discourses: even though they are both bound up in the psychology of creation, they tend to be posited separately, and to be relegated to different parts of the narrative structure of the story of Adam and Eve. Thus it is possible to speak of discrete narratives of prohibition and permission, which are respectively (if somewhat roughly) correlated with the pastoral-dramatic and romance aspects of the Adam and Eve narrative. The ethic of prohibition is the more official ethic of the poem, allied as it is with doctrinaire hexameral drama. In reference to Adam and Eve's story situation, it takes the form of an ethic of passive waiting, whose principal aim is to repress creation's surplus energy and the lack it posits and is linked to. This ethic makes an interesting appearance at the end of the cosmological dialogue in Book VIII, where it is more or less forced upon the unruly material of creation. The problem of cosmological grounding assumes a symbolic ethical significance in Raphael's discourse. The poem implicitly argues, from what is made to seem the permanent indeterminacy of cosmological or scientific systems, not for ethical experimentation, but rather for a conservative skeptical ethic: Raphael concludes from the fact of scientific confusion that Adam should be "lowly wise," should attend more to matters domestic than scientific. The poem at this point attempts to close off the ethic of permission or of aggressive suspense, which is centered on or inherent in the creative profusion of which the planets and stars are one significant symbol. This ethic is nonetheless surreptitiously figured in Raphael's speech, in the surplus energy that he necessarily centers upon in deflecting. The ethic of permission is immediately attached to physical creation, and is hence dominant in the narrative and in the psychology of creation itself, which may thus be said, in exciting Adam and Eve, to motivate the fall.

The ethic of permission is most evident in the individual creation stories and in the fall. Since it is necessary to separate both creation and fall stories, let us consider Adam first. I have noted that Milton has Adam voice and test his need for a companion in dialogue with the Son. I will add now that Adam, in giving symbolic expression to this need, is transforming his primal need, the positive desiring-motion of romance, into (meta-romance or utopian) lack. His relationship with Eve, then, "fills up" this original lack. The consubstantiality of paradisal marriage seems almost to deny the abstract or symbolic character of lack, to translate it back into a physical need; but it also serves to stress the direct basis of Adam's desire, and of marriage, in creation itself.

Marriage thus epitomizes the conflict between surplus energy and lack in utopian creation; for marriage is a kind of secondary or surplus creation which works to cover over the original lack that marks Adam's primal need. Adam's fall stresses the consubstantiality of marriage, and hence dramatizes the conflict inherent in creation: the choice presented to him by the fallen Eve is between fulfilling an undeniable need that now appears plainly as a dysfunction or living with a lack that has been intensified and rendered wholly determinate, given a habitation and name. The strongest explanation for his fall comes at the end of his long soliloquy:

> I with thee have fixt my Lot,
> Certain to undergo like doom; if Death
> Consort with thee, Death is to mee as Life;
> So forcible within my heart I feel
> The Bond of Nature draw me to my own,
> My own in thee, for what thou art is mine;
> Our State cannot be sever'd, we are one,
> One Flesh; to lose thee were to lose myself.
>
> (Bk. IX, ll. 952–9)

We cannot read this, at the romance level, as mere rationalization; or rather, if it is rationalization, then it is creation speaking through Adam that is mainly responsible for it. It follows that the narrative in a sense (that is, at its romance level) justifies Adam's action; the permissive ethic imbedded in the gesture of romance creation would have him embody or consummate his need. But whether this be the case or not, Waldock was certainly right to say that the narrative voice's official gloss on Adam's action – that he falls "fondly overcome with female charm" – is patently inadequate to his situation.[25] Romance and hexameron are flatly at odds here, and their incompatibility highlights the separation between theology and ethics that is crucial to the poem's representation of the fall.

I would not be taken to be arguing that the foregrounding of the ethical by which this separation takes place is itself to be understood from some ultimate and coherent ethical perspective. The romance framework forces us instead to understand Adam's fall in terms of an insuperable ethical contradiction. Adam is simply confronted with, and acts out, an ethical dilemma intrinsic to, indeed constitutive of, romance psychology. It is impossible for him to choose in such a way as to preserve his station within the pure romance framework of positive sublimation or gradual wish-fulfillment. This is to say that the ethical situation in romance itself – partly, but not only, because of its dramatic overdetermination – is contradictory. Romance justifies Adam's action, true, by giving it body; at the same time, however, it presents it as evil. Adam in falling is a failed romance hero:

> On th' other side, *Adam*, soon as he heard
> The fatal Trespass done by *Eve*, amaz'd,

> Astonied stood and Blank, while horror chill
> Ran through his veins, and all his joints relax'd;
> From his slack hand the Garland wreath'd for *Eve*
> Down dropp'd, and all the faded Roses shed.
>
> (Bk. IX, 11. 888–93)

His reaction to the fallen Eve is that of the quester bewildered by the sudden shocking appearance of the lower world. His fall delivers him over to that world, as the romance of which he is the passive agent reveals itself to be a dark one. Romance undermines ethics as a self-sufficient explanatory system even while breaking ethics free from theology. Or rather ethics is only explanatory insofar as its antinomies are visibly determined by the ambivalent production of creation and thus figured in a generalized romance psychology.

The romance "world" motivates the fall not only by way of the physical or sexual connection between the paradisal couple, but also through the corresponding symbolic attachment. Romance psychology assumes its securest station in the domestic drama by putting a peculiar emphasis on the discursive nexus between Adam and Eve. For Adam and Eve are constituted in mutual discourse, as a dialogical couple. One hesitates, in fact, to make a distinction between their physical and discursive dependence on each other: the physical itself (that is, marital sex) is best and most consistently figured in dialogical terms; Adam speaks, for instance, of the "sweet intercourse / Of looks and smiles" as a kind of necessary sustenance which complements "talk between, / Food of the Mind" (Bk. IX, 11. 237–9). Dialogue serves as the privileged dramatic figure for the positive reciprocity, the "alimental recompense" that governs the gesture of Milton's creation. We can say that the gesture of recompense dominant in the paradise books, and paradigmatic for the whole poem, is dialogical in kind, or is cast in the mode of dialogical signification. The discursive tie between Adam and Eve represents then but an intensification of this larger natural discourse or signification. Original sin is perhaps most cogently presented as a transgression against this essentially symbolic tie; Tillyard's argument that the separation dialogue marks the point of the real fall has its greatest force in this context.[26] Adam and Eve both fall in soliloquizing by withdrawing into the inner speech of meditation. The first lines of the two fall speeches noticeably disengage themselves from their contexts, and retreat into private musing.[27] The dramatic and singular interiority thus asserted is unnatural, it is implied, and separates Adam and Eve further from their dialogical constitution.

But dialogue itself is not unproblematical. Eve's fall, perhaps more than Adam's, exemplifies the conflict inherent in the dialogical dimension of the psychology of creation. If Eve is the weak point in the chain of alimental recompense, of sublimation, she is nonetheless in a sense its representative: we might almost say that the chain itself speaks through her. As spokeswoman of creation, Eve brings positive sublimation into opposition with the prohibition. She herself bears a formal resemblance to the prohibition (or to the tree that bears its name) because she stands at the apex of earthly creation, as its present "end," and figures as God's last word on creation. Yet she contrasts sharply with the Tree in that the word that brings her into being is a responsive word: she is the issue of Adam's dialogue with the Son, and hence of an ultra-softened fiat, the most sublimated and dialogical of God's creative words.

As the ultimate representative of positive reciprocity, Eve is paradoxically the most independent or "individual" of the creatures. This, we may note, is not incompatible with her being lower in the natural hierarchy than Adam; on the contrary, Eve's independence is conferred on her just by virtue of her being Adam's object (the object of his dialogue as well as of his desire, for there is of course no pretense of equality in their dialogical constitution). Since she is defined as Adam's object, as the utopian sign and repository of his surplus energy, Eve's desire is relatively unattached and undirected. Therefore, she appears to be uniquely self-possessed. In her personal creation story in Book IV (11. 449–91), she is reluctant to give herself to Adam, and must be drawn from Narcissus-like fixation on her own image by a superior voice (which, as relocated in Adam, remains essential to her constitution). Eve's later fascination with Satan and with the tree further testifies to the relative freedom of her desire. Adam is excessively attracted to Eve precisely because of her relative detachment or self-possession. It is not just her "fair outside" that makes Adam's superior powers sink in admiration; it is rather Eve's whole demeanor or bearing:

> Yet when I approach
> Her loveliness, so absolute she seems
> And in herself complete, so well to know

> Her own, that what she wills to do or say,
> Seems wisest, virtuousest, discreetest, best.
>
> (Bk. VIII, 11. 546–50)

Adam is vulnerable to what he sees as Eve's gestural centeredness, her utter self-possession, whereas that centeredness is itself but a sign of Eve's creative and dialogical decenteredness, of the excess, within her, of free or undirected desire.

We can now interpret the moment of Eve's external fall. Satan's strategy is to attach the lack he knows Eve feels to the prohibition. To do this, he must place Eve strictly on the plane of creation, so as to redispose or clarify its internal logic and show that the surplus energy or desire that so troubles Eve is a function of a determinate lack (the apple). This he accomplishes, I think, not so much by any of his individual arguments as by the projection of a self-contained character or rhetorical ethos. Satan tempts Eve precisely by dramatizing his speech, by making gesture itself speak. The passage that introduces Satan's temptation, in which Satan is cast as a classical orator, underscores his true strategy. As orator, Satan appears to contain and control surplus energy. He thus represents, from our generic point of view, the logical fulfillment of epic romance; oratorical gesture appears to absorb into the material language of character the absence at the center of epic action and culture. Before speaking, Satan

> Fluctuates disturb'd, yet comely, and in act
> Rais'd, as of some great matter to begin.
> As when of old some Orator renown'd
> In *Athens* or free *Rome*, where Eloquence
> Flourishd, since mute, to some great cause addrest,
> Stood in himself collected, while each part,
> Motion, each act won audience ere the tongue,
> Somtimes in highth began, as no delay
> Of Preface brooking through his Zeal of Right,
> So standing, moving, or to highth upgrown
> The Tempter all impassion'd thus began.
>
> (Bk. IX, 11. 668–78)

The arguments that follow enforce, in their ready abundance, this image of the classical orator whose ethos is its own argument. The centered Satan thus represents for Eve the culmination of creation's utopian drive.

ychology on its own terms. The ethical antinomy written into the
uple's utopian purificatory drive is posited as an effect of the paradoxical
ll to closure imposed by the introduction of lack into creation.

This is the point, then, at which theology itself is evidently controlled
ɔm without by the ethical psychology of utopian romance, and in
hich the coherence and clarity of theology is imperiled by the
ɔpearance of a discrete ethical problematic within the fall narrative. If
e positive sublimation of creation is always in fact motivated by an
ɩposed absence, by a lack, then the category of predestination itself
kes on an ambivalent psychological status because its "work" appears
ɩcessarily to accord with the constitution of creation's desirous move-
ent. The prohibition merely gives determinate symbolic foundation to
ɩ absence that preexisted it. Theology is decentered by the neutral
ɩychological narrative which the epic form, working through the
ɩbstitute genre of romance, selects as the dominant narrative of the fall.

But if the epic occludes theology, its own formal integrity is modified
ɩd imperiled in the same gesture. The unique suspenselessness of epic
ɩrrative gives way in the paradise books, as the monistic narrative of
eation comes to the fore, to what might be called cognitive neutrality.
his transformation may perhaps be most conveniently understood in
rms of the constitutive role of *lack* in the psychology of creation (and in
ɩilton's monist narrative). For this new and neutral category replaces the
ɩore positively defined *fate* of classical epic. The positive homology of
ɔic narrative, its unique suspenselessness, is founded in the positive
ɩdependence of the various forms of classical laboring activity, which
ɩas made possible by the absence of any general concept of labor. The
ɔgnitive neutrality of Milton's epic narrative, on the other hand, is
ɩtermined finally by the lack at the heart of the form of capitalist labor,
ɔon the distance from experience determined by the reification of the
ɩpitalist subject. Miltonic fate (which is to say, predestination) is
ɩstinguished from the fate of the principal classical epics in that it is at
ɩce more abstract and more internal both to gesture and to narrative
ɔtion than is the latter. This abstract internality of fate with regard to
ɔic action not only determines the inadequacy of the external theological
ɔint of view on paradisal action and on the fall. It also conditions the
roblem of heroism (or of the lack thereof) in the paradise books, since
ɩe concreteness of gesture is sapped by the presence of abstract fate
·ithin it. And beyond this, in thus reducing the momentary quality of

He figures a post-prohibitional nature, a creation now con
thoroughly in control of its productions. Eve is lured to fal
creative centeredness in which lack no longer exists, in
energy is not wasted.

Satan's gesture of temptation, then, completes the narr
in usurping upon the utopian end projected by paradise
and inherent in the movement of creation. We should all
there is a propriety about this usurpation. For on the on
gesture is but a "type" of creative gesture: the controlled
the temptation and of Satanic gesture in general is but a
creative overproduction, and precisely through this affini
signifies the liberation of the anarchic powers at the basis
make for its unruliness. In this respect, that is at the ges
precisely the principle of plenitude at work in Satan's con
permits him to tempt Eve and bring about Creation
represents the triumph of pure production and the we
powers within the body of creation of which it is compos
then, to the possessive moment of Milton's monism at it

On the other hand, Satanic gesture distinguishes
dialogical gesture of creation by its self-contained com
unique control or oneness with itself. Satan seems to be
desire, to experience no lack. In making this finish out t
eating the apple, he implicitly makes the prohibition into
abstract lack that is the other side of creative surplus en
is thus rendered determinate, it appears to *constit*
production of creation, in the sense of providing it with
paradoxical figurative consequence of Satan's accusati
reduce the prohibition itself, and the predestination for
to the plane of creation, to lodge them in the very
figuratively determine. Thus does Satan complete the l
by exposing the open-endedness of its utopian narrativ
the pre-given closure of lack; by revealing the dependen
ethic of permission on an abstract and initial ethic of pro
likewise, that temptation and fall reunite the halves of N
revealing the hidden form of monistic purification at v
narrative logic even as they put a period to it. Moni
figures predestination itself onto the plane of creation
inherent lack, thereby assuring the comprehensibi

heroism, the entrance of lack into gesture accords the category of suspense a qualitatively different and more important place within epic narrative.

Yet there is still a sense in which Milton's epic may be spoken of as suspenseless. For if, as I am arguing, Adam and Eve are framed by creation to fall, then it is not too much to say (as has of course been done) that they are always already fallen from the moment of their first appearance in the poem. The psychology of lack is finally a psychology of transgression; it implies that creation, and hence the paradisal couple, proceed by repressing and refiguring lack itself, committing ever purer imaginary transgressions against the arbitrary proscription to which they are linked. Creation moves by translating temptation into strength, and hence relies on temptation. Such an implicit dynamics of temptation is the basis for the poem's most powerful theodicy, for God's best fallback. This defense is already present – though of course in a more militant register – in *Areopagitica*: God had good (ethical) reason for inserting lack into creation. He did it to make men move and aspire:

> Many there be that complain of divin Providence for suffering *Adam* to transgresse, foolish tongues! when God gave him reason, he gave him freedom to choose, for reason is but choosing; he had bin else a meer artificiall *Adam*, such an *Adam* as he is in the motions. We our selves esteem not of that obedience, or love, or gift, which is of force: God therefore left him free, set before him a provoking object, ever almost in his eyes; herein consisted his merit, herein the right of his reward, the praise of his abstinence. . . . This justifies the high providence of God, who though he command us temperance, justice, continence, yet powrs out before us ev'n to a profusenes all desirable things, and gives us minds that can wander beyond all limit and satiety. (pp. 527–8)

Eve's sin is that she transgresses against paternal temptation by attempting to contain or control the lack that it signifies. But it is, of course, rather pointless to blame her for this: Eve, at the deepest level of the epic, is fashioned in such a way as to be able to resist anything but temptation. Milton's epic believes in temptation as firmly as it believes in God. Its original couple comes into the world driven by a dynamic of temptation that even God does not control.

Conclusion

I should emphasize, in conclusion, the social significance of the generic process that we have now drawn to its logical end. For the psychology of transgression projected by the utopian intersection of the subgenres of romance and pastoral, in which romance desire strives for what it is forbidden, for what is constitutively absent from the pastoral world, is the final symbolic form taken by the counterplot. Predestination is thus figured as an ethical psychology at work in creation, and this logic provides the dominant generic explanation of the fall, hence of the failure of political desire in the revolution.

The social message of the generic process that culminates in this explanation is a contradictory one, and may be read both at the level of content and of form. On the one hand, we must interpret the purification of monism as a tacit confession of subjective conjuncturality, of the fragmentary character of the material experience from which ethos is drawn. The ethical explanation of political failure cannot cover over the imperturbable *difference* of political desire or ethos, any more than can the theological explanation that is generically dominant only in the heavenly portions of the poem. Nonetheless, the poem does make a direct allegorical statement in its assertion of an ethical ethos. For this is what the psychology of transgression amounts to for Milton's fit reader: it is a way of living predestination as temptation, of incorporating prohibition as a kind of metaphysical lack against which one tests and purifies oneself in ever subtler ways. The natural psychology of paradise asserts the cultural revolution by celebrating its displaced result: the ethical subject of emergent capitalism, whose narrative dynamic is determined by its paradoxical distance from itself, or in other words by constitutive lack.

This same revolution in the subject is conveyed at the level of form. But it is conveyed, not through a militant wrenching of genre to revolutionary ends, but rather through the cognitive dispassion of the generic purgation of political desire. What strikes us most when we stand back from the generic process by which Milton's monistic sense of the subject undergoes allegorical purification is the passivity with which the poem records its transitional contradictions in fighting against them. We may regard it, perhaps, as the partial result of the poem's elision of collective agency from its explicit horizons that it can view the results of that agency as if from afar, that it can be written from what appears to be a godlike perspective: its trust in its own generic representations, its willingness to let narrative have its own way, is the trust and willingness of the postrevolutionary subject, ensconced now in its own domain beyond representation, the domain from which representation takes its narrative force. The cosmic passiveness of *Paradise Lost* in the face of its own contradictions may be taken as a statement in its own right of the emergent subject's confidence in the security of its Imaginary integrity vis-à-vis the social symbolic representations that it manipulates, hence in the security of its own class position. Insofar as meta-generic practice in *Paradise Lost* appears secure, it takes on the force of an institution, and serves as a sign of control rather than of power, or casts the power of the subject as control. Such detachment, I would suggest, spells the beginning of a transition in the nature of aesthetic production itself, whereby the meta-genre of the empowered revolutionary subject is transformed into the ironic imitation and the satire of the ethically entrenched Restoration subject.

Nonetheless, in spite of its figuring of control, the exasperation undergone by the subject in this passive generic process is immense, and this exasperation is duly recorded in the poem's finale. The harshness of Milton's depiction of the historical quotidian in the last two books is transparently motivated by his political disappointment, which proves too unruly to be successfully purged or controlled. It is impossible to discuss these books here, if only because doing so would require the construction of a whole new genre, that of biblical epic, which vies with classical epic for dominance over the typological narrative. It is sufficient to say that the fall is a fall into biblical epic and predestinary theology;

and in this context political libido enjoys a rather grim and paradoxical consummation after the fireworks of its repression and dispersal. All the elements of Milton's overt politics – for example, the theory of the struggle between tyranny and liberty in man; the belief in direct divine intervention in history through the prophet or great man; the prophetic distrust of the multitude – all these doctrines spill out to lay at Restoration's door a rather explicit diagnosis of its present evil state. For all the admirable nerve of this diagnosis, it is difficult to see how to reconcile the political-theological pessimism of Milton's postlapsarian history with the ethical explanation of the fall and the secure confidence of the ethical subject that it asserts. But perhaps there is no better way to usher the subject into capitalism than by exposing the grinding contradiction between its own ethical freedom and the world of necessity of which that freedom is itself a part. It is surely one of the reasons for the haunting quality of the last lines of the poem, in which the ethical ethos of transgressive classical epic is revived for one last time, that they give this contradiction the form and force of an emblem.

Notes

Chapter 1: Introduction (pp. 1–16)

1 See Alastair Fowler's edition of the poem in *The Poems of John Milton*, ed. Alastair Fowler and John Carey (London: Longmans, 1968). I do not mean to question the *value* of Fowler's notes, which is formidable, but rather their presupposition of a static and seamless Christian tradition as the ultimate context in which the poem should be read.

2 My formulation is intentionally close to the definition of class favored by E.P. Thompson, who is perhaps the best known modern historian of collective agency. See his classic *The Making of the English Working Class* (New York: Vintage Books, 1966), p. 9.

3 This definition of "problematic" is derived from Louis Althusser's use of the term. See Ben Brewster's definition in his glossary to *For Marx*, trans. Ben Brewster (London: New Left Books, 1977), p. 253: "A word or concept cannot be considered in isolation; it only exists in the theoretical or ideological framework in which it is used: its problematic." (This glossary is revised and approved by Althusser.) Althusser is the Marxist philosopher of "structural determination" *par excellence*, and my own consideration of transition is heavily dependent on his theory.

4 Karl Marx, *The Eighteenth Brumaire of Louis Bonaparte*, in Karl Marx, *Surveys from Exile*, ed. David Fernbach (New York: Random House, 1973), vol. II, p. 146.

5 The seminal text in this literature, and still central in my opinion, is Maurice Dobb's *Studies in the Development of Capitalism* (London: Routledge and Sons Ltd, 1946). Dobb's work was taken issue with by Paul Sweezy, and their argument turned into a full-scale debate within Marxism. The major essays from this debate are collected, with an important introduction by Rodney Hilton, in *The Transition from Feudalism to Capitalism* (London: New Left Books, 1976). For important recent contributions, see Robert Brenner, "The origins of capitalism," *New Left Review*, 104 (1977), 25–92, and Perry Anderson, *Lineages of the Absolutist State* (London: New Left Books, 1974), esp. ch. 1. For stimulating work on the general *theory* of transition, see Etienne Balibar's chapter, "Elements for a theory of transition," in Althusser and Balibar, *Reading Capital*, trans. Ben Brewster (London: New Left Books, 1970).

6 See Dobb, *op. cit.*, p. 18.

7 Translated by Ben Fowkes (New York: Vintage Books, 1977), pp. 873–942.

8 Dobb, *op. cit.*, ch. 2, esp. pp. 41–2.

9 John Merrington's "Town and country in the transition to capitalism" (*The Transition from Feudalism to Capitalism*, pp. 170–95) shows that feudalism was the first mode of

production to allot urban trade an autonomous role within the economy, and thus gives particularly convincing refutation to the notion that trade is external to feudalism.

10 Dobb, *op. cit.,* pp. 44 ff. Also see Anderson's impressive résumé of the feudal system in *Passages from Antiquity to Feudalism* (London: New Left Books, 1974), pp. 147–53, 182–212. Anderson emphasizes the imbrication of the contradiction between lord and serf with the legal autonomy of towns in the West, and casts this connection as the decisive factor in the disintegration of Western feudalism.

11 See Rodney Hilton, *Bond Men Made Free* (New York: Viking Press, 1973), and esp. Brenner, *op. cit.*

12 See Eric Kerridge, *The Agricultural Revolution* (London: Allen and Unwin, 1967).

13 Lawrence Stone, *The Causes of the English Revolution 1529–1642* (London: Harper and Row, 1972), pp. 68–9.

14 Dobb, *op. cit.,* pp. 123–51.

15 Stone, *op. cit.,* p. 69–70.

16 ibid., p. 69.

17 See Anderson, *Lineages,* pp. 113–42, for a summary description of the move toward absolutism in England.

18 The dominant Marxist position is of course that the mid-century crisis *was* a successful bourgeois revolution because it irrevocably altered the distribution of political power in capital's favor. I agree with this position. I do not think it too much of an oversimplification to say that it was in the main a locally oriented and basically capitalist class of gentry which brought down the monarchy in 1640, engulfing the nation in civil strife; that this strife turned into a civil war between capitalist and neo-feudal factions of the ruling class, factions which represented two distinct modes of production; and thus what began as a battle over particular interests turned into a revolution, or revealed itself to have been a revolution all along.

19 Quoted from Christopher Hill, *The Century of Revolution 1603–1714* (New York: Norton, 1961), p. 106.

20 See, for an influential study of Puritan politics, Michael Walzer, *The Revolution of the Saints: A Study in the Origin of Radical Politics* (New York: Atheneum, 1970). Walzer's book rewrites the Weber thesis in political terms: the Puritans were not the first capitalists, but the first revolutionary politicians; Puritanism indeed made possible the modern concept of political revolution (see, for example, pp. 304–7). It should become obvious in the course of this introduction that I do not think Weber's and Walzer's interpretations are mutually exclusive or opposed; nor do I think either is entirely correct. Taken all together, Christopher Hill's work remains the best appreciation of Puritanism as a revolutionary culture. See particularly *Puritanism and Revolution* (London: Panther, 1969), *The World Turned Upside Down* (New York: Penguin Books, 1972), and *God's Englishman* (New York: Harper and Row, 1970), ch. 9.

21 It is surely no accident that Protestantism's transitional role is nowhere so prominent as in the period of the revolution itself, with the shattering of the Protestant ranks into factions and heretical sects. Christopher Hill's *The World Turned Upside Down* is fascinated with the radical sects partly because of the lucid secular impulses expressed in them.

22 It is assumed here that ideology, in the form of theology, formed the dominant instance of the feudal mode, in the sense that it was allotted the role of assuring the reproduction of feudal relations. See Marx, *Capital,* vol. I, pp. 175–6.

23 Max Weber, trans. Talcott Parsons, *The Protestant Ethic and the Spirit of Capitalism* (New York: Scribner's, 1958).

24 I should allow that Weber's notes nuance this position considerably (see, for example, pp. 197–8, 273). Still I think it is fair to say that the reputation of *The Protestant Ethic* as

a refutation of Marxism is accurate, and that the main burden of the book is to cavil with the view of Protestantism latent in Marx's writings on the transition.

25 See Anderson, *Lineages*, pp. 173–85.

26 See J.B. Broadbent, *Some Graver Subject* (New York: Shocken Books, 1960), pp. 24–35, for an interesting if casual psychological reading of Milton's emphasis on chastity in the 1630s.

27 See Maurice Kelley's introduction to *De Doctrina* in *Complete Prose Works of John Milton*, VI (New Haven: Yale University Press, 1973), pp. 43–102, for a systematic historical exposition of each of the heresies in turn. Of the other critics and expositors of Milton's theology, Arthur Barker has best understood the unity of the heresies. See *Milton and the Puritan Dilemma* (Toronto: University of Toronto Press, 1942).

28 Raymond Williams, *Marxism and Literature* (Oxford: Oxford University Press, 1977), pp. 128–35. Williams tends to reserve the term "structure of feeling" for emergent and inchoate ideological units; the term "semantic figure" designates then the definite expression of these inarticulate structures. "Structures of feeling can be defined as social experiences in *solution*, as distinct from other social semantic formations which have been precipitated and are more evidently and more immediately available ... Yet this specific solution is never mere flux. It is a structured formation which, because it is at the very edge of semantic availability, has many of the characteristics of a pre-formation, until specific articulations – new semantic figures – are discovered in material practice: often, as it happens, in relatively isolated ways, which are only later seen to compose a significant (often in fact minority) generation."

29 Milton, *Complete Prose Works*, VI (New Haven: Yale University Press, 1973), pp. 307, 310. Page numbers given in the text are also from this edition.

30 For the relation of Milton's materialism to Aristotle, see John Reesing, "The materiality of God in Milton's *De doctrina christiana*," *Harvard Theological Review*, 50 (1967), 159–73.

31 *Complete Prose Works*, II, p. 403. The quotation is from *Of Education*.

32 Terry Eagleton, *Criticism and Ideology* (London: New Left Books, 1976). I should point out that Eagleton rarely uses the term "genre," preferring "mode," presumably because of its less literary and more productive connotations; a literary mode, for him, is a mode of production.

33 Jameson's essay on romance, now presented in *The Political Unconscious* (Ithaca: Cornell University Press, 1981), pp. 102–50, may be taken as an exemplary construction and lineage of one such original relation inscribed in generic form. It should be noted that genres are more free-floating for Eagleton than they are for Jameson, whose "practical" constructions of definite genres do not have their equivalent in Eagleton's work. Perhaps Eagleton's "productivism" is partly determined by his being more focused than is Jameson upon the nineteenth-century novel, whose use of a barrage of genres encourages their consideration as floating signifiers of a kind. For one writing on the Renaissance, Jameson is surely the more valuable theorist, as my indebtedness to his specific constructions of epic and romance will testify.

Chapter 2: Areopagitica (pp. 19–51)

1 "Hegemony" in this sense is associated with the name of Gramsci, though it is of Leninist origin. See Perry Anderson, "The antinomies of Antonio Gramsci," *New Left Review*, 100 (Nov. 1976–Jan. 1977), 5–78.

2 For a more detailed description of the tract's situation of intervention, see Ernest Sirluck's introduction to vol. II of the *Complete Prose Works* (New Haven: Yale

University Press, 1959).

3 See Sirluck, pp. 164–78. I am much indebted to Sirluck's groundbreaking study.

4 See Barker, *Milton and the Puritan Dilemma*, p. 63.

5 Milton, *Complete Prose Works*, II (New Haven: Yale University Press, 1959), p. 491. Page numbers given in the text hereafter are from this edition of the tract.

6 Milton tells us in the first lines of his tract that at the beginning of his endeavors he "may have been variously affected" with the transitory moods or "dispositions" incidental to such undertakings, and that he "likely might in these formost expressions now also disclose which of them sway'd most, but that the very attempt of this address thus made, and the thought of whom it hath recourse to, hath got the power within me to a passion, farre more welcome then incidentall to a Preface" (p. 487). He thus shows an awareness of (indeed he practically thematizes) the conventional exorbitance of his aspirations in the tract. "Passion" is used here both as a stock rhetorical term for the appeal to the emotions in oratory, and as a term from corporal theory designating that state in which all the dispositions and affections act spontaneously in unison to form one common power.

7 See John Illo, "The misreading of Milton," in *Radical Perspectives in the Arts*, ed. Lee Baxandall (Penguin Books, 1972), pp. 178–92.

8 The citation may refer to Ovid's story of Cadmus (*Metamorphoses*, III, 101–30) or to that of Jason (VII, 121–42). The first of these stories has imperialistic overtones which dovetail well with the intense "nationalism" of Milton's tract; if it is this story which is referred to, then the admonitory function of the citation is a secondary one.

9 See Morris W. Croll, "The Baroque style in prose," in *Style, Rhetoric and Rhythm*, ed. J. Max Patrick *et al.* (Princeton: Princeton University Press, 1966), pp. 207–36.

10 For a stimulating discussion of French Renaissance prose as writing, see Terence Cave, *The Cornucopian Text* (Oxford: Clarendon Press, 1979).

11 I am here endorsing K. W. Stavely's suggestion that Milton's anti-Ciceronianism is politically "radical." See *The Politics of Milton's Prose Style* (New Haven: Yale University Press, 1975), p. 42.

12 The phrase "figuration of incorporation" is meant to refer to the (just noted) centrality of the human body in the pamphlet's "imagistic framework", without, however, excluding figures displaying the characteristic "referential" activity but not directly based on the human body.

13 See Alan F. Price, "Incidental imagery in *Areopagitica*," *Modern Philology*, XLIX (1952), pp. 217–22, and John X. Evans, "Imagery as argument in Milton's *Areopagitica*," *Texas Studies in Language and Literature*, VIII (1966), pp. 189–205.

14 I will return later to the passage advocating knowledge of evil (it is quoted below, page 45). For Jesus' apocalypticism see Ernst Bloch, *Man On His Own*, trans. E. B. Ashton (New York: Herder and Herder, 1970), pp. 123–4.

15 See Evans, *op. cit.*, pp. 194–205, for an exposition of these three patterns.

16 Barker, *Milton and the Puritan Dilemma*, p. 318.

17 For the "potency of matter," see pp. 11–12 above.

18 See the OED for early uses of the word in this sense of "lineage" or "descent."

19 K. G. Hamilton, "Structure of Milton's prose," in *Language and Style in Milton*, ed. Emma and Shawcross (New York: Frederick Ungar, 1967), p. 329. See Stanley Fish, "Reason in *The Reason of Church Government*," in *Self-Consuming Artifacts* (Berkeley: University of California Press, 1972), pp. 265–302, for a very different interpretation of this anti-discursive bias as it appears in *The Reason of Church Government*.

20 See Lacan's article, "The mirror-phase as formative of the function of the I," trans. in *New Left Review*, 51 (1968), pp. 71–7. Fredric Jameson's essay, "Imaginary and Symbolic in Lacan," in *Literature and Psychoanalysis* (Yale French Studies, 1977), pp. 338–95, is the

clearest and most cogent exposition that I have seen of the Lacanian orders and the uses to which they might be put. Also see Anthony Wilden's long introductory essay in *The Language of the Self* (New York: Dell, 1968), pp. 159–311.

21 See Jameson, *op. cit.*, p. 357.

22 This is the main burden of Jameson's article on Lacan. I should allow that this is one reading of Lacan, and that the more technical expositions of his texts do not stress the possibilities opened up for historical psychoanalysis.

23 See Paul Bénichou's discussion of the aristocratic ethic of purification in France during the early seventeenth century in *Man and Ethics*, trans. Elizabeth Hughes (New York: Anchor Books, 1971), pp. 1–45 and *passim*.

24 See Sartre's analysis of the nineteenth-century bourgeois in terms of a bodily respectability neither of nature nor of blood in *Critique of Dialectical Reason*, trans. Alan Sheridan-Smith and ed. Jonathan Rée (London: New Left Books, 1976), pp. 770–80.

25 I will crudely define "mode of production" by saying that it refers to a historically distinct economic formation, without going into the grinding paradoxes involved in the concept's definition; these paradoxes stem from the fact that the term "mode of production" must be thought of as a historically variable concept whose elements undergo substantial change (thus the modes of production variously delimit the very sphere of the socioeconomic in terms of which we have just defined the notion of mode of production itself). There are traditionally thought to be five modes of production after the original communal society: the Asiatic, the ancient, the feudal, the capitalist, and the communist.

26 In order to render concrete the determinants of Milton's immanent sense of the subject, it would be necessary to study the development and interactions of political, legal, religious, and other spheres of social reality, and to specify the contribution of each of these spheres to the definition of the subject. It is obviously impossible in this study to go into anything approaching such detail. By stating, in such a general way as I have done, the relationship between capitalism and the subject, I realize that I run the risk of appearing to assume that the juxtaposition of analogous phenomena deriving from different spheres of social reality demonstrates their mutual status as aspects of the same process. Given the demand for social reference or explanation written into the letter of the text itself (see p. 36 above), I do not see how this risk of "adjacentism" can honestly be avoided.

27 "Overdetermination" is a crucial Althusserian term (arrived at by way of Freud), designating the distinctness and the complexity of interaction of the various levels of the social structure. For Althusser, social determination is always multiple and complex, always a conjunctural phenomenon: no single contradiction or level determines or is determined in isolation; each occupies its determining place in the social whole by virtue of its mode of interaction and cohabitation with the other contradictions and levels. Technically speaking, it is improper to say that any place or level is peculiarly overdetermined, for everything must finally be equally overdetermined. The monistic ethos is extremely overdetermined only in the sense that it represents a peculiarly dense fusion of antinomies deriving from different levels of social contradiction (the obvious analogy here is with the Freudian symptom, which can appear as such because of its condensed displacement of contradictory desires). For discussion of the concept, see especially Althusser's essay "Contradiction and overdetermination," in *For Marx*, pp. 87–128. For a lucid presentation and critique of the concept and its associated categories, see Norman Geras, "Althusser's Marxism," in *Western Marxism*, ed. *New Left Review* (London: Verso, 1977), pp. 232–72.

28 Although I will not deal with the reference to Spenser which follows hard on the passage about to be quoted, in which Milton commits the error of ushering the Palmer

into Mammon's Cave with Guyon, I should note that my view of Milton's temperance is indebted to Ernest Sirluck's interpretation of Milton's revision in "Milton revises the *Faerie Queene*," *Modern Philology*, 48 (1950), 90–6. Sirluck argues that Milton's revision of Spenser, which places an added emphasis on reason at the expense of temperance, is also a revision of Aristotle. I think that the relation between reason and temperance, however, is more problematical than Sirluck allows.

29 For the contradiction between nationalist and Congregationalist positions, see Michael Fixler's discussion of the tract in *Milton and the Kingdoms of God* (Evanston, Ill: Northwestern University Press, 1964), pp. 121–30.

Chapter 3: Possessive individualism, genre and ethics (pp. 55–77)

1 It will be clear by now, I hope, that when I write "subject," I mean the "individual subject" unless the context indicates otherwise, this in what I would call a logical rather than a strict linguistic sense. I choose the term, in preference to more traditional ones such as "individual" or "self," because of its implication that "individuality" is not a natural but always a constituted category, always a sociocultural phenomenon. I assume that the subject is ultimately determined by a definite social conjuncture, and thus created by a combination of levels of ideological "interpellation"; yet I also assume that the subject is in some sense – at least a functional sense – *one*, so that my resort to such categories as "economic subject" and "ethical subject" to designate discrete levels of interpellation should be understood to make use of metonymic license. For the late Althusserian theory of ideology as interpellation, see the essay "Ideology and ideological state apparatuses" in *Lenin and Philosophy*, trans. Ben Brewster (New York: Monthly Review Press, 1971), pp. 127–88.

2 I adopt this phrase from C. B. MacPherson's *The Political Theory of Possessive Individualism* (Oxford: Clarendon Press, 1962), upon whose lucid construction of the philosophical tradition beginning with Hobbes my own presentation is based.

3 This is not to say that the division between rhetoric and ethics was not a source of worry and embarrassment for classical rhetorical theory (see Terry Eagleton's "small history of rhetoric" in his *Walter Benjamin* [London: Verso, 1981], pp. 101–13), but only that classical theory never presupposed the necessity of real virtue's manifesting itself beneath speech.

4 See, for example, the meditation on the law in Romans 7 and 8.

5 See Christopher Hill, *The Century of Revolution*, pp. 28–35.

6 See Dobb, *op. cit.*, pp. 193 ff., for how anti-monopoly sentiment was only free market ideology "in effect." One may look in vain for such movement in other tolerationist tracts, a representative selection of which have been collected in *Tracts on Liberty in the Puritan Revolution, 1638–1647*, ed. William Haller (New York: Columbia University Press, 1934), vols. II and III. Much of Milton's implicit theological argument for toleration reduplicates Lord Brooke's argument in *A Discourse Opening the Nature of Episcopacie*, in *Tracts*, pp. 38–163. Brooke and his tract are of course given an accolade in *Areopagitica*, pp. 560–1. But Brooke does not evoke the process of ethical cognition in the way that Milton does. Note that such a "radical liberal" argument as that of Roger Williams for complete religious liberty hinged upon the utter separation of religious cognition from any form of civil activity or process (see Barker, *op. cit.*, pp. 98–122). I will shortly address the question that arises of *why* anti-monopoly sentiment did not typically lead to a valorization of the free market.

7 In other words, I am shifting here from what has been a more Lukácsian definition of reification, according to which reification is conceived virtually as the ontology of the

capitalist system (see Georg Lukács, "Reification and the consciousness of the proletariat," in *History and Class-Consciousness*, trans. Rodney Livingstone [Cambridge: MIT Press, 1968], pp. 83–222), to a more Althusserian definition of reification, according to which it is the "general ideological effect" of the dominant capitalist relations of production (see Nicos Poulantzas, *Political Power and Social Classes*, trans. Timothy O'Hagan [London: New Left Books, 1973], pp. 293–314). Note, however, that Althusser himself favors the abolition of the term (it is explicitly conjured in a long note in *For Marx*, p. 230).

8 See, for example, Eric Hobsbawm's major article, "The general crisis of the seventeenth century," in *Crisis in Europe*, ed. Trevor Aston (New York: Basic Books, 1965), pp. 5–58.

9 See, for example, Brenner, *op. cit.*, 77–8.

10 See Dobb, *op. cit.*, p. 199. For an updated and political point of view, see Anderson's description of mercantilism as absolutist economic ideology in *Lineages*, pp. 33–5.

11 For the long-term effects of this political subordination, see Tom Nairn's *The Break-Up of Britain* (London: New Left Books, 1977), pp. 11–91.

12 Dobb, *op. cit.*, pp. 217–19.

13 Anti-monopoly sentiment goes back to peasant resentment against noble exactions (*banalités*) upon the means of production. See Anderson, *Passages*, pp. 184–5.

14 This was especially true of the attack as carried on by the industrial city population; see Brian Manning, *The English People and the English Revolution* (London: Heinemann, 1976), pp. 138–62. The Levellers, for instance, who concentrated in the city, spoke for the immediate productive rights of various sorts of smallholders (Manning, pp. 279, 287, 297–8).

15 MacPherson, *op. cit.*, pp. 22–3.

16 ibid., pp. 19 ff.

17 ibid., pp. 76–7. MacPherson well emphasizes the revolutionary significance of this equation of political right with bodily power: "In ... deriving right and obligation from fact, Hobbes was taking a radically new position. He was assuming that right did not have to be brought in from outside the realm of fact, but that it was there already: that, unless the contrary could be shown, one could assume that equal right was entailed in equal need for continued motion."

18 Again, at a more intimately personal level, Hobbes' notion of natural ability (that is, of *eminent* ability), presupposes that the individual's qualities define themselves *against* the qualities of others and thus tends to naturalize market competition.

19 See, for instance, MacPherson, p. 62, and Dobb, *op. cit.*, ch. 6.

20 See Christopher Hill, "Pottage for freeborn Englishmen: attitudes to wage labor," in *Change and Continuity in Seventeenth-Century England* (Cambridge: Harvard University Press, 1975), pp. 219–38.

21 Thus MacPherson himself shows, in other chapters in his book, how the possessive individualist framework set out originally by Hobbes undergoes successive recastings to accord with different class and situational interests.

22 See Anderson, *Passages*, pp. 147–8, for the parcelization of feudal property rights.

23 See, for example, Stavely, *The Politics of Milton's Prose*, pp. 23–4, and Barker, *The Puritan Dilemma*, pp. 80–8. Both texts, it should be noted, make Milton's humanist idealism partly phenomenal to developments in Puritan politics.

24 See Gilles Deleuze and Felix Guattari, *Anti-Oedipus: Capitalism and Schizophrenia*, trans. Robert Hurley, Mark Seem, and Helen R. Lane (New York: Viking Press, 1977), *passim*, but particularly the section on "capitalist representation," pp. 240–61. I am greatly simplifying this rich and suggestive book in extracting its thesis in this way.

25 As quoted in Geoffrey Hartman, "Milton's counterplot," in *Beyond Formalism* (New Haven: Yale University Press, 1970), p. 125.

26 See Jameson, *The Political Unconscious*, pp. 106–7.
27 Angus Fletcher makes highly sophisticated use of this conventional definition in his brilliant study of *Comus: The Transcendental Masque* (Ithaca: Cornell University Press, 1971).
28 See, for instance, Cicero's treatment of the appeal to the emotions, *De Oratore*, trans. H. Rackham (Cambridge: Harvard University Press, 1942), pp. 331 ff. "The power of passionate reflections and commonplaces, discussed and handled in a speech, is great enough to dispense with all make-believe and trickery; for the very quality of the diction, employed to stir the feelings of others, stirs the speaker himself even more deeply than any of his hearers" (p. 335).
29 Burton's *Anatomy of Melancholy* will perhaps stand as sufficient illustration of the "textual" and parodic bent of the anatomy form. No adequate work on the Renaissance anatomy has yet appeared.
30 See above, pp. 22, 29, 44, for oscillations formerly noted, and pp. 543–58 of *Areopagitica*. Milton moves in this stretch of prose through three "characters," the moral fable of Truth quoted above (p. 29), and a short history of the English people, to the sustained staging ("Behold now this vast City," p. 553) of contemporary London at work in the manufacture of Truth, ending in the prophetic vision of reformed, "noble and puissant" England.
31 The most authoritative discussion of the tract's parts is to be found in Sirluck's introduction, pp. 170–1; note that he must multiply subdivisions in order to make traditional nomenclature apply (but also note his point that this nomenclature is better suited to forensic than deliberative rhetoric). For differing views as to the tract's rhetorical structure, see Wilbur E. Gilman, *Milton's Rhetoric* (Columbia: University of Missouri Studies, 1939), pp. 9–44, and G. K. Hunter, "The structure of Milton's *Areopagitica*," *English Studies*, XXXIX (1958), 117–19.

Chapter 4: God: epic, hexameron and predestinary theology (pp. 81–147)

1 For representative readings of the poem as classical epic, see C. M. Bowra, *From Virgil to Milton* (London: Macmillan, 1945), John Steadman, *Milton's Epic Characters* (Chapel Hill: University of North Carolina Press, 1959), and Joan Webber, *Milton and his Epic Tradition* (Seattle: University of Washington Press, 1979). C. S. Lewis, who classifies the poem as secondary epic, may also be described as a main partisan in this trend, though his description of the formal ideology of epic is such that it need not be erased by Christianity; see *A Preface to Paradise Lost* (London: Oxford University Press, 1942). Francis C. Blessington's *Paradise Lost and the Classical Epic* (Boston: Routledge and Kegan Paul, 1979) follows Lewis in assuming the easy adaptability of classical form to Christian content. One of the best discussions of *Paradise Lost* in the context of epic tradition is that of Thomas M. Greene, in *The Descent from Heaven* (New Haven: Yale University Press, 1963); Greene (indebted, as I am, to post-Victorian ethical criticism of the poem) is highly sensitive to the formal difficulties posed by the writing of Puritan epic.
2 See Maury Thibaut de Maisières, *Les Poèmes Inspirées du Début de la Genèse à l'Epoque de la Renaissance* (Louvain, 1931); Grant McColley, *Paradise Lost: an Account of its Growth and Major Origins* (Chicago: Packard, 1940); Sister Mary Irma Corcoran, *Milton's Paradise Lost with Reference to the Hexameral Background* (Washington: Catholic University Press, 1945); Frank E. Robbins, *The Hexameral Literature: A Study of the Greek and Latin Commentaries on Genesis* (Chicago: University of Chicago Press, 1912); and (though with a broader theological focus) J. M. Evans, *Paradise Lost and*

the *Genesis Tradition* (Oxford: Clarendon Press, 1968). Watson Kirkconnell has collected and translated the most influential of the hexameral works; see *The Celestial Cycle* (Toronto: University of Toronto Press, 1952). The tradition of Biblical commentary on Genesis is hardly separable from the hexameral tradition; see Arnold Williams, *The Common Expositor* (Chapel Hill: University of North Carolina Press, 1948), for an extended discussion of *Paradise Lost* in the context of the commentaries.

3 *Milton: Complete Poems and Major Prose*, ed. Merrit Y. Hughes (New York: Odyssey Press, 1957), p. 210. This is the edition of the poem cited throughout.

4 See E.M.W. Tillyard, *The Miltonic Setting* (Cambridge: Cambridge University Press, 1938), pp. 141–204, for a discussion of *Paradise Lost* and traditional epic "patriotism."

5 The structural importance of "nationalism" is demonstrated more fully, if indirectly, later on, in my discussion of epic fate in its relation to gesture (pp. 107–11).

6 See Christopher Hill, "The Norman Yoke," in *Puritanism and Revolution*, pp. 50–122. The myth of the Norman Yoke projected a democratic and popular constitution as the form of society native to England before the Conquest; the attack on the Stuart despotism was thus an attack on a *foreign* state and state of affairs. The Norman Yoke was standard Puritan propaganda; note, though, that the Independent version was always less "popular" than that of the Levellers.

7 I am suggesting here Milton's affinity, and not his association, with the Independents. For an extremely impressive and well informed "Goldmannian" reading of Milton as a representative of Independent "philosophy," see Andrew Milner, *John Milton and the English Revolution* (London: Macmillan, 1981).

8 ʿFor concise formulations of the contradictions obstructing the successful installation of absolutism in England, see Anderson, *Lineages*, pp. 113–30, and Stone, *Causes of the English Revolution*, pp. 58–67.

9 There is evidence for this in Milton's posing of the question, in *The Reason of Church Government*, as to "what king or knight before the conquest might be chosen in whom to lay the pattern of a Christian hero." *Before the conquest*: the theory of the Norman Yoke was very much alive at the time of writing, and I do not think it far-fetched to suggest that Milton's chivalric epic might have made typological play with this myth of archaic English strength and freedom, using it to shadow the end of reformation. One supposes that the style of such an epic would have been equally anti-absolutist and anti-Spenserian, and have figured native strength in place of the Spenserian stability.

10 At least this would seem to hold true of the later mercantilist school (from approximately mid-seventeenth century on); see Dobb, *op. cit.*, pp. 198 ff., and Anderson, *Lineages*, pp. 35–7.

11 *Complete Prose*, I, ed. Don M. Wolfe (New Haven: Yale University Press, 1953), pp. 810–16.

12 *Complete Prose*, VI, p. 367.

13 See Dobb, *op. cit.*, p. 183.

14 See John Guillory's excellent discussion in his *Poetry and Authority: Spenser, Milton, and Literary History* (New York: Columbia University Press, 1983), pp. 150–1. I am indebted to this work for the category of "political libido."

15 Christopher Hill, *Milton and the English Revolution* (New York: Viking Press, 1977), pp. 365–75.

16 ibid., p. 366.

17 See Malcolm M. Ross, *Milton's Royalism* (Ithaca: Cornell University Press, 1943), for an excellent study of this problem.

18 See Michael Fixler's article on the "apocalyptic structure" of the poem, "The apocalypse within *Paradise Lost*," in *New Essays on Paradise Lost*, ed. Thomas Kranidas (Berkeley: University of California Press, 1971). I am suggesting that epic form induces such a

typological reading.

19 The context makes it unclear whether God predestines the Elect through all time. See pp. 134–5 below.

20 See Hill, *God's Englishman,* ch. 9, and Stone, *Causes,* p. 100.

21 This entire section is based and attempts to expand upon Fredric Jameson's brief description of epic in his book on Wyndham Lewis, *Fables of Aggression* (Berkeley: University of California Press, 1979). See the chapter "The epic as cliché, the cliché as epic."

22 Erich Auerbach's *Mimesis,* trans. Willard Trask (Princeton: Princeton University Press, 1968), pp. 3–23, and Georg Lukács' *The Theory of the Novel,* trans. Anna Bostock (Cambridge: MIT Press, 1968), contain what I consider the two best descriptions of this distinguishing formal effect.

23 See, for instance, Northrop Frye, *Anatomy of Criticism* (New York: Atheneum, 1965), p. 319. "The discovery of the epic action is the sense of the end of the total action as like the beginning, and hence of a consistent order and balance running through the whole. This consistent order is not a divine fiat or fatalistic causation, but a stability in nature controlled by the gods, and extended to human beings if they accept it."

24 *The Aeneid of Virgil,* trans. C. Day Lewis (New York: Doubleday, 1953), p. 310.

25 Auerbach's essay, cited above, on the Euryclea passage in Homer (*The Odyssey,* Book XIX), may be taken as a study of paratactic narrative syntax by way of an analysis of the heavily subordinate syntax of epic style.

26 See James Whaler's interesting series of articles for description of the peculiarities of the Miltonic simile, esp. "The Miltonic simile," *Publications of the Modern Language Association of America,* XLVI (1931), 1034–74; "Grammatical nexus of the Miltonic simile," *Journal of English and Germanic Philology,* XXX (1931), 327–34; and "Compounding and distribution of similes in *Paradise Lost,*" *Modern Philology,* XXVIII (1931), 313–34.

27 We touch upon something crucial to Milton's Hell. For Hell is defined in large part, and most vigorously, in terms of metonymic overflow, as the place of gesture; which I would suggest goes far toward explaining its curious absence from the poem, at least in memory, as a place. But if Hell is Satanic overflow, is uniquely figured as a place of gesture, then this suggests something important about Satan and his cohorts as well; they are delivered most adequately in gestural terms, especially in the great similes of the opening books. Satan is indeed preeminently a figure of gesture, and thus observation will serve as our starting point when we come to his drama.

28 See Jameson, *Fables of Aggression,* pp. 76–8.

29 Tsvetan Todorov well emphasizes the miraculous character of the bard's activity as it is presented in Homer; see "Primitive narrative," in *The Poetics of Prose,* trans. Richard Howard (Ithaca: Cornell University Press, 1977), pp. 53–65.

30 I rely here upon Fredric Jameson's influential construction of romance in *The Political Unconscious,* pp. 103–50.

31 See Jameson's exposition of romance evil as a category of the Other, *The Political Unconscious,* pp. 114–17.

32 See J. P. Vernant, *Mythe et pensée chez les Grecs* (Paris: François Maspero, 1965), ch. 4, esp. pp. 185–96.

33 See Perry Anderson, *Passages from Antiquity to Feudalism,* the chapter on "Rome," esp. pp. 67–8. If we were to pursue our construction of epic into a consideration of the macronarrative or legend, we would find, I think, that one of its important functions was symbolically to address the tension between the state and the military which Anderson shows to have been a structural consequence of the Roman peasant-based imperialism; the pious Aeneas providentially combines civic and military functions.

34 *The Aeneid of Virgil,* p. 232.

35 For the notion of the utopian figure employed here, and its relation to ideology, see Jameson, *The Political Unconscious,* pp. 281–301.

36 I should emphasize that this is a partial construct, and many aspects of epic structure remain untreated: to cite a main example, the obviously important function of epic legend, of the macro-narrative itself as a kind of pre-given content, has not been discussed.

37 These formulations are influenced by Terry Eagleton, "Ideology, fiction, narrative," *Social Text,* II (Summer 1979), 52–81.

38 The classic example of this assumption is to be found in C. S. Lewis's amusing defense of Milton against Saurat's "accusation" that the heresies were operative in *Paradise Lost*: "In *Paradise Lost* we are to study what the poet, with his singing robes about him, has given us. And when we study that we find that he has laid aside most of his private theological whimsies during his working hours as an epic poet. He may have been an undisciplined man; he was a very disciplined artist. Therefore, of his heresies – themselves fewer than some suppose – fewer still are paraded in *Paradise Lost.* Urania had him in hand. The *best* of Milton is in his epic: why should we labour to drag back into that noble building all the rubble which the laws of its structure, the limitations of its purpose, and the perhaps half-conscious prudence of the author, have so happily excluded from it? Must Noah *always* figure in our minds drunk and naked, never building the Ark?" *A Preface to Paradise Lost,* p. 92.

39 For lucid presentation of the argument that God is willful simply by virtue of epic narrativization, see, for example, A. J. A. Waldock, *Paradise Lost and its Critics* (Cambridge: Cambridge University Press, 1961), and H. W. Swardson, *Poetry and the Fountain of Light* (Columbia: University of Missouri Press, 1962), pp. 115–17.

40 *Complete Prose Works,* VI, pp. 130–8.

41 The dichotomous view of God is of course "representative" of a secret fissure within Protestant theology. See Weber's note on how both Luther and Calvin "believed fundamentally in a double God," in *The Protestant Ethic and the Spirit of Capitalism,* p. 221.

42 For translations of these works, see Saint Basil, *Exegetic Homilies,* trans. Sister Agnes Clare Way, C.D.P. (Washington D.C.: The Catholic University of America Press, 1963), and Saint Ambrose, *Hexameron, Paradise, and Cain and Abel,* trans. John J. Savage (New York: Fathers of the Church, Inc., 1961).

43 Kirkconnell's *The Celestial Cycle* is particularly useful for offering translations of the reading-plays thought to be most influential upon Milton. By far the most important narrative hexameron before Milton is that of du Bartas, to which Milton is demonstrably indebted in Sylvester's translation (see George Coffin Taylor, *Milton's Use of Du Bartas* [Cambridge: Harvard University Press, 1934]). My construction of hexameron takes du Bartas, accordingly, as its primary referent. I should note that the narrative hexamera were not limited to "the first things," but extended indefatigably into biblical (typological) history; Books XI and XII of *Paradise Lost* represent a traditional hexameral incorporation of history.

44 The terms here, and the formulations throughout this section, are indebted to Michel Foucault's construction of the sixteenth-century "referential" or "analogical" episteme, in *The Order of Things* (New York: Vintage Books, 1973), pp. 17–45. (This book is a translation of *Les Mots and Les Choses* [1966] from the French; the translator's name is not given.)

45 This is from Sylvester's translation, *The Complete Works of Joshua Sylvester,* ed. Alexander Grosart (Edinburgh University Press, 1880), p. 112, ll. 534–41.

46 Note that in Grotius' play, however, there is no cognitive uncertainty, and little real speculative interest in the cosmos; Satan's address to the wonders of creation in Act I,

for example, is simply stock awe (see *The Celestial Cycle*, pp. 101 ff.). In Basil and Ambrose, on the other hand – whose works were republished, and popular, in the early sixteenth century – the main focus is on cognitive matters.

47 See Anderson, *Lineages*, pp. 15–42.

48 For evidence of this popularity, see Kirkconnell's introduction and descriptive catalogue of analogues to *Paradise Lost*, pp. xi–xxiii, 481–682.

49 See Foucault, pp. 46 ff. Foucault argues that the "classical episteme," which appears with Descartes and Cervantes and replaces the episteme of "resemblance," was an analytical episteme. Analysis operates in terms of identity and difference, measure and order, and repudiates ontological resemblance. Analytical knowledge is founded upon the epistemological question – it is the orderly movement of thought or discursive representation, and not that of things, which is analyzed – even though that question does not yet appear as a problem. Thus "language has withdrawn from the midst of beings themselves and has entered a period of transparency and neutrality" (p. 56). It is evident that Foucault implicitly motivates the shift from referential to classical episteme in terms of the consolidation of (French) absolutism; see, for instance, his chapter on *Las Meninas*, in which the sovereign is shown to be the founder of the sign, the absent power behind representation. It is because of the more continental and political reference of his brilliant construction of ideological transition that I think Foucault offers a particularly appropriate context in terms of which to grasp the decidedly international and late feudal genre of the hexameron. It will not be thought ungracious, I hope, if I add that the more political focus of Foucault's work, and its militant repression of any form of socioeconomic determination other than the merely *ad hoc*, represents a major weakness from my own point of view; and my argument in what follows, that the analytical nature of commentary in *Paradise Lost* responds finally to an emergent capitalism, may be taken in part as expressing my reservations at this aspect of Foucault's system.

50 See Darko Suvin's authoritative definition of science fiction in these terms, in *Metamorphoses of Science Fiction* (New Haven: Yale University Press, 1979).

51 William Empson has argued, I think admirably, that the lucidity with which he presents sacrificial logic is the chief redeeming feature of Milton's God. See *Milton's God* (London: Chatto and Windus, 1961), pp. 229 ff.

52 Note, however, that nothing that God says is explicitly out of harmony with Milton's "official" (if private) pronouncements on predestination in *De Doctrina*, pp. 168–202.

53 H. R. McCallum, "Milton and figurative interpretation of the Bible," *University of Toronto Quarterly*, 31 (1961–2), 397–415, shows that Milton the theologian typologizes all of biblical history; no part of biblical narrative is exempt from typological transformation. For an interesting application of this principle to *Paradise Lost*, see John Guillory, *Poetry and Authority*, pp. 232–47.

54 I should emphasize that in explicitly dissolving God's will into creation, hexameral commentary exerts a function parallel and complementary to that performed by epic with regard to predestination: commentary is Arminian insofar as it is a non-narrative mode, and casts God's will in non-narrative form. While it seconds epic in negating predestination, its defense is neither so important nor so forceful as that of epic – as should be especially apparent in the heavenly sections – for it cancels rather than expels God's "personality"; it casts God as non-narrative rather than extra-narrative.

55 It seems to have been highly unorthodox to motivate Satan's revolt by means of the exaltation (see McColley, *Paradise Lost*, pp. 24–9), though this narrative invention was by no means original with Milton. Fowler's note to this passage, in his edition, claims that there was a vogue for starting Satan's revolt in this way, but he gives no evidence. Vondel's *Lucifer* (1652) is the only other hexameral work, known to me, that makes

Satan's revolt seem so *provoked.*

56 See above, pp. 126-7.
57 This is to put into generic terms Stanley Fish's argument about the presentation of God in *Surprised by Sin* (Berkeley: University of California Press, 1971), pp. 56 ff.
58 See below, pp. 213-14.
59 See "Milton's counterplot" in *Beyond Formalism* (New Haven: Yale University Press, 1970), pp. 113-23.
60 ibid., especially p. 15. For another interesting analysis of Miltonic suspense or delay, see Leslie Brisman, *Milton's Poetry of Choice and Its Romantic Heirs* (Ithaca: Cornell University Press, 1973), pp. 152-68.
61 See, for example, Leon Trotsky, *The History of the Russian Revolution,* trans. Max Eastman (Ann Arbor: University of Michigan Press, 1957), pp. 3-16.
62 See T. M. Greene, *The Descent from Heaven,* p. 404, who takes it as a commonplace that "Milton's faith in the goodness of matter" underlies "the profusion of Paradise" and "the unconventional refusal to follow Tasso, Marino, and Cowley in dressing up his angel [Raphael] with a temporary body."

Chapter 5: Satan, epic, and allegorical tragedy (pp. 148–178)

1 To say that Satan is both extremely epic and extremely dramatic is in itself to express a conventional view of the poem. See, for example, Hughes' introduction to his edition of the poem, pp. 177-8, and references there.
2 *Some Versions of Pastoral* (New York: New Directions, 1974), ch. 5, especially pp. 163-75.
3 I am agreeing here, then, with the view of theological critics of the poem that Satan is by definition inconsistent. See, for one of the best expressions of this view, B. J. Rajan, *Paradise Lost and the Seventeenth-Century Reader* (Ann Arbor: University of Michigan Press, 1967), pp. 93-107.
4 See John Armstrong, *The Paradise Myth* (London: Oxford University Press, 1969), pp. 104-23, for an interesting mythic analysis of Satan.
5 In view of my later argument, it is important to stress that the epic strength and splendor of Satan as a military leader conveyed in the first two books strike one before the dramatic strength of his moral position does: the more Blakean defense of Satan as a symbol of libidinal integrity impresses before the Shelleyan or Empsonian defense of Satan as a moral figure raises itself as a possibility.
6 This is the tenor of much Milton criticism. See, for example, John Steadman, *Milton and the Renaissance Hero* (Oxford: Clarendon Press, 1967), p. 1, C. M. Bowra, *From Virgil to Milton,* p. 228, and Sanford Burdick, *Poetry of Civilization* (New Haven: Yale University Press, 1974), p. 61. Blessington's *Paradise Lost and the Classical Epic* is refreshing for debunking the notion. Nonetheless, it seems to me patent that the rejection of classical epic is really there, as especially the Christians say. But this is just a moment in Milton's classical epic, and should be understood as such, rather than being globalized into the moral message of the whole work. To saturate Satanic gesture with theological and ethical anathema, in the manner of Lewis or Fish (to name perhaps the two best practitioners of this school) is to miss the autonomy and ambivalence of the literary structures which produce that gesture, to cover over the Imaginary of Milton's text with an equally Imaginary moral judgment.
7 It was A. J. A. Waldock who coined the term degradation for Satan's decline. See his excellent chapter, "Satan and the technique of degradation," in *Paradise Lost and its Critics* (Cambridge: Cambridge University Press, 1947), pp. 65-96.

8 See Barthes, *S/Z*, trans. Richard Miller (New York: Hill and Wang, 1974), especially p. 19.

9 Empson, *Milton's God*, pp. 57 ff.

10 See, for example, Book V, ll. 642–7, Book VI, ll. 1–15.

11 My reading here is indebted to Waldock's discussion of the poet's interventions into the Satan saga, pp. 78 ff., though it is of course Satan's manipulability that Waldock finds disgusting.

12 See Arnold Stein's essay on Satan in *Answerable Style* (Minneapolis: University of Minnesota Press, 1953), pp. 3–16.

13 For an interesting and sensitive discussion of the relation between scientific and poetic space in the work of Marvell, see Rosalie Colie, *"My Ecchoing Song"* (Princeton: Princeton University Press, 1970), *passim*, but especially pp. 192 ff.

14 *The Origin of German Tragic Drama*, trans. John Osborne (London: New Left Books, 1977). "Allegorical tragedy" is my translation of *Trauerspiel* (which is literally rendered in Osborne's translation as *mourning-play*). Note that though *Trauerspiel* is centered in Germany it is still, for Benjamin, a continental phenomenon. Calderon and Shakespeare (mainly *Hamlet*) are used, throughout his analysis, as reference points who transcend *Trauerspiel* in exemplifying certain of its laws.

15 I should note, before beginning, that Benjamin himself argues – in what seems to me a very elliptical context (see *Origins*, pp. 226–33) – that the Satan narrative represents exemplary mourning-play content. Evidence for this may be found in what seems in translation one of the best hexameral plays, Vondel's *Lucifer*, which falls fairly clearly into the category of the *Trauerspiel*. In this play, the war between the angels is the outcome of an initial state of emergency in heaven, a state which has been triggered by God's elevation of man; Satan leads a heavenly battalion against God in the name of a law which transcends God's acts. One can hardly overemphasize the directly political implications of this: the play was written in 1652, and clearly alludes to the conflict between law and monarchical power that was one of the main themes of the English Revolution. Vondel, a Catholic Royalist, would have had little reason to elevate Satan and republican law; yet the moral questions raised by the play remain unsettled, and Satan is cast as a martyr-tyrant. Milton probably read Vondel, but the resemblances of narrative content between the Satan narratives of *Paradise Lost* and *Lucifer* are hardly overwhelming. I would take the adherence of both renditions of Satan to the paradigm of allegorical tragedy chiefly as sign and effect of the preexisting ideological-generic determination of the Satan narrative.

16 The following brief summary of *Origins* is based on a reading of the whole book, but see pp. 80–6, 131–8, and 174–82. It should be evident from this summary that Benjaminian allegory is a very different thing from the traditional notion of allegory – in terms of which I have partly cast hexameron – as a social didactic mode.

17 Benjamin, pp. 132–8.

18 The anti-Catholic allegory written into this image of epic city-building – which is part of the programmatic attempt at the dramatic level to debunk Satan by casting him as a tyrant – seems to me to be undermined by the reminiscence of the great millennial passages in the early prose tracts (most notably, of course, of the vision in *Areopagitica* of the entire city of London busy to be born).

19 Oriental despotism was favorite subject matter for the *Trauerspiel*. See Benjamin, p. 68.

20 Waldock, *Paradise Lost and Its Critics*, pp. 65–96.

21 Benjamin, p. 71.

22 Benjamin, pp. 145–58.

23 For an interesting structuralist reading of Satan as a peculiarly "written" character, see Donald F. Bouchard, *Milton: a Structural Reading* (Montreal: McGill-Queen's University Press, 1974), pp. 63 ff.

24 Benjamin, pp. 54–68.

25 Job 38. 4–5.

26 See Empson, *Milton's God*, pp. 76–8.

27 For the literalist basis of Milton's monism, see George Newton Conklin, *Biblical Criticism and Heresy in Milton* (New York: King's Crown Press, 1949), pp. 75–85.

28 "Another inconvenience of Milton's design is, that it requires the description of what cannot be described, the agency of spirits. He saw that immateriality supplied no images, and that he could not show angels acting but by instruments of action: he therefore invested them with form and matter. This being necessary, was therefore defensible; and he should have secured the consistency of his system, by keeping immateriality out of sight, and enticing his reader to drop it from his thoughts. But he has unhappily perplexed his poetry with his philosophy. His infernal and celestial powers are sometimes pure spirit, and sometimes animated body." Quoted from *The Six Chief Lives from Johnson's "Lives of the Poets,"* ed. Matthew Arnold (London: Macmillan, 1907), p. 112.

Chapter 6: Garden and fall (pp. 179–215)

1 See Walter Clyde Curry, *Milton's Ontogeny, Cosmology and Physics* (Lexington: University of Kentucky Press, 1957), ch. 2, for discussion of the neo-Platonic background of Milton's Chaos.

2 For subtle and extended meditation upon this Miltonic "gradualism," see Geoffrey Hartman, "Adam on the grass with balsamum," in *Beyond Formalism*, pp. 124–50. W. B. C. Watkins has remarked well upon the momentum of Milton's creation in *An Anatomy of Milton's Verse* (Hamden: Archon Books, 1965), pp. 54–60.

3 The definitive work on the sources of Milton's angels is Robert H. West's *Milton and the Angels* (Athens: University of Georgia Press, 1955).

4 I am using here the model of the ideological unit developed by A. J. Greimas, and termed by him "the elementary structure of signification." I take it to be the chief virtue of his work to have demonstrated that significant oppositions always involve not two but four initial terms, in that the terms of any such positive opposition or antinomy imply also their simple negations or contradictories. The initial opposition then may be worked upon at a remove by way of the narrative manipulation of the various possibilities of combination opened up by the initial signifying movement. See A. J. Greimas and François Rastier, "The interaction of semiotic constraints," in *Yale French Studies*, 41 (New Haven: Eastern Press, 1968), pp. 86–105.

5 We may represent this shift on the diagram, accordingly, by attaching place names to the sides of the rectangle, as follows:

It is a counterclockwise slippage because the characters are first posited as epic, then as hexameral.

6 For an extended discussion of this diagrammatic utopian movement, see Fredric Jameson's essay on Louis Marin, "Of islands and trenches: neutralization and the production of utopian discourse," *Diacritics*, 7 (1977), 2–21.

7 See Suvin, *Metamorphoses of Science Fiction*, ch. 3, and Jameson, "Islands and trenches," *passim*. My treatment of utopia, as of romance, is most indebted to Jameson's work. Considerations of scope prevent my introducing these paradisal subgenres as historically determined semantic constructs here.

8 C. S. Lewis, *A Preface to Paradise Lost*, p. 49.

9 Arnold Stein, *Answerable Style*, pp. 78–92.

10 Friedrich Engels, *The Origins of the Family, Private Property, and the State* (New York: Pathfinder Press, 1972).

11 For sensitive presentation of paradise as pastoral, see Frank Kermode, "Adam unparadised," in *The Living Milton*, ed. Kermode (London: Routledge and Kegan Paul, 1960), John R. Knott, *Milton's Pastoral Vision* (Chicago: University of Chicago Press, 1971), and Louis Martz, *The Paradise Within* (New Haven: Yale University Press, 1964), pp. 122–6.

12 See Empson, *Some Versions of Pastoral*, pp. 173–4.

13 See Raymond Williams, *The Country and the City* (New York: Oxford University Press, 1973), pp. 13–15, 46–54, and William Empson, *Some Versions of Pastoral*, especially ch. 1, for the relation between nostalgic urbanity and archaic rusticity which seems inherent to the pastoral form. It is beyond my scope here to give pastoral the kind of explicit construction given above to the main genres of epic and hexameron, though such a treatment is clearly a theoretical prerequisite to any comprehensive generic reading of the poem, at least according to the scheme I am setting out here. Empson's and Williams' works seem to me to constitute the best that has been done on pastoral so far; the view of pastoral adumbrated in my own remarks is particularly indebted to Empson. For an interesting and subtle interpretation of pastoral as a Stoic genre, see Thomas G. Rosenmeyer, *The Green Cabinet* (Berkeley: University of California Press, 1969).

14 Milo Kaufman, *Paradise in the Age of Milton* (Victoria: University of Victoria, 1978), pp. 12–16.

15 See Jameson, "Islands and trenches," pp. 4–5 and *passim*.

16 It might be useful at this point to return to the Greimassian rectangle and map the generic rendition of the paradise narrative according to its coordinates. This is not an easy thing to do. Since, as I have emphasized, each of the characters is represented by way of generic dislocation, it is impossible to define any individual semantic place solely in terms of one genre. Nonetheless it does seem that we may speak of the *relative* dominance of a particular genre in the constitution of each place or character. When we fill in the corners of the rectangle with these relatively dominant genres and subgenres, it takes the following form:

This gives us a generic code in which to speak of the management of the monistic antinomy. The wishful drive of romance attempts to give the diffuse movement of creation a quasi-epic finish, while pastoral projection attempts to cast epic fate or closure *outside* the simple and random plenitude of hexameral creation. The virtue of imaging the generic situation in this way is that it shows that the substitute genres which move to the fore in the paradise books represent a negation of and reaction against the original generic construction of monism. The utopian intersection between romance and pastoral, which will be crucial in my reading of the paradise narrative, attempts to overcome what now appears as an ideological antinomy between epic and hexameron in striving to lift paradise into Heaven.

17 Stanley Fish, in *Surprised by Sin*, has perhaps best made this argument, though he is following a path laid down by much neo-Christian and liberal criticism. See, for instance, Joseph Summers' influential *The Muse's Method* (Cambridge: Harvard University Press, 1962), esp. pp. 30–1, and Ann Ferry's *Milton's Epic Voice* (Cambridge: Harvard University Press, 1963), pp. 44–66.

18 See *De Doctrina*, VI, pp. 351–2.

19 Book VIII, ll. 380–450.

20 Book IV, ll. 336–7; Book IV, l. 800; and Book VII, ll. 412–15.

21 Book VII, ll. 237–9.

22 See Fish, *Surprised by Sin*, pp. 130–50, whom I take as giving a rather harsh summary of the dominant critical view of "wandering" before the fall.

23 Book V, ll. 658–9; Book VIII, ll. 25–38.

24 Book IX, ll. 205–11.

25 Waldock, *Paradise Lost and Its Critics*, pp. 43–64.

26 Tillyard, "The crisis of *Paradise Lost*," in *Studies in Milton* (London: Chatto and Windus, 1955), pp. 8–52.

27 Book IX, ll. 743 ff., ll. 896 ff.

Index